Mounted Archery in the Americas

Edited by

David Gray and Lukas Novotny

Copyright © David Gray and Lukas Novotny

All rights reserved. Without limiting the rights under copyright reserved above, no part of this publication may be reproduced, stored in or introduced into a retrieval system, or transmitted, in any form or by any means (electronic, mechanical, photocopying, recording or otherwise) without the prior written permission of the authors and The Long Riders' Guild Press.

This book is part of "The Equestrian Wisdom and History" series produced by The Long Riders' Guild Academic Foundation, a division of The Long Riders' Guild, the world's first international association of equestrian explorers.

www.thelongridersguild.com
www.lrgaf.org.
www.classictravelbooks.com
www.horsetravelbooks.com

ISBN: 1-59048-262-X

Cover image courtesy Guy de Galard.

All the royalties from this book will go directly to the Mounted Archery Association of the Americas to help promote the discipline.

Prefacing comments and acknowledgements

The reader who wants to read selectively may of course pick from the Table of Contents. After reading or scanning a chapter of first choice, there is often the question, "who is this author?" Having just written the "About the authors" section, I am impressed with the rich array of contributors to the story of this book. The common strand throughout the group is they are nearly all practicing horseback archers, trainers, and promoters of this great martial art. Eleven of the 13 have been associated with the training school at the International Horseback Archery festival in Fort Dodge, Iowa.

Beyond the commonalities of the authors, their backgrounds are widely different. They come from Canada, China, Japan, Turkey, and the United States. Professions and vocations include academics, bowyers, business persons, a dentist, entrepreneurs, government personnel, home makers, a medical doctor, a lawyer, and a radiology technician. The editors owe a debt of gratitude for the time, effort, and creativity of each of the authors; their toil was a work of love because any royalties will go directly to the Mounted Archery Association of the Americas to promote the discipline. The generous sharing of the authors' wide experience and expertise is immensely appreciated.

The editors set a few ground rules and then let the authors speak with very little altering of content. The guidelines were to sketch as accurately as possible the older, and in some cases ancient, roots of their tradition, give an up-date on modern revival, and to include liberal personal experience. While the tone and style of each chapter reflects the particular author, we did actively try to make the formal structural elements of things like headings and paragraph structure and references to be somewhat uniform.

Our great thanks go to the Long Riders Guild for their imaginative publishing enterprise. Their inspiration, guidance, and encouragement on this project was superb and most helpful. David gratefully thanks Phyllis, his wife, for reading the text, reducing errors, and providing wisdom and perspective. Final errors are of course the responsibility of the editors.

www.lrgaf.org

About the Authors

Todd Delle, Big Fork, Montana. Owner of Auto Specialists. Todd is the U.S. representative for the Kassai School of horseback archery which involves training, directing competitions, and promoting the discipline. He is also the U.S. representative for the Horseback Archery World Association. horsearcher@centurytel.net

David Gray, New Wilmington, Pennsylvania. Co-owner of Krackow Company, promoting the arts of international traditional archery. David is the author of a number of archery magazine articles and the book Bows of theWorld (sold out). He is a retired professor of social and organizational psychology. He performs, trains, and promotes the discipline. gray@pathway.net

Erik Hildinger, Ann Arbor, Michigan. Lecturer at the University of Michigan. Erik is the author of Warriors of the Steppe: a Military History of Central Asia, 1996, and of Swords Against the Senate, 2003. A previous work is a translation from the Latin of Giovanni di Plano Carpini's The Story of the Mongols Whom We Call the Tartars. He was a practicing lawyer for many years. eshild@umich.edu

Dana Hotko, Milan, Indiana. Radiology tech. Dana is a dedicated and accomplished horseback archer and trainer. His horse experience is longstanding; he has bred, raised, and trained BLUE STAR Arabian horses for many years. Dana's training of other horseback archers is especially marked with patience and effectivness. ronin@seidata.com

Barb Leeson, Jarvis, Ontario. Barb is involved in medieval mounted arts. She has brought the same skill and devotion to performing and promoting horseback archery. Her technical and artistic bent has enabled her to launch Era Equestrian and the re-creation of Hungarian-style horseback archery saddles and accessories. era@look.ca

Holm Neumann, Bend, Oregon. Holm is an orthodepic surgeon and anthropologist. He has transferred his nationally recognized skills in

www.lrgaf.org

cowboy action shooting to the discipline of horseback archery. His ranch in Bend has become an attractive mounted archery training center in the northwest region of the States. He has distinguished himself by taking gold medals at the annual mounted archery competitions in Korea. He and his wife Susan import the coveted Marchador horses from Brazil. holmsusan@aol.com

Lukas Novotny, Liberty, North Carolina. Lukas is a full time bowyer and very successful trainer. He is a serious traveler and student of Asian archery and is the author of archery magazine articles. Lukas is a major world-wide performer, demonstrator and competitor. He also owns the Saluki Bow Company and makes some of the most refined and high performing modern interpretations of Asian bows. Lukas was raised in the former Czechoslovakia and was originally trained as a glass sculptor. info@salukibow.com

Murat Ozveri, Istanbul, Turkey. Murat is a Dentist and Peridontal Ph.D. Murat has worked systematically to collect and save knowledge of the rich Turkish archery tradition, and to coordinate enthusiasts. He has established the first modern archery team, and with others has founded the Society for Archery Research (OKADER). Murat gives archery lectures and demonstrations and is the author of a traditional archery book, Okculuk. mozveri@kemankes.com

Jay Red Hawk, Whitewood, South Dakota. Jay is a rare modern mounted buffalo hunter and thus an accomplished horseback archer in the Lakota Sioux tradition. He is also a bowyer and a key leader in the movement of Indian youth archery programs. Jay is an effective preservationist of Lakota Sioux culture, and champion of protecting and improving the quality of life among his people. cetanduta@yahoo.com

Ed Scott, Grants, New Mexico. Ed is a highly accomplished full time bowyer of primitive bows of all kinds, but especially those inspired by the southwestern United States. He has working experience in African countries and has lived in close contact with Native American tribes in Florida, Montana, and New Mexico. Ed unstintingly cooperates with American Indian workshops on Native bowmaking. 505-287-8134.

www.lrgaf.org

Stephen Selby, Hong Kong, China. Stephen has worked in Hong Kong for over 20 years. He holds an Honors MA from Edinburgh University in Chinese. He is the author of the scholarly Chinese Archery, 2000, and the highly illustrated Archery Traditions of Asia, 2003. He established the respected Asian Traditional Archery Network to exchange information and support the revival of the discipline. Stephen also currently practices horseback archery, trains others, and promotes that branch of the tradition. srselby@atarn.org

Pat Stoddard, Libby, Montana. Pat is a professional maker of outdoor gear. He is indefatigable in a daily regime of training himself in rapid mounted shooting with either hand and related martial arts. When not training himself, he is training others for horseback archery, training horses for mounted archery, and giving demonstrations at major venues such as the Denver Stock Show. He is part American Indian and has lived around the Blackfoot Indians for a long time. dogrt102@libby.org

Misa Tsuyoshi, Brookfield, Wisconsin. Misa is a superb and colorful practioner of Yabusame, one of the ancient Japanese horseback archery traditions. She has been trained under TAKEDARYU in Japan, which is responsible for maintaining the very traditional horseback archery during the past fifteen centuries. Even on a fast horse, her grace and skill are striking. Misa performs in authentic and dramatic ancient costume, and uses authentic ancient tack. misa_tsuyoshi@yahoo.co.jp

Table of Contents

Mounted Archery in the Americas

Page

Introduction: Uniting mind, body, horse, and bow - David Gray 7

Part I. Eurasian roots
Chapter 1
The Eurasian steppe: Nomadism and horse archery
Erik Hildinger 21
Chapter 2
Turkey and Persia
Murat Ozveri 35
Chapter 3
Japanese traditional horseback archery
Misa Tsuyoshi 57
Chapter 4
Horseback archery in China and Korea
Stephen Selby 78

Part II. American Indian roots
Chapter 5
Lakota Sioux
Jay Red Hawk 92
Chapter 6
Blackfoot and the northwest
Pat Stoddard 119
Chapter 7
Native American horse archery in the southwest
Ed Scott 128

Part III. The revival of mounted archery in the Americas
Chapter 8
Founding and growth
David Gray 175
Chapter 9
Training the horseback archer
Lukas Novotny and David Gray...198

Chapter 10
Horseback archery in South America
Holm Neumann and David Gray...213
Chapter 11
The bows for horseback archery
Lukas Novotny..221
Chapter 12
Horses in horseback archery in the Americas
Dana Hotko 233
Chapter 13
Tack for horseback archery
Barbara Leeson...241

Part IV. Associations and organizations
Chapter 14
The Mounted Archery Association of the Americas (MA3)
The Officers 257
Chapter 15
Horseback Archery World Association (HAWA) and Kassai USA
Todd Delle..265

www.lrgaf.org

Introduction

Uniting mind, body, horse, and bow

by David Gray

Why the revival of the ancient discipline of horseback archery, and why produce a book about it? One current equestrian offers a list of reasons for sports and games of all sorts; the list includes: tension, passion, joy, entertainment, aesthetics, and stimulation (Bjarke Rink, 2004). If I had to choose a master motive from that list, it would be stimulation. The need for stimulation of the human senses is basic, universal, and profound. One can trudge through a flat and unvaried atmosphere for a very long period of time, but a lack of variety and challenge eventually takes its toll by dulling the senses, the mind, and the human spirit.

The universal need for stimulation

Sensory deprivation experiments have been conducted to intentionally shut down the senses by severely depriving the participants of nearly all outside stimulation. After a luxurious opportunity of uninterrupted sleep and extended relaxation, people in the experiments started to feel anxious, disturbed, and even hallucinatory. For a brief period after the experiments, participants experienced mild cognitive deficits. For example, they made more mistakes on simple fifth-grade arithmetic problems than they would normally. Much more tragically, in the famous Lubiyanka underground prison in Moscow many prisoners placed in solitary confinement for long periods of time went insane. Stimulation is not a luxury, it is a necessity. It is a necessity for mental health, productive lives, and constructive societies. The universal need for stimulation is at least one reason why nearly all cultures have, and have had, forms of art, music, dance, and games. Persons or cultures deprived of these forms may actually be in danger of personal or national decline.

Many people in this age find themselves in inherently boring and non-stimulating situations. Some have to hold two low-level, tedious, brain numbing jobs just to make ends meet. Nor does this leave much time or energy to create a vital and stimulating family life. Child abuse and spousal abuse, or neglect all too often get woven into this scenario.

Boredom plays some role in many antisocial and destructive behaviors. Take for example a lack of purpose among our youth; it may be part of the catalyst in juvenile vandalism. Picture three or four kids walking home from a Friday night basketball game at their high school. They are marginal, disengaged kids with no commitment to sports, academics, music, or drama. They have made their eating stop and hangout at McDonald's. As they walk on toward home, still dissatisfied, bored and unfulfilled, one says "now what are we going to do?" Spotting a brick lying in the middle of the sidewalk, he picks it up and sails it through a window. The others join in; glass is cracking and smashing with thrilling sound effects. Adrenaline is flowing; they are finally effective and making their mark. Great excitement! As they run for home, police tires are squealing and sirens are screaming. They are delivered from their boredom.

Gang formation, some types of adult crime, and even warfare may be partially triggered and maintained by boredom and purposelessness. There is an exciting side to war which delivers one from boredom and routine. I remember as a child during the Second World War rushing to see huge headlines in the evening newspapers about a successful invasion of our troops, or crowding around the radio with the family to get the latest news flashes. Air raid practices with screaming sirens and imposed blackout conditions in our community were exciting to me as a child. There were watch towers on the hills with 24-hour binocular surveillance for enemy planes. It was exciting, anything but boring. These feelings were intense for our family because my oldest brother was in combat on a PT boat in the Pacific Theatre. Soldiers may experience times of tedium, routine, and boredom outside combat, but if war was overwhelmingly and consistently boring for all parties at all levels of command, there would probably be fewer wars. Many war movies are smash hits because the mixture of intrigue, tension, death and bravery are intensely stimulating, and unfortunately glamorized.

www.lrgaf.org

Aesthetic stimulation, a unity of physical and mental

I will not argue that horseback archery offers more stimulation than the major American sports, but I will argue how it is different and how its stirs the human spirit in unique and very far reaching ways. Let us start with aesthetics. The horse has been seen and celebrated for centuries as a creature of exceptional beauty, whether standing still or in full action. It is one of the fastest, strongest, most graceful, spirited, and agile living art forms. This celebration of beauty has been widespread through most all cultures and far back into antiquity. As moderns we often think the ancients were aesthetic clods, but nothing could be further from the truth. Careful adornment and decoration of humans and animals has received full attention from very ancient times. The Scythians, maligned by moderns until recently, had sophisticated gold plaques and vases with realistic and beautifully executed scenes, as well as semi-abstract and stylized subjects. They dressed their horses in extravagant and brilliant red, gold, and blue cloth adornments (Rolle, 1980).

In hard times the horse was eclipsed by survival needs and the regal creature came through only as a beast of burden. In better times, the eclipse passes and there streams the proud head held high, and flairing tail, in full gallop. For one of the really great records of this widespread celebration of the horse feast your eyes on the pages of *Man and Horse, An Enduring Bond* by Fulvio Cinquini, a life-long horse photographer capturing images and lore from around the world. The horse has been an exquisite subject of the great painters and sculptors whose renderings have arrested our gaze. But these masterpieces fade into dimness beside the living, breathing form in motion.

The bow can also be a striking form of sculpture. Elegance and refinement of line and ornamentation are written all over bows such as Persian and Turkish horn bows of a century or two ago. And like the horse, it is sculpture that comes to life in beautiful dynamic action. What other piece of traditional sculpture builds and stores large amounts of kinetic energy, and then releases it in silky smooth fashion?

The game is to join the human, the horse and the bow in a seamless Centaur. The mounted archer has his or her full burning concentration on the bulls-eye of the targets from the beginning of the course to the very end. The rest of the world is shut out. The arrows must be nocked onto the bow string on a running horse in a second or two without the luxury of looking. The horse must be trained to canter the course at a steady rate without any rein control. Subconsciously, the rider may give the horse some leg cues while total concentration is being given to the shooting. A trusting cooperative partnership must be established between the horse and the rider. This is especially critical in the backward or parting shot when one mis-step by the horse could result in serious injury to the rider. Uniting the human with the horse involves complex physical cues in order to communicate with the horse, but much of the communication is more subtle, nuanced, feeling oriented, and largely mental. For this reason, and many others, we consider mounted archery a martial art similar to the Japanese approach to archery called Kyudo.

The beauty of games is often most intense in high speed and risky maneuvers. All in all, mounted archery is a relatively safe equestrian sport, and is safe compared to many other sports as well. To be sure, any time one is around horses there will be some injuries. Even on the most highly trained, gentled, and trusting animal, the age old and highly developed emotional defenses of fear and flight can be set off by a simple misperceived object. Or more simply, horses stumble, fall, kick at flies, etc. It is most interesting that any sport and many performing arts involve rapid interaction with other performers, animals, mechanical devices, or the physical environment. The beauty is often most salient in the high risk interactions.

Football may be wrongly dismissed by some as merely a macho game, but one often hears the spectator say "that was a beautiful play." A long forceful but graceful pass perfectly timed and precisely guided to the receiver 30 yards downfield and skillfully caught by the intended receiver, running at top speed, between two defenders about to hit the receiver hard from both sides is a high risk picture, and it is beautiful. You can take your own favorite sport or performing art and paint your own scenario of how high-risk action and beauty are organically linked — figure skating, baseball, ballet, soccer, and on and on. The stimulation from the action of mounted archery is centered in the unique and beautiful dynamic that unites human, horse, and bow. This dynamic fires the passion of the horseback archer, and the spectator as well.

www.lrgaf.org

Inspiration for the story of the discipline

Ideas for this book have been simmering in my mind and imagination for a long time, but there was one last minute surprising excitement. As we started to approach publishers, Lukas Novotny said he knew a group which would definitely be interested — The Long Rider's Guild Press. I started to correspond with the head of this amazing and unusual publisher. CuChullaine O'Reilly was not only open to the idea of our book, he was ecstatic because he sensed the excitement and challenge of the discipline immediately. That enthusiasm for our project, coupled with cutting edge electronic publishing on demand and the relative ease of publication that this technique entails, led to a formal contract.

How could CuChullaine respond so positively and so quickly? What prepared him to be instantly receptive? He is a journalist turned equestrian, a convert to Islam, and familiar with parts of the Islamic world. He is one of the Long Riders celebrated in one of the many books which are the specialty of the Long Rider's Guild Press. In the early 1980s when Russia was at war in Afghanistan, and a life was of little value on the Pakistani northwest Peshawar region, he set off on a thousand-mile long ride. His book cover says, "His mission was to ride over some of the world's highest mountain ranges, thread his way back through untamed tribes, and miraculously get back to war-torn Peshwar." He ate luke-warm goat fat, drank sullied ditch water, was kidnapped, tortured, and was imprisoned in an infamous Pakistani prison. His horse died and was eaten by hungry tribesmen. Against all odds and every life threatening danger, he found another horse and journeyed on and on, and finally completed his course. This long-ride story is told in his book Khyber Knights. The book was written from his travel notes, maps, and journals. It contains a unique collection of eye-witness descriptions of life in Pakistan's northwest frontier Province of Peshawar.

As though that were not enough, his wife Basha, accomplished equestrian, a publishing partner, mother, and writer, completed a 2,500 mile ride from Russia to London. Her Cossack stallion, Count Pompeii, carried her the whole distance, meeting many unanticipated barriers and problems and she and her horse solved them all along the way. Basha tells her story in Count Pompeii which is designed for pre-teen readers, but is a great adult book as well. Basha edits other children's books in the Little Long Riders Series. Basha and CuChullaine have recharged my spirit of adventure, and have confirmed the importance of launching this book on <u>Mounted Archery in the Americas.</u>

The long-term inspiration to promote mounted archery comes from one man in Hungary. He started all alone with occasional encouragement from some friends. He had loved the bow for a long time but he was not a horseman. His first horse was a sick and unpromising animal. He nursed his horse back to health, became emotionally connected, but was not well connected to its back. He fell off many times. After several years of lonely struggle he became a rider and eventually a mounted archer. He played a crucial role in recreating and disseminating the ancient Magyar bow. He went on to capture the attention of his countrymen, all of Europe, and much of the world. Kassai's love of his ancient roots in the Scythians, Huns, Avars, and Magyars, and his vision to recapture this heritage in a modern standardized competitive discipline have drawn many including myself to visit his enchanted archery valley and see his achievements. The narrative of his role in planting the sport in the United States is set forth in the chapter on Founding and Growth. We salute you Kassai Lajos for your pioneering adventure and for the endless inspiration you provide. His book, <u>Horseback Archery</u>, is yet another delightful way that he shares with us the adventure he has been pursuing.

The story of this book is a narrative of reviving the ancient practice of mounted archery in the Americas. But the story first needs to backtrack to its ancient roots to see the places of its origin, and to appreciate the proportions of our inheritance.

A colossal inheritance from Eurasia

Genghis Khan's Mongol horseback archers who thundered across the great steppes to shake Europe in its boots and set up one of the largest kingdoms of all time nevertheless left little physical legacy. No cathedrals, no castles, no viaducts or paved roads, and certainly none of us have ever inherited a billion dollar estate from a rich Uncle in Ulan Batar, Mongolia's capital city. In fact modern historians until the last two decades would have us believe that the Mongols and the hordes preceding them in the westward migrations and conquests were all barbaric savages and scarcely within the human race. There is nothing of value that they contributed for our inheritance, only mass butchery, terror, and devastation. Gradually the fog of our western bias and ignorance has been clearing away. The discovery of sources such as The Secret History of the Mongols, and other original research on the horse tribes of the steppes reveals a very different picture.

The truth of the matter seems to be that the general conquest strategy of the Mongols was to send advanced emissaries into a new town and impose taxes and conscript slaves and skilled craftsmen. If the town complied and avoided later betrayal, the town was spared. No one was forced to accept a strange ideology, religion, or ritual. If they did not comply, or later showed betrayal, the town was swiftly obliterated in its entirety. The rich cultural inheritance that the Mongols did leave to us is a surprisingly advanced set of social principles and organizational insights. Genghis and his sons and grandsons took big strides in replacing autocracy and inherited tribal status with open advancement by merit — that is demonstrating intelligence and exceptional skills. So this is the part of the larger and attractive social context within which our mounted archery inheritance comes to us. This kind of revolutionary and democratic-like thinking was unfolding when Europe was still well locked into rule by inheritance, and fiat; and social mobility was not within the dimmest reaches of western European mentality.

There is also something profound here about identity. Many of us want to know our genealogies as far back as possible. Adoptees often struggle valiantly to find their biological parents. We do not want to be constricted to creatures who just appear, live, and die. We yearn to be bigger, to be more lasting with continuity, community, and connections, and thus more significant and stimulated rather than diminished. The value of being strongly connected to family, tribe, nation, and nations is hard to overestimate.

But our inheritance goes well back and beyond the times of the Mongols in the 1200's to the Magyars, the Avars, the Huns, the Scythians around the time of Christ, and several centuries before that. The better we make these connections, the more enrichment we extract from our ancient roots.

Well before 6,000 years ago truly wild horses were plentiful on the great plains of Eurasia that we call the steppe. They were trapped and driven over cliffs to be killed for food, clothing, shelter, and bone-based tools. Later, they were domesticated enough to be herded, milked, and more readily slaughtered, or used as beasts of burden. Then 5,000 or so years ago some brave souls mounted them and the domestication became more complete. It is believed by some that because the people of the steppes lived with the wild horses and observed them daily first in the wild then in captivity that they have been some of the greatest equestrians ever. They mastered the horse, but they did it by riding in sync with the flow of the horse. They were great equestrians because they knew the power of working with the horse, and had a keen savvy of tapping into their natural herd behaviors.

It would be difficult for any one writer to cover the broad scope of this book. Erik Hildinger, an historian and experienced writer, tells the expanded story of these steppe people, their culture, achievements, evolution, and migrations to the west. Murat Ozveri, from Istanbul, leads us through the contributions of the Persians and Turks. Although equipment, including the horse bow, appears toward the latter part of the book, we will sketch an introduction here because of its origins in the steppe and related deserts. The bow in probably all cultures started with a simple straight one-piece stick of wood and gradually progressed to being composed of several materials and in very sophisticated shapes and designs. People like Adam Karpowitz, Kassai Lajos, Lukas Novotny and others have done extensive research internationally on these highly developed composite bows. This research has been tested in many replicas he has made patterned after the bows of the western steppe and desert tribes. These are truly horn bows and may take a couple of years to make—multiple pieces of wood forming the core, buffalo horn on the belly, sinew on the back, and the lever-like siyahs on the ends of the limbs.

Excitement from China, Japan, and Korea

Beyond the eastern edges of the steppes Japan and Korea have given us a rich treasure of horseback archery which is relatively newer than that of the steppes. The fully developed bows and the horseback archery cultures of the steppes reach back at least a millennium before the time of Christ, whereas the Japanese and Korean horseback archery disciplines in their present non-war oriented form may only be calculated to be five or so centuries old; however a big difference is that they have been in continuous practice all that time up to today as martial arts whereas mounted archery disappeared from the steppes in any form a century or so ago depending on the area.

The Japanese martial art of Yabusame is incredibly colorful and dramatic. If people speculate that it would have been impossible for the English to use their longbows on horseback, how is it possible that the Japanese could be so skillful with their great Yumi bows which tend to be about a foot and a half longer than the English longbow? The highly asymmetrical bow with the radically shorter bottom may alleviate the length problem somewhat. But any way one cuts it, the Yumi in and of itself is high drama. Added to that towering bow is elaborate costuming and highly adorned saddles and harness. Misa Tsuyoshi is a superb performer even on a fast and spirited horse, and she authors the unique Japanese chapter. The Korean style is a little more subdued in appearance and their bow is small, shaped somewhat like the Persian bows, and used on standard ground ranges of over 150 meters. Their great mounted archery tradition lives on today in international competitions in their homeland. Several North American performers have competed in Korea for the last several years. Stephen Selby is steeped in all things Asian and gives a fine account of the Chinese and Korean mounted archery history and current practice of mounted archery.

The horse archery culture of the American Indians

Several chapters are devoted to the fascinating horseback archery culture of the North America Indians. Jay Red Hawk, a Lakota Sioux from South Dakota, covers that part of the country, Pat Stoddard from Montana looks at the Blackfoot contribution, and Ed Scott from New Mexico discusses the Apache and other tribes from the southwest. These are all authors with wide experience, either Native Americans themselves, or archers who have lived closely with Indian cultures from childhood. Jay and Pat are accomplished horseback archers, and the third author, Ed Scott, is a highly respected bowyer, especially of southwest ground and horsebows.

These archery traditions rose to a great pinnacle of development relatively rapidly with the coming of the Spanish horse in the southwest in the 1500s, but unfortunately basically disappeared with the passing of the buffalo in the late 1800s. The specially trained buffalo pony, the unsurpassed equestrian skill of the rider/archer, the spiritual nature of the buffalo and all the ritual and culture encompassing it has captured the imagination not just of North America but rivets people's attention around the world to this very day via special magazines and international organizations. The paintings of Bodmer, Caitlin, Russell, and many others of the Buffalo hunt hanging on our walls will forever remind us of adventure and downright pandemonium.

Most fortunately, these horseback archery cultures are currently being revived. We are very happy to have these authentic accounts of the past glories of American Indian milestones as well as the emergent revivals.

The big revival in the Americas

In 1998 the standardized discipline of horseback archery founded by Kassai Lajos was brought to the States for the first time. David Gray was instrumental in that move and writes the story of the founding and growth of the discipline to date. Lukas Novotny who trained under the master Kassai eventually emerged as one of the lead performers and trainers in the United States, and internationally. Thus a chapter by Lukas (with David Gray) on the basic elements of training for horseback archery.

The pivotal role of the International Horse Archery Festival (IHAF) in Fort Dodge, Iowa must be fully acknowledged and is described in the chapter on founding and growth. The Festival has strong name recognition and is known and appreciated internationally.

In the last two years, a nice breakthrough into South America has occurred. Holm Neumann, a surgeon and our leading mounted archer from Oregon has taken small groups to Brazil to a major horse center there to introduce the discipline to that country. Holm and his wife have the Brazilian contact by importing the wonderful gaited Marchador horse which is the national horse of Brazil. This Brazilian center is world renowned and is deeply committed to planting the

www.lrgaf.org

discipline in that country. Holm takes the lead in writing this special chapter.

Horses and equipment

One could not have a book on horseback archery without a special treatment of the topics of the horse and tack. As we all know volumes have been written from time immemorial about the horse, but very little has been written about the horse in horseback archery. Dana Hotko has bred, raised, and trained BLUE STAR Line Arabs most of his life and currently uses his Arab, Murphy, in serious horseback archery. He not only tells us about the appropriate use of the Arab breed but of other breeds and will include his criteria of necessary natural characteristics in selecting a horse. He lays out the rudiments of training of the horse for mounted archery.

We have already briefly described the composite bow in the introduction regarding the steppe because of its origin there. Lukas Novotny's extensive research and pioneering work in re-creating the ancient horn bows and designing creative modern versions enable him to bring us a superb chapter on the composite and modern horseback archery bows. Saddles, bits, bridles, auxiliary harness and adornments deserve a space of their own. Barb Leeson, a medieval mounted arts specialist from Ontario traces the evolution of tack for mounted archery up to and including pieces used by mounted archers today. She not only has a great love for playing detective in order to get back to origins of saddle trees, stirrups, and bits, but she is a skilled mounted archery saddle maker.

A couple of shorter chapters on newly formed archery associations will close the book. These associations are designed to educate the public, promote the discipline, and expand the performing core of mounted archers in the Americas. The Mounted Archery Association of the Americas (MA3) is described by the officers, and Kassai's outreach in the United States (Kassai USA) is explained by Todd Delle. Todd is Kassai's official representative in the States.

A final reason for the book and the revival of the discipline is that it has rich potential to help build inner character. In all times and cultures, the negative human characteristics are usually plentiful—greed, jealousy, impatience, aggression, deception, and the worst kinds of competition and desire to impugn and destroy the other person or group. All the martial arts, in their purer forms, celebrate non-aggression and restraint based on inner strength and spirit. Force is reserved for self-defense. The following statement of personal development is taken from the Mounted Archery Association of the Americas.

Mounted Archery as a Martial Art
Discipline and Personal Development

Similar to Kyudo, Yabusami, and Korean Archery traditions, the western discipline of mounted archery strives for <u>grace</u>, <u>accuracy</u>, and <u>character development</u>. Western sports generally celebrate grace and accuracy, but character development tends to be somewhat less emphasized.

Mounted archery calls for personal characteristics often referred to as "soft" and "hard," the yin and the yang, and a productive balance between the two. The "hard" characteristics of the discipline include things such as healthy ambition, courage, assertiveness, persistence, very hard work, and seeking continual improvement and striving toward perfection.

The "soft" characteristics involve such things as restraint, gentleness, humility, patience, cooperation, and a spirit of giving. What does it mean to pursue the hard and the soft with vigor but to keep the two in balance in the best of martial arts mentalities?

The "hard" guidelines lead the archer to expect every shot to be perfect, to have the imagery and expectation that the target will suck the arrow into the heart of the bull's eye. The archer works for a lifetime in perfecting form and performance. Each shot that fails instructs about accuracy as well as one's character. We learn to do things better, but we forget the bad shot and totally forgive ourselves as we approach the next shot which we expect to be perfect. The hard competition is with ourselves.

The "soft" aspects of cooperation are with each other. We support, give feedback tactfully, and encourage others. It is said that some of the Korean archery groups chant "A very good shot!" after each of their long 145 meter shots is taken. So part of our task in our formal mounted archery competitions is to help other archers to do their very

www.lrgaf.org

best always. We are not trying to suppress or beat their score, we are thinking of all we can do to improve all contestants. We are only competing against ourselves. Thus the hard and the soft are in balance, and an attractive personality is being fostered.

In other words, there is no place for winning and losing, dominating, attitudes of superiority or supremacy, or arrogance. Never do we wish the other archer to do poorly, and never do we do anything to diminish the other's performance. Rather an archer strives towards higher self goals — to be more graceful and consistent, or to pursue the next higher level of performance. At the same time we work just as hard to share our knowledge and support others toward an enhanced performance and an enriched character.

The character of the ever maturing archer will also show up in his or her relationship with the horse. In training and caring for one's horse, the spirit of cooperation and respect are essential in mounted archery. We should embrace the lifetime challenge of understanding and communicating with the horse in the very best, humane, and timeless traditions.

****

References:

Cinquini, Fulvio. 2003. Man and Horse: An Enduring Bond. San Francisco: Chronicle Books.

Kassai, Lajos. 2002. Horseback Archery. Budapest: Puski Kiado, kft.

O'Reilly, Basha. 2006. Count Pompeii. The Long Rider's Guild Press.

O'Reilly, CuChullaine. 1999. Khyber Knights. The Long Rider's Guild Press.

Rink, Bjarke. 2004. The Centaur Legacy: How Equine Speed and Human Intelligence Shaped the Course of History. The Long Rider's Guild Press.

Rolle, Renate. 1980. The World of the Scythians. Berkely: University of California Press.

www.lrgaf.org

Chapter 1

The Eurasian Steppe: Nomadism and Horse Archery

by Erik Hildinger

Horse archery, with its origins and history, makes an immense topic; though it has been treated in detail in other books, only the broadest remarks can be made here. Still, they should be enough to give interested readers or horse archery enthusiasts enough context to understand the Eurasian origins of their sport.

Nomadic horse archers

Horse archery, as its name implies, arose when men had mastered two things: the riding of horses and the manufacture of bows. The domestication of the horse for food began on the steppes and was followed by its training in order to pull chariots: chariot-borne archers formed the mainstay of middle-eastern armies until the end of the first millennium BC. Some time during the second millennium the horse was actually ridden, and it was natural that the rider would use the bow just as the elite chariot warriors did. He had advantages over the charioteer, however: he could operate in rougher terrain, he didn't depend on a delicate chariot (itself the expensive product of an elaborate palace economy), and the injury of one animal didn't immobilize him as it did a chariot-warrior with his pair of horses.

The riding of horses made nomadic life on the steppes of Asia possible and practical. Men could cover great distances quickly, and they could manage large herds of animals. More precisely, they could now practice nomadism: the shuttling between two large areas of pasture, often hundreds of miles apart, depending upon the season. In the winter, herds could be moved south, and in the summer north, where the cooler temperatures allowed the growth of enough food for the animals. Nomadism, in other words, is not senseless wandering about: it is the regular movement between two areas each of which is suited at different times of year to the raising of animals.

dates back to the Neolithic. However, some time during the second millennium both in the Near East and the Far East it was discovered that a better bow could be made if different parts of it were made of different materials. Whereas a simple self-bow is made of a single stave of wood, a composite bow is made of wood, horn and sinew. The core of the bow is made of wood, and then strips or plates of horn are glued against the belly of the bow (that part which faces the archer when he shoots). Sinew, usually from cattle, is glued along the back of the bow (that part turned away from the archer when he shoots.)

This combination produces a much more efficient bow than the simple self-bow. The horn can stand much more compression than wood, and the sinew can stand much more tension. This means the bow can be smaller and lighter than a self-bow, and its manufacture results in a recurved shape which permits a smoother draw. These facts mean that it can cast an arrow further with a given draw weight, and minor differences in draw length don't result in marked differences in arrow speed and, hence, accuracy. Although phenomenal and often imaginary distances are attributed to these bows, they had an effective range of about 60 to 80 meters and a maximum range of about several hundred meters. Shooting at opponents from the saddle with any accuracy would, of course, have taken place at much closer ranges, probably 10 to 20 meters if the experience of expert modern horse archers is any indication.

Different nomadic peoples used bows of different shapes, though all were recurved. Scythians used the classic "Cupid's bow" which passed through Greek art to us. Huns used asymmetric bows with the lower limb somewhat shorter than the upper. Tatar bows were quite large, and Turkish bows of the 16th and 17th centuries were some of the most graceful and efficient.

Other horse archers

All of this might suggest that horse archery was limited to nomadic people. This is untrue, though they were its best and most common practitioners. The ancient Persians, whose ancestors must have come off the steppe, were also horse-archers. The elite of the Persian army which the Greeks faced at Marathon and Platea, were the horse-archers posted on the Persian wings, ready to sweep forward and disrupt the Greek charge. Terrain, timing and the disconcerting Greek habit of fighting face-to-face in heavy armor, undid the Persians. A hundred years later Alexander the Great met and defeated the Persians with his combined-forces army of disciplined infantry and cavalry, but all the same he enrolled horse-archers in his army as he proceeded with his conquests.

By about 250 BC, the Parthians, once a subject people of the Persians, came down from the steppe, and established an empire on former Persian territory, and its main strength was mounted archers, though the nobility were heavily equipped with armor and lances. They destroyed a Roman army on a plain near Carrhae in 54 BC.

The Romans, always willing to adopt military innovations from their enemies, began to turn to horse-archery during the latter days of empire. A hundred years of dealing with Huns and with the revived Persian Empire of the Sassanids convinced them of their value, particularly in the east. As a result, by the fifth century AD many of the Roman cavalry were mounted archers and this tradition continued in the East Roman or Byzantine Army for centuries. The small but highly successful sixth century armies of the Emperor Justinian which took North Africa and Italy back from German invaders were well-equipped, armored cavalry using both lance and bow.

Similarly, mediaeval Muslim states such as Egypt and Syria established corps of mamluks, or slave soldiers, trained in horse-archery, and these formed the elite of their armies. The slaves were bought as boys, first from the steppes and later from Circassia, and then formally trained in the arts of horsemanship and archery. Using these skills, Egyptian mamluks under their general Baybars defeated Mongol invaders in 1260; this was the first significant defeat the Mongols had suffered since their rise to prominence some fifty years before. Here were sedentary people facing a nomad army and fighting fire with fire.

And the Russians must not be forgotten either. They suffered the Tatar Yoke for two hundred and fifty years. As subjects of the Mongols (whom they called "Tatars") for so long, both subject to their military incursions and forced to join their armies in support of the campaigns of the Golden Horde, the Russian armies changed from sword and axe wielding infantry forces on the Viking model, to pony-riding mounted archers in conical helmets, quilted coats and pointed boots. When the Russians faced down the Tatars along the banks of the Kalka River in 1480 the two armies resembled each other closely in composition, equipment and tactics.

Scythians, Parthians against major powers

Nonetheless, horse-archery is the hallmark of the steppe nomad, and those interested in the history of this activity naturally turn to him. The earliest of those that we know about appear briefly in the work of Herodotus, a fifth century Greek, and the first true historian. He mentions the Cimmerians, but they are a dim people and we aren't told much about them. On the principle that all steppe nomads are much alike we can guess that their culture was of the sort common to those who followed them: trekking between different pasturage at different seasons, living in mobile encampments and fighting on horseback with the bow. We know little more than that they lived on the steppe about the Black Sea and were troublesome to their neighbors.

The Cimmerians were followed and displaced, however, by a people that we do know about: the Scythians. They made their home on the Black Sea steppe and were famous for their archery. Athens, in fact, hired them, particularly during the sixth century, as mercenary archers and, oddly perhaps, as police. They appear on Greek vases of the period, often peeping out between heavily armored Greek foot soldiers, drawing their bows at the enemy. They must have shot a few arrows and then slipped back through the ranks as the battle was joined in earnest. These illustrations show them clearly in their national costume: the pointed Phrygian cap with flaps over the cheeks and neck, and a snug long-sleeved tunic. The men wore beards and long hair.

Other vases show the rest of their costume: trousers, short capes and tall boots, all boldly patterned and doubtless brightly colored. Herodotus mentions less appealing equipment: horse trappings decorated with their enemies' scalps. They were also known to make goblets from their enemies' skulls, a custom found centuries later among the Bulgars.

The Scythian often carried his bow in a case at his right hip. It was a large affair known as a *gorytus* that held both his bow and a large clutch of small arrows. A particularly fine example of one, covered in gold, was found in the tomb of Phillip II of Macedonia, father of Alexander the Great; it was no doubt a diplomatic gift from a Scythian tribe.

Although Scythians are typically shown in Greek art shooting the bow, they might use other weapons as well, such as their peculiar battle-axe, the *sagaris*, which had its blade mounted transversely across the haft, like that of a modern ice-axe, or the *akinakes*, a short, often curved, sword. The common Scythian did not wear armor, though a noble might; grave finds of scale armor have been turned up. The Scythians also used round or oblong shields of wickerwork and fought with lances.

The Scythians were not a Turkic people, as were so many nomads. Instead they were of Indo-Iranian extraction like the Persians and like the Sarmatians, another steppe people with whom they would struggle for the steppe for some centuries before being displaced.

This linguistic affinity did not necessarily lead to peaceful relations with the Persians. While some Scythians were subjects of the Persian Empire, others were free, and in the early sixth century the Great King Darius (known better for his unsuccessful attempt to bring the Greeks to heel at Marathon) went into the steppe to punish them. His army chased them about the steppe unsuccessfully, never able to bring its strength to bear on them. For their part, the Scythians contented themselves with attacking Persian foraging parties and sending them to the protection of the Persian infantry with which they wouldn't fight. As a stratagem the Scythians would retreat across the steppe, sometimes leaving a few cattle behind for foraging parties to seize, all in the hope of drawing the Persians deeper into the steppe where, far from their supplies, an opportunity might arise to destroy them.

Although Darius may have shown poor judgement in attempting an expedition against these people with whom he couldn't close, he did realize in time the danger of his situation and retired back across the Danube and into this dominions without losing his army.

Alexander the Great conquered the Persian Empire after a series of remarkable battles and, upon his death in 323 BC, his empire was shared out among his generals. The eastern satrapies of Persia, includeing Parthia, fell to Seleucus. The Parthians, cousins of the Persians from off the steppe, were to seize power from the Seleucids in about 250 BC and establish the Parthian Empire, a state that would contend with the Roman Empire for centuries. In spite of their nomadic origins, however, it was a settled state with its capital at Ctesiphon. Their army, however, betrayed their nomadic origins: mounted archers, well-suited to the terrain and famous for the "Parthian shot", taken by the archer over the back of his horse at a pursuer.

Nomads were creatures of the steppe, or the east, and for centuries, even as Rome's ambit grew, it had little business with them and little to fear from them.

Rome had fought barbarians of one stripe or another since the late fourth century BC: Gauls, Germans, Britons, Dacians and so on. By the fourth century AD, however, a change was coming. Throughout her history most of Rome's enemies had fielded predominantly infantry forces, and none could match her infantry. Even enemies such as the Goths, who did fight on horseback with lance and sword, could be met effectively by balanced Roman forces of infantry and cavalry. But by the late 300s it had become apparent that Goths trying to enter the empire were doing so to seek refuge from a people they dreaded: the Huns.

The Huns

The Huns were illiterate and no trace of their language remains. Furthermore, they had the habit of giving their children Germanic or Sarmatian names from the Goths and Alans who were their subjects and in a higher state of culture. What Hunnic names we have were forced into Latin or Greek forms with grammatical endings that obscure them, thus even their names don't give their language away. Still, it was likely they were Turkic.

They were certainly Asian and so differed in appearance from earlier steppe people who had come west, and they were primitive and tough in the extreme. They terrified the west: the name of their most famous king, Attila, is still a byword for destruction. These people came into the Hungarian plain, in its way the westernmost extension of the Asian steppe, and made it their home. On the way there they put a number of people under subjection, most significantly the Germanic Ostrogoths, the Gepids and the Alans of Sarmatian origin, and this swelled their numbers. It was the usual steppe approach: subdue a people and make them a subordinate and fighting part of the community.

The Hun way of life was like that of other nomads; not much need be said about it. From the standpoint of the Romans, what was significant was their military prowess: as light cavalry they moved fast, and their men and horses were extremely tough. They fought with the bow, of course, and with a light lance and round shield. They used swords if they could get them, and were known to use the lasso in battle.

Like all ancient nomads on the borders of a settled people, they raided or threatened raids for economic gain, and a clear indication of this is Attila's demand, as a condition of peace with the Empire, not only of a heavy tribute in gold, but also the maintenance of a market along the border between their domains. Neither is particularly a surprise because nomads, for all their toughness and aptitude for survival on the steppe, still need some of the products of the civilized world, such as agricultural products and easy access to metals. What this meant for a civilized people with nomads on their borders was a constant threat, either minor or major depending on how unified the nomads were.

www.lrgaf.org

The Huns lived along the borders of the Roman Empire for about a hundred years, alternately raiding or serving the Empire. For example, the Emperor Theodosius I used Hun mercenaries to defeat a usurper from the western provinces in civil war in 394. The Roman general Flavius Aetius hired troops of them decades later in connection with another civil struggle and used them extensively to fight Burgundians and Visigoths and to maintain order in Gaul.

Rome, however, found things going less her way with the accession of Attila to power in the mid fifth century. Before that time the Huns had not been very united, though many of them had been the subjects of a king named Rugilas or Ruas, whose nephews Attila and his brother Bleda were. Upon the death of their uncle the two brothers divided the people among them and ruled together for a while. Shortly, however, Attila killed Bleda and assumed sole kingship in 443 or 444 AD. With this unified base Attila was in a position to seriously trouble Rome for a decade.

During his reign Attila raided the Empire and extorted gold on a large scale until, in 450 Marcian, the Eastern Emperor (the Empire was at this time had two capitals and two emperors, one in Ravenna and one at Constantinople), declined to pay the tribute. In 451 Attila descended upon the western half of the Empire with a view to devastating Gaul. On April 7 of that year he destroyed Metz and proceeded west toward Orleans. Flavius Aetius marched north out of Italy to meet him with a small Roman army made up of barbarian auxiliaries and, doubtless, of his own personal troops.

When he reached Gaul, Aetius joined forces with his ally Theodoric, king of the Visigoths, whom the Romans had allowed to settle around Toulouse and establish a kingdom there. The combined Roman-Visigothic army advanced on the Huns, who abandoned their siege of Orleans and withdrew east. On the plains near Troyes the two armies met in June of 451 and fought what is generally known as the Battle of the Mauriac Plains or, sometimes, the Battle of Chalôns-sur-Marne.

The Romans took up position on the left wing, the Visigoths on the right. In the center was a force of Alans under their king Sangibanus. Though nominally Roman allies detailed to protect the city of Orleans, Aetius did not trust them entirely and so put them where he reckoned they would have to fight. The battle was hard-fought and, at the end of it, Attila retreated to the protection of the waggon-laager which served as his camp and fortress on campaign. There he prepared to commit suicide if his enemies should succeed in breaching this defense. In the end, Aetius decided not to attack. Instead, he decided to let the Huns slip away home. This may seem an odd decision, but he almost certainly had decided that he might need the Huns as allies once again in order to keep the Visigoths obedient in Gaul. Roman power was no longer overwhelming, and he needed one barbarian to play off against another.

Attila, stopped and with his prestige badly damaged, returned to his home in Hungary from which he planned another invasion for the following year, this time of Italy itself. He passed into northern Italy, destroyed the city of Aquileia and was met by an embassy which included the Pope. A treaty was made, money promised, and Attila returned home once again, his decision to do so doubtless influenced by the Eastern Emperor Marcian's plan to send an army against him. The next year, 453, Attila died after marrying a German princess; the usual fate awaited his nomadic state: dissolution.

The Huns were divided like property between several of his sons, but within a year their Germanic subjects had revolted and defeated their former masters in battle and the Huns practically disappear from history.

Avars, Bulgars, and Magyars

Their place was quickly taken by another steppe tribe which was to harass Europe and the Eastern Roman Empire: the Avars. These people were much like the Huns and were made up of two main tribes, the Var and the Hunni, the latter of whom may have been Hunnic. They had the boldness to attack the city of Constantinople on two occasions: in 626 and 762, though with no great success. They were finally brought to heel by Charlemagne in 796 when his army, under his son Pepin, attacked and sacked the Avar capital, a large permanent encampment on the Hungarian Plain known as The Ring.

Although the Bulgars were the next to come off the steppe and establish themselves in Europe, they converted to Christianity and were absorbed by the local Slavs. Before this happened, they raided Byzantine territory and even managed to kill the Emperor Nicephorus, who was on a campaign against them. However, they were quickly overshadowed by a much larger threat, the Magyars.

The Magyars now settled themselves in Hungary and were, in fact, the ancestors of the modern Hungarians. Between 899 and 954 they raided France and Northern Italy on a huge scale. The German King Otto I defeated them decisively at the Battle of the Lechfeld in 955 and ended their raiding. They subsequently became Christian and settled down as a part of Europe.

www.lrgaf.org

The Mongols

Though western armies next met mounted-archer armies when they faced Seljuk Turks during the Crusades, Europe's greatest danger lay in the future: the Mongols. A minor steppe tribe related to the Naimans, Tatars and Merkits, their territory lay in what is now Russia and China. Their prominence was due to the rise of one Temujin who united the Mongol peoples and their Turkic neighbors, ruling over them as Chinggis Khan.

Temujin was born about 1160 to a Mongol chief of the Borjin clan named Yesugei. While Temujin was still young, Yesugei was murdered by Tatars (a people whom he had previously fought), and Temujin watched his father's followers drift away now that they no longer had a strong chief to lead them. At this point Temujin's life became hard and precarious. The immediate family stayed together and survived as best it could through hunting and fishing.

Over time, however, Temujin was able to attract followers, claim Borte, the bride his father had chosen for him and put himself in the service of Toghrul, Chief of the Keraits, with whom his father had been associated. He was beginning to rise.

At this juncture Temujin's new wife Borte was snatched by raiding Merkits in revenge for his father's seizure of Temujin's mother years before. She had been slated to marry a Merkit before she was seized by the Mongol chief. Toghrul, in order to aid Temujin, ordered another of his followers, Jamuka, the young Khan of the Jadarats, to help him. Together the young men rescued Borte. As a result the two became very close, though they were eventually to fall out, probably because Temujin was willing to take anyone competent into his service, while Jamuka felt that close followers should be noble, like themselves.

Temujin was astute in choosing his followers this way; not only were they chosen for competence, they depended upon him for their place precisely because they were not nobles with their own independent followings. This meant that as Temujin rose, he was not as subject to the wishes of powerful men around him as he would have been had his father died later and left him surrounded by powerful, relatively independent, supporters.

Years of fighting followed, and a good deal of it is unclear. In much of it Temujin was successful, though he seems at one point to have taken refuge in China for about a decade. In the end, however, due to the force of his personality and general military success, he was able, in 1206, to make himself "Khan of All Who Live in Felt Tents", the effective ruler of all Mongolia and the various tribes living there. It was at this time that he took the name "Chinggis Khan".

He could not sit still though; he needed activity and wealth for himself and his followers, and that meant conquest. Between 1205 and 1209 he conquered Xixia, a Tangut state under Chinese cultural influence. He turned his attention to Khwarezm (now Iran and part of Iraq) between 1219 and 1221 and destroyed it utterly despite its apparent military strength and great wealth. After the campaign, two of Chinggis Khan's generals took a roundabout way home and passed through southern Russia with an eye to future conquest.

Chinggis Khan, however, was more interested in China, against which he conducted wars until his death in 1227. The conquest of China would not be completed for another fifty years, but it would be done. In the meantime the Mongol Empire was divided among Chinggis Khan's relatives, though the different divisions of the empire were subordinate to the Great Khan at Karakorum in Mongolia. This Great Khan was Occodai, Chinggis's brother. Chinggis's youngest son, Tolui, was given the appanage of Siberia while his grandson Batu was given the westernmost lands. To these were added the various Russian states which had fallen to the Mongols in a series of horrific campaigns between 1236 and 1238.

This Russian conquest made the princes and dukes of Russia vassals of Batu Khan and his state, The Golden Horde for the next two hundred years. And Western Europe had a taste of the same horror in 1240 and 1241 when Mongol armies campaigned in Hungary and Poland with great brutality, speed and efficiency. It seemed, after a series of western armies were virtually annihilated, that Western Europe might suffer the fate of China and Khwarezm, but the death of Occodai thousands of miles away in Karakorum brought the campaign to an end. Batu had to be satisfied with his Russian holdings; the Mongol regiments that had been lent to him for conquests in Europe headed back east, as did many of the nobles, for the election of the next Great Khan. Batu settled into a splendid reign over his people, whom the Russians would call Tatars because so many of these Turkic people had been absorbed into the Mongol Horde and fought in the Russian campaigns.

The Mongols' unmitigated successes continued with the conquest of Persia in 1258. This Mongol state was known as the Ilkhanate.

In fact, the Mongols were never checked until the Battle of Ain Jalut in 1260 when a Mongol army met an Egyptian force of mamluks and were finally halted. The mamluks were better prepared than many of the Mongols' enemies to resist them: they were trained horse archers of Turkic extraction and used to this method of fighting. They were closer to home and perhaps better equipped as well.

Mongol successes continued, though, in a general way, with the Great Khan Kubilai moving his capital to Beijing in 1276; by 1279 the conquest of China was complete and Kubilai established the Yuan Dynasty.

In time, however, the Mongol Empire broke into a number of separate khanates that no longer even pretended loyalty to each other: the White Horde, the Little Horde, the Krim Khanate were some of them. The inability of the steppe nomads to create lasting political institutions was their undoing. Their military power was phenomenal, particularly when united under a single khan, but they had little staying power when compared with the states and political institutions of sedentary people. In 1480 the Grand Duke of Moscow led his Russian army (equipped and fighting like Tatars) against the Tatars of the Golden Horde in a stand-off on the Kalka River and, though there was no battle, the Tatars pulled away, tacitly acknowledging that they were no longer masters. The Tatar khanates were troublesome for more than another 200 years, but they would slowly be marginalized.

Mongol power did not last as long in China: the Yuan Dynasty fell and the Mongols were driven out in 1368, and the Mongols of the Ilkhanate converted to Islam and faded into their subject population. The last of the steppe peoples to trouble a settled country, the Manchus, were able to seize Beijing in 1644 and rule China until 1912, but they, like the Mongols of the Ilkhanate in Persia, became largely absorbed into the dominant Chinese culture. The day of the steppe nomads had passed.

References:

Hildinger, Erik. 1997. Warriors of the Steppe: A Military History of Central Asia 500 B.C. to 1700 A.D. Cambridge, MA: Da Capo Press.

Hildinger, Erik. (Translator, from the Latin of Carpini's) The Story of the Mongols We call the Tartars.

Maenchen-Helfen, Otto J. 1973. The World of the Huns: Studies in their History and Culture. Berkley: University of California Press.

Man, John. 2006. Attila: The Barbarian King Who Challenged Rome. New York: Saint Martins Press.

Rolle, Renate. 1980. The World of the Scythians. Berkely: University of California Press

Weatherford, Jack. 2006. Genghis Kahn and the Making of the Modern World. New York: Crown Publishing Group.

Chapter 2

Turkish and Persian Mounted Archery

by Murat Ozveri

Turkish Archery

Turkish traditional archery can be examined in three time intervals: Archery of pre-Islamic Turkish and Turkic tribes, archery of Turks of Early Islamic era and Turkish Archery in the Islamic time frame.

Pre-Islamic Turkish archery has its roots in the first millennium BC, in the Scythian, Parthian, Hun and other early Asian archery traditions. The horseback archers of Central Asian steppes have used very similar archery tackle and fighting strategies throughout their entire history and the nomadic life style avoids making a clear, distinctive categorization of the tribes and nations. These people have lived on the same geography, shared many values and influenced each other's religion, language, tradition and undoubtedly genetic code. In this complex cultural and genetic pool of Central Asia the historians try to find their way in tracing different linguistic tracks which are not very reliable. Although there is a consensus about the relation between the tribes that speak Ural-Altaic and Finno-Ugrian languages, it is well-known that some "other" tribes that spoke Aryan or Indo-European languages lived here as a part of this common culture. This common culture consists of social life, religious beliefs, taboos, and art, as well as hunting and fighting techniques. Numerous civilizations appeared and disappeared from the history scene throughout centuries and left behind a common thread – the Asian school of archery.

No need to tell about the fact that history has been used (or misused) by various political foci and the truth was sometimes distorted by historians. If watched thoroughly it will be seen that many false impressions are the consequence of prejudices and misinformation. A good example is that the historians categorize nomadic armies according to the tribal identity of their warlords. Even in Genghis Khan's army there were thousands of non-Mongol groups, including

Turks and even Chinese. Although the ethnic continuity is questionable, the Asian horseback archery tradition passed from Scythian to Parths, Huns, Avars, Magyars, Mongols, Seljuk and Ottoman Turks with a gradual development in the tackle.

Mounted Archers of Archaic Turks

Some authors believe that Turks originated from Huns, but the word "Turk" was first mentioned in Chinese sources in the 6th century for a Turkish nation called "Blue Turk Empire" (Gokturks). Although the archaic Turkish archery has not been very well documented specifically, the information about the steppe people gives an idea about it. Other than old Greek, Roman and Byzantian scripts, archaeological excavations made by the former USSR scientists enlightened many points of the nomadic life and culture. Despite the fact that there are different kinds of nomadism, in the current context, nomads are pastoralists who follow their animal herds, as they search for food and water. Nomadic steppe peoples were tribal or clan-based entities and their leaders achieved their status and political power by their personal abilities. The unification of tribes of different ethnic origins under the command of such leaders was fairly common. Cultural, genetic and military interactions made it possible to talk about a "common mounted archery culture" which can easily be representative of early pre-Islamic Turkish horseback archery. This cultural complex, widely known as "Scythian Triad", is typical as seen from the content of their tombs: weapons made of bronze and iron, equipment of horsemanship, and the so-called "animal-style" art. Warriors were buried with their weapons and horses, so the tombs offer great information.

The earliest written sources of other cultures about the steppe folks were dated to the first millennium BC and these steppe people were referred to as Scythians. The historian Herodotus called them Scythians, but the Iranians called them Saka. After the Scythians, historically we next encounter the Sarmatians who came as aggressors and finally occupied all Scythian land. Both groups of steppe people were speaking Iranian languages (at least their leaders were) and closely related to the Medes and Persians who themselves originated on the steppe. The Scythian culture became widespread among Altai people from which the Turks originate. This is quite important and may be the earliest example of the interactions between the Turkic and Persian cultures.

The domestication of the horse, riding, and selective breeding appeared by 4000-2000 BC, in the steppe between today's Ukraine and Russia. Horses were initially herded for meat, milk, hair and other animal products. Horse breeding has been practiced from very early in the history of horse domestication. Breeding for type would continue unabated as long as the horse was needed for specific tasks. Iranian-speaking peoples are known to have bred selectively for size in order to carry a warrior into battle as early as 1000 BC. By the time of Parthians, the region around the river Amu Darya in Central Asia was well known for horse breeding. Breeders were mixing the blood of the wider steppe horse with taller and faster horses of the oasis and desert fringe, such as the *Karabair* and the *Akhal-Teke*, the latter having been used as a fast cavalry horse for the last 3000 years.

Riding probably arose with the need for herding. The herders might have realised that it was easier to care for the herds when mounted. The importance of the horse increased with time and the horse became a cult object as indicated by burial deposits. A good horse could make the difference between life and death on the steppe and this culture gave the horse the status it deserved. It was the same for the main weapon of this culture. Other than being an important weapon combination, the bow and arrow have been ceremonial objects that sometimes became a sacred or religious item. Mounted archer figurines found in the archeological excavations are believed to have been used in shamanist rituals.

The most important developments in the Scythian era were the ones that made the rider become more effective in a military sense: composite bow, the small and tough steppe horses. Unlike the taller horses that could carry armored men but were unable to survive without stables and sufficient food, this breed could survive under the hard conditions of the steppes. Later the Mongols, who invaded all of Eurasia under the reign of Genghis Khan, rode these steppe ponies. On the other hand, there is strong evidence that archaic Turks rode horses of a different breed that were taller with thinner legs and longer neck.

Scythians invented sophisticated saddlery as well as weapons made of bronze and iron. Higher saddles and stirrups enabled the rider to sit more comfortably and handle the weapons, especially the bow and arrow. Success on the battlefield was the only way to be respected socially. As an extension of this cultural criteria, Turkish adolescents "deserved" and got their names by a heroic accomplishment in the battle or hunt. The social roles of men and women were differentiated but women did all the work men were doing, including fighting.

The retreat-and-attack strategy that pulls the enemy to its death was another Scythian invention. This strategy was supported by the horseback archer's amazing skill, turning back and shooting backwards in the saddle, known as the *Parthian shot*. In pre-Islamic Turks, only those warriors skilled at shooting both forward and backward among *tarkan* or "heroes", were permitted to put white falcon wings or feathers in their helmets, as a mark of rank. This technique was adopted by Mongols and Turks in the following centuries but the given name proves that this technique was created by Indo-European-speaking tribes. Parths, the ancient owners of today's Turkmenistan, may not be remembered, but their influence on today's English can still be seen in phrases like "parting shot".

After the appearance of Gokturks another story began. Within time, the word "Turk" became a term independent of ethnicity, a common name of tribal confederations. Later, during the Ottomans, it even became the name of a severely mixed population of one of the world's greatest empires. The Turkish language spread with the Turkish-speaking warriors to the south and southwest, towards Anatolia with gradual "turkification" of the land and people. As a result of the Islamization of Turkic tribes, this term gained another meaning associated with Islam, especially after the Ottoman sultans got the Khilafate from Mamluks in the 16th century.

Within the social context of the typical nomadic life in which heroic behaviours were highly appreciated, hunting was the main and a very important activity. It was not only a way to harvest the daily food but also a war-practice and a social activity with ceremonial aspects. Hunting was also an opportunity to prove and improve skills in riding and weaponry, especially the bow and arrow, a weapon combination prominently and effectively used by all Central Asian tribes. Turks, like the other nomadic people, preferred the drive hunt in which the game animals were driven on horses and killed mainly with sword and bow. This hunting method required great skill in riding and archery that could only be acquired with years of daily, hard training. Riding and archery training started early childhood. Kids shot birds and rats from on sheepback. When they grew older they became skilled riders and hunted edible foxes and rabbits. As a result of this, all the young men were mounted archers in battle. In times of peace they lived by herding and hunting, but when an economic crisis arose they armed and went looting. They carried the famous composite bow as long range weaponry and preferred sword and lance for close-quarter fighting.

In an 8th century Arabic text the mounted archery skills of Turks are well described. The skills of Turkish mounted archers, especially their ability for shooting in any direction from horseback at full gallop and with pinpoint accuracy, are explained in detail. Their dependence on their horses and bows were noticed as well and it was mentioned that the Turkish warriors always had a back-up bow and a horse. They were known not only for their skill in archery but also for their ability to make and repair their own equipment. The manufacturing of bows has been in the hands of the professional bowyers from Turkish times but the Muslims who first encountered Turkic horse archers were amazed at this ability of individual warriors. Gumilöv claims that there was no infantry class in Turkish armies, as the sculptures of Turkish warriors in Ermitaj Museum indicate. He also mentions that the warriors wore lamellar armor and carried a light lance as the major weapon. His thesis is supported by some Chinese sources which highlight "the Turkish mounted warriors with their lances and the Iranian with their horseback archers had become a nightmare for the Chinese". Gumilöv also claims that horseback archers in Turkish armies were adopted from the tribes or nations defeated by Turks. Anyway, archaeological findings support the fact that in the 7th century Turkish armed forces consisted of both heavy and light cavalry armed with bow and arrow. While heavy cavalry were equipped, beside bow and arrow, with lance, sword and mace, the unarmored light cavalry were using a recurved composite bow with a reflex grip. Other findings about the 8th century Blue Turk Empire (The Second Khaganate) show that the Kaghan's army had a small number of foot soldiers but the majority was mounted and their main weapon was the composite bow.

Mounted archery is in some ways like any archery, but in critical ways it is quite distinct. The mounted archer has to be not only the best archer possible, but also a high-skilled horseman. When shooting from horseback, both hands are used in shooting, leaving control of the horse

www.lrgaf.org

to leg pressure alone. Any competent rider will naturally learn to do this to some extent, but few could be comfortable with releasing the reins entirely while riding at full speed under battle conditions. For most cavalry, losing the reins could be disastrous but for the steppe archer, riding without reins was a practised skill needed in herding and hunting. Another theory/method of riding without the control of reins is training the horses not to "swerve aside" but remain running in a straight line until turned by a touch of the bridle.

The most important written source that includes many details about the pre- and early post-Islamic stage of Turkish archery is *The Book of Dede Korkud*. This book is sometimes called "The Turkish Iliad" and contains epic stories of the 12th century Turks, probably written in the 15th century but with roots hundreds of years before. It covers the stories of recently Islamized Oghuz Turks who moved to North-eastern Anatolia in the early 13th century. However, many authors agree that the Islamic motifs have been inserted later into these stories. Together with the characteristic of the language, social life and beliefs exhibited in the stories, they reveal a nomadic life style that is associated with a "passing phase" rather than an established Islamic life. The Islamization of Turkish tribes occurred in Maveraunnehir, as a result of 300 years of military, commercial and cultural interaction with the Islamic armies. The frontiersmen who lived in this region in the 8th-11th centuries created and adopted a mixed military culture that was sharply differentiated from their native cultures. Dramatic changes occurred in the life of Turkish nomads and hereby Iranian mystics played the lead role through systematic missionary activity. Most likely there has been some further exchange in military tactics and strategies as well as the weaponry between two cultures, while Turks adopted Islam and the Arabic alphabet.

In *The Book of Dede Korkud*, life is mainly based on hunting and war. In one of the hunting scenes a hunter "erects [stands] pressing up on his stirrups prior to drawing his bow", an action that emphasizes the importance of stirrups in horseback shooting. However, many enthusiasts believe that the stirrups are not essential for this purpose and that they played a more important role in the use of close-quarter weapons in the saddle. Still, stirrups provided a solid "stance" for shooting the bow and probably increased the ease and accuracy, especially when shooting to the rear. Like in all the epic narrations the actors in the stories are hard to beat, and it is noticeable that the Oghuz heroes could be defeated, killed or imprisoned only when they are dismounted or asleep. This is another indicator of how "unbeatable" the mounted warrior was from the point of view of the storyteller.

One of the secrets behind the military success of steppe people has been undoubtedly their metallurgical know-how that enabled them to make metal equipment for horsemanship, like bridles and stirrups, as well as high quality weapons like swords, daggers and arrowheads. But the most important invention of steppe people was certainly the composite bow. The amazing composite bow of steppe horseback archers was, as the name suggests, made of several different materials. With the clever combination of wood (or bamboo) with horn and sinew, this bow acquires incredible physical specifications. These three materials are glued to each other by using collagen-based glues derived from animal tissues. In addition to the shortened overall length of the bow that makes it more comfortable on horseback, this Asian invention provides some mechanical advantages over the "old standard" selfbow. First of all, the early draw weight is higher than that of straight-limbed bows. It produces more stored energy in the same poundage and same draw length. Secondly, the leverage effect of the so-called "ears" avoids the stacking problem of shorter limbs and allows longer draw lengths. The typical all-wooden rigid tips, the "ear" of some earlier Asian-type composite bows was the common feature in Hun, Magyar and Mongolian bows. In the later bows, like Ottoman and Persian, the all-wooden tips disappeared as will be explained later in this chapter.

Turks encountered the Byzantian army in the 9th and 10th centuries when the Byzantian army was at its height. While in western Europe the fighting tactics were still based on the individual skill and ability of the heavily armored knights, the aristocratic warrior of eastern Europe was not satisfied with proficiency in using weapons and added theoretical knowledge to his empirical accomplishments by reading the books of Mavrikios, Leon, and Nikeforos about war strategy and philosophy. One of these books, the *Tactica* by Leon, included suggestions for fighting against Turks. According to Leon the Byzantian infantry must not get into an arrow-combat against Turkish mounted archers and should close up the distance between them. The Turkish cavalry wore light armor but their horses were unarmored, and the steppe warrior was totally helpless when he lost his horse.

www.lrgaf.org

The Turkish tactic was that of harassing the enemy by the hit-and-run action, dividing his forces by pretending retreat and enticing pursuit but then turning unexpectedly back and showering the enemy with deadly arrows, and, finally when he was reduced in number and courage, to surround him and destroy him with volleys of arrows.

Post-Islamic era: Mounted Archers of Seljuk Sultanate

The first remarkable Islamic Turkish sultanate was that of *Seljuks*, a clan of the Oghuz Turks, who lived north of the Oxus River (present-day Amu Darya). The Turks must have noticed and admired that their new religion gave importance to archery, a martial art that already had priority in their lifestyle. There is one verse in the Koran which orders "to feed horses and prepare force for a possible war", this "force" being "shooting arrows" as interpreted by the Prophet Muhammad himself. In addition to this verse there are 40 Hadiths in which Muslims are encouraged to practise archery. In the 11th century, Seljuks conquered the Iranian cities adjacent to their borders and invaded the country with no serious resistance. The Great Seljuk Sultanate in that Turkish invasion reigned over the Iranian land with the co-operation and acquiescence of Persian bureaucrats, and established a tax collection system called *"iktâ"*, which constituted the base of the feudal cavalry. This system continued and was improved under the Ottomans.

The historians of that time described the Seljuk army as "an effective and moving force with long-range weaponry". In 1071 *Alp Arslan* defeated the powerful Byzantian army under the command of *Roman Diagones IV*, in Manzikert (Malazgirt). The historians agree that it was the outstanding leadership of Alp Arslan as well as the fighting skills of his fast and lethal mounted archers that played an important role in the victory. Seljuk light cavalry hesitated to "impact" the enemy and to get into close-quarter fighting. What they preferred was the lightning-fast "attack and retreat" strategy of steppe mounted archers. The Byzantians had known the enemy well and made some tactical modifications in its troops, including adopting horseback archers and equipping the infantry with long-range bows, but it did not help to defeat Alp Arslan. This battle started a process which led the Muslim Turks in making Anatolia home. Another Seljuk Sultanate was established in Anatolia afterwards.

It is documented that in the Manzikert battle each warrior was carrying about 100 arrows, in the quiver, the bowcase and even in the boots. In a battle against the first Crusade, the Crusade army knights had to suffer a 3 hour uninterrupted arrow attack from the Seljuk army. It was *Count Raymond* who came to help with his army and saved them from a total destruction.

Eastern Turk armies relied increasingly on heavily armored cavalry, though the bow remained as their main weapon. We know that Seljuk warriors have used recurve bows with "ears", being identified as "East Turkmenistan type bows" by Yucel. It's quite possible that other Asian style bows too were used by Seljuks. There is an old picture of a Seljuk atabeg *Bedreddin Lulu* in *Kitâbü'l-Agânî,* written in 1218-1219, showing the atabeg holding a shorter bow with "siyahs" (Siyah is the entire rigid end of the bow including "kasan" and "bash" in Turkish bow, different than the "ear", the rigid all-wood extremity of the limb). But unfortunately there is no strong evidence such as surviving bows or other archeological findings. All the other pictures of the same time era prove that the rigid-tipped longer bows were more common.

Another document from the Seljuks is a coin produced during *Sultan Rukneddin*'s (or *Kılıçarslan IV*) reign (note the Turkish and Islamic name of the Sultan). Here is a short, recurved horsebow and two more arrows in the drawing hand using the typical thumb release of Seljuk archers.

Military Structure in the Ottoman Empire

The Ottoman Empire was supposedly founded in 1299 by an insignificant tribal leader, *Osman Bey,* from the *Kayı* tribe of Oghuz Turks. Ottomans ended the Roman Empire and became an Empire that ruled on three continents. This Empire refined and developed archery to unprecedented and still unsurpassed levels.

The final stage in development of the composite bow was in the hands of Ottoman Turks who in the 15th and 16th centuries improved it by refining the shape and materials used. Evolving from centuries-old Turkish cavalry-based military experience, Ottoman bows and arrows had been made with the minimal size and weight possible to provide a perfect maneuvering capability to the warrior on the horse. Yet these slim, light, beautifully ornate tools were armor piercing weapons of pure Hell!

In spite of the strong influence of Islamic culture, the Ottoman army and military life reveal their Asian origin in many aspects. The symbolic value of both the horse and the bow were maintained. The political executions, especially the ones within the dynasty have been held with a bowstring, an application that binds the "blood taboo" of Central Asian past with a "honorable death" concept, similar to that of some other military cultures. The presence of a horse-related military symbolism was another link to Central Asian steppes: the so-called *"tug"*, a banner made of horsetail, was erected in the middle of barracks prior to warfare to make the soldiers aware of the sultan's decision of war. This was a good example about what the "horse" meant to them. This symbolism originated from the archaic Turks who employed elaborate tug "tailed" banners or horsetails carried separately or attached to the ruler's great drums. Horsetail banners indicated a commander's status.

Different from the Central Asian military structure, the Ottoman army had infantry troops, the famous *Janissaries*. The attack-and-retreat tactic was unfavourable to close combat operation, and inefficient in laying siege to forts and walled towns; nor could the steppe warriors sustain long campaigns, especially in the winter months. The logistics of the infantry opened the way for conquering new land. In the 14th century the Ottoman army was superior to the 11th-13th century armies of other Muslim countries. In this new structure, mounted archers were still the most dominant component. Additionally, there were *timarlı sipahi*, or "feudal cavalry", who were native-born Turks and armed not only with bow and arrow but also with close-fighting weapons like sword and lance. Feudal cavalry was the result of *iktâ* of Seljuks, as mentioned above. This tax collection system was based on excluding some of the taxes of local leaders, the so-called *"beg"* (or "bey"), and demanding them to feed and equip a certain number of mounted forces. *İktâ* is completely different from the European feudal system in which the property belonged to feudal barons. With Seljuks and Ottomans the land was offered by the sultan in exchange for military service and its owners were changed from time to time. In the second half of the 14th century the army consisted mainly of these *timarlı sipahi*.

www.lrgaf.org

The advantages to a warrior being mounted are numerous; mobility in the famous retreat-and-attack strategy is only one of them. Fighting the pedestrian opponent from a higher position; the physical and psychological effects of the large and powerful animal itself; and the possibility of the individual warrior using the fighting tactic or the weapon that the situation demanded. Sipahi warriors were typically cavalrymen using a sword, spear, javelin, and mace for close-quarter fighting, plus their very dangerous composite bows.

Beside the timarlı sipahi there was another mounted component of the army, the *"Cavalry of Sublime Porte,"* that consisted of the specially educated and trained elite warriors of the Sultan. They were skilled in using many weapons, including the famous Ottoman bow. They were graduates of the *Palace School* that was founded in the 15th century.

Ottoman Sports Archery

Before taking a closer look at the Palace School, it is helpful to remember that the most remarkable part of Ottoman archery is a well-established sports archery that begun in the early 15th century. Despite the classical Anglo-Saxon literature that claims the sports archery to have begun in 16th century England, Ottomans had *Okmeydanı* (literally "Place of Arrow") and *"tekye-i rumât,* (literally "tekke of shooters") where systematic archery education was given and competitions were held, a hundred years before the foundation of *"The Guild of Saint George"* under the order of Henry VIII. The three main disciplines in Ottoman sports archery were *puta* (target) shooting, *darb* (piercing hard objects), and flight or distance shooting. After firearms became dominant on the battlefield, the Ottoman licensed archers (*kemankeş,* cam-un-cash*),* focused mainly on flight shooting and reached incredible distances over 800 metres. The war-related disciplines lost their popularity after the 17th century but they were not totally ignored.

Okmeydanı was like the modern sports fields and the tekye was not too much different than a modern sports club. However, in spite of the closeness of riding and archery in Turkish culture, horses were not allowed in Okmeydans since these sports fields were regarded as holy

www.lrgaf.org

places which cannot be "polluted". Even for the archers the Islamic cleaning ritual was a must prior to entering these fields.

Naturally, there were other sports fields dedicated to another archery discipline in which horses were involved: the *"Kabak meydanı"*. The Kabak (qabak) game was a "game" which in fact was a demonstration of skill, rather than a sport discipline. Although kabak is a "gourd", a vegetable set as target, many other objects like cups, balls etc. were used as targets. The target was put on the top of a tall pole that the archer was approaching with full speed. As the archer galloped past the pole, he turned backwards and upwards and shot at the very high target. This was incredibly difficult.

The Kabak game was not only a war-related practice but also an occasion for demonstrating skill and for entertainment. It had its peak in popularity in the 15th-17th centuries but its tracks can be followed back to the steppes of Central Asia. This archery game was played in many other Middle Eastern countries and known under the same name, indicating the Turkic origin of it, since the word "kabak" is etymologically Turkish. A very interesting clue about its origin can also be found in the *Epic of Oghuz Khan*. At the end of the text the alliance of Turkish tribes is declared and celebrated by an interesting "swearing ritual" which involves riding around tall poles and shooting live chickens put on the top of them.

Kabak fields disappeared in time, probably because riding was the privilege of elites and of the members of *Cavalry of Sublime Porte* (Kapıkulu Sipahileri) in Istanbul. The need to find proper land to feed the horses made many of the Kapıkulu sipahi move outside the city after the 17th century. It may be one of the reasons that the Kabak game lost its popularity in the capital city after the 17th century.

While the horse was still in the centre of life in the countryside where feudal cavalry (timarlı sipahi) was accommodated, in the Ottoman capital riding was accepted as a status symbol and restricted by law. But in the Palace there was a school, named *Enderun-ı hümayûn,* where riding and other martial arts together with the sciences of the time were taught. The Palace School, founded by Mehmed II "The Conqueror", deserves to be examined thoroughly to understand the professional horseback warriors of the Sultan, the *Cavalry of Sublime Porte* (*Kapıkulu sipahileri*).

www.lrgaf.org

Cavalry of Sublime Porte: Mounted Archers of the Palace

To understand the system of education in the Palace School it must be kept constantly in mind that for more than three centuries the despotism of the Ottoman dynasty was based almost exclusively upon a deliberate policy of government by a slave class. This method of government seems to have been developed by the Turkish rulers as a defensive mechanism designed to exclude native-born subjects from the government, to eliminate the rise of aristocracy of blood or of a hereditary official class.

It must be remembered also in considering this system of government by a slave class that slavery in Muslim lands was greatly different than that in Europe and often proved to be the most direct road to fortune and honour. The teaching of the Prophet was that slaves should be treated with kindness and generosity, and that they should be fed and clothed in the same manner as the members of the master's own family. In the Muslim East, slavery has never had the meaning that was attached to it in the West. As an example, the Georgians and Circassians who found the slave trade with Constantinople so profitable and maintained slave farms to meet the demand, reared their own children, because they were considering the Palace service the best possible opening for a brilliant career.

During the centuries when the slave system of the government was at its height among the Ottoman Turks, the only posts for which native-born Turks were eligible were commissions in the timarlı sipahis and Kapıkulu Sipahis, to which latter only the slaves of Christian origin, or Turks in the first generation were admitted.

Slaves for the Palace service were supplied through capture, purchase, gift and *Law of Tribute Children* or the *Law of Draft (Devshirmeh)*. This law was about drafting the recruits for the army from the conquered European provinces. The law denied to the people of these provinces the usual right accorded Christians of payment of the capitation tax in lieu of military service, and instead exacted as tribute a stipulated number of male children every three or four years. By the same law these youths were required to serve a novitiate of seven years in military schools, in the royal palaces provided for the purpose or in the household of provincial governors and of high officials in the capital, or upon the timarlı sipahis of Anatolia.

www.lrgaf.org

The second important source of supply for Palace slaves was prisoners of war. One-tenth of these became the property of the Sultan and were usually attached to the Palace service. The most physically perfect, the most intelligent, and the most promising in every respect were set aside for the Palace service. The remainder who were distinguished mainly because of their physical strength and dexterity were assigned to the Janissary corps. Those who had been set aside for the Palace service were separated in two classes. The cleverest of mind or genius types were destined for a high education as student pages (*ich oghlanlar*). The remainder who were classified as apprentices (*ajemi oghlanlar*) were put through a stiff training program as gardeners or gatekeepers. The boys received instructions in the liberal arts, geography, mathematics, in the art of war and physical exercise, and in vocational training.

Physical training started with gymnastic exercises including lifting and carrying weights. The exercise progressed from these to sports of various kinds, especially cavalry exercises, and other "arts of war". As a result of the systematic and long-continuing training which they received, the students of the Palace School are said to have developed amazing strength and agility of body, perfect health and unusual skill in arms. The high standard of physical development which they attained resulted in the finest army in Europe during the centuries when the palace system of education was at the peak of its efficiency. Practically all the officers of the Sublime Porte, and many of the officers of the feudal cavalry, had been trained in the Palace School.

There are documents available about what kind of physical exercises the student pages had done and the extraordinary level they have reached. Initial weight lifting exercises for which a bag was lifted one-handed with the help of a pulley and a cord, reminds one of a modern fitness work-out. A second exercise was lifting and carrying various kind of weights in the arms and upon the shoulders. From time to time the size of weights was increased until, the pages were frequently able to carry as much as 370 or even 380 *oqas* (470-482 kg), for a distance of 150 or 160 paces. Later iron weights of various kinds were substituted. It is said that pages were able with one arm to lift weights ranging from 40 to 100 pounds, and that those which they were able to raise above their heads were incredibly heavy.

More advanced physical exercises were archery, wrestling and sword practice. *Cirit* is another traditional horseback martial art/sport that still survives in modern Turkey. The members of two teams throw wooden darts by hand at the opponents. The darts have no points but the game is still too dangerous, and serious injuries, even death is not uncommon.

Archery training started with bows of moderate draw weights. The draw weight was increased gradually. Yet even with the largest and the heaviest of these bows the record of two hundred draws without stopping is said to have been frequent in the school matches and tournaments. I would like to remind the reader that in a recent research of Adam Karpowicz, the draw weights of many bows in Topkapi Palace Museum have been estimated well over 130 pounds. Heavier bows made for the purpose of improving or demonstrating strength might have been made also.

Since the majority of the students were destined for the cavalry service, one of the main lines of physical training was fine horsemanship. Not only did the students become skilled cavalrymen, but they also excelled in feats of horsemanship. While running their horses at full speed, they would unsaddle and resaddle them without slackening their pace; they would ride standing on the seat of the saddle; they would ride two horses at the same time with one foot on each saddle; two pages while riding at top speed would exchange horses with one another; and they would slide under the bellies of their horses and remount from the other side.

The literary education that the boys received consisted of the Arabic and Persian languages. While the Arabic language was the key to the Koran, the Persian language was the courtly language of the Near Orient and the key to the literature of chivalry and romance. It was the aim of the Turkish sultans to discover and to train youths of exceptional ability for leadership in the state. A part of their education was learning "some art and occupation according to the capacity of their spirit". All Turks, except Janissaries, were formerly accustomed to learn some art or science, by means of which they could earn a livelihood in case they should fall upon evil days. Sultans were no exception and many of them excelled in their chosen craft.

The student pages who completed their novitiate were promoted from the Palace to the reserve corps of the cavalry, a custom which was known as "the Deliverance" (*Chiqmah*). Some of the students became high ranking bureaucrats, including viziers but most of them left the Palace as professional elite mounted warriors. In warfare they were in charge of protecting the sultan, the royal standard, and the treasure. In times of peace they accompanied the sultan, armed with sword and bow; but while going to the mosque with the sultan for Friday prayers, they were armed with a sword only.

The majority of their horses were tough and agile Anatolian breeds. They were bred in Cukurova in South Anatolia and their export was strictly prohibited. Other sources were Epir and Teselia in Greece, but after the 17th century Arabian, Tatar and Magyar horses were used also.

The Ottoman army had a crescent shape while moving. Sultan and the treasure were located in the centre, protected by Kapıkulu sipahis on the right and left sides. The "tips" of this crescent consisted of timarlı sipahis. In the centre, in front of the sultan there were Janissaries who follow the *Azaplar*, the light infantry. Another component of the army, *Akincilar*, was the light cavalry armed with the composite bow and who moved as pioneers, a few days prior to the whole army. After the 16th century, Akincilar were replaced with Crimean Tatars, another nomadic nation with deadly skills as mounted archers. Crimean Tatars were using bows that were longer than that of Ottomans but looked very similar to them. They kept using these weapons until the end of the 18th century, long after the Ottoman army has completely switched to firearms.

The Roots of Persian (Iranian) Mounted Archery

In the Neolithic era, Indo-European speaking people of Central Asia started to migrate to the south. The Neolithic horse culture of the steppes spread to the Iranian plateau with this immigration. The reason that both Indians and Iranians name themselves "Aryan" would make one think that these two folks had been living as one unseparated nation in the steppes of South Russia and Siberia once upon a time.

The well-preserved, dried bodies that were found in the graves in Tarom basin and dated back to 2000-400 BC with radiocarbon dating method, reveal the physical type of white race. These findings support the position that Indo-European people had lived in the land which is today a part of China's Shin-giyang State. Among some artifacts found in these graves there are black, conical, "wizard" hats, similar to that worn by very early Iranians. In the Iranian plateau it is possible to come across some civilizations in the prehistoric era by 7500 BC. But the first Indo-European-speaking immigrants supposedly came to this area by 2000 BC and contacted the Semitic and non-Semitic people of Mesopotamia, the natural geographical extension to the west. The Median Empire was the first Iranian dynasty corresponding to the northeastern section of present-day Iran, Northern-Khvarvarana and Asuristan (now it is known as Iraq), and South and Eastern Anatolia. The inhabitants, who were known as *Medes*, and their neighbors, the *Persians*, spoke Median languages that were closely related to Aryan (Old Persian). Historians know very little about the Iranian culture under the *Median* dynasty. After *Median* and *Achaemenid* dynasties, the *Parths* ruled over the Iranian plateau by 284 BC-224 AD and intermittently controlled Mesopotamia.

Parthia, due to its invention of heavy cavalry, was a serious enemy of the Roman Empire in the east and it blocked Rome's expansion beyond Cappadocia. The Parthian Empire lasted five centuries, longer than most eastern empires. Experience had shown that light cavalry armed with the bow and arrow and probably also the sword was suitable for skirmishes that fought with the attack-and-retreat strategy, but could not sustain close combat. For the latter task, Parths formed heavy cavalry (*cataphraoti*), which wore steel helmets, a coat of mail reaching to the knees and made of rawhide covered with scales of iron or steel that enabled it to resist strong blows. For offensive weapons the cataphract had an unusually thick and long lance and a bow. The Parths were followed by the *Sassanids* whose mounted forces were formed under strong influence of Parthians. They retained Parthian cavalry, and employed new-style armor and siege-engines, thereby creating a standing army which served for over four centuries. The Sassanids defended Iran against Central Asiatic nomads and Roman armies. This army was called "*spah*", from which the "*sipah*" or "*sipahi*" in the Seljuk and Ottoman military structure originated. The Sassanian army had two types of cavalry unit, *Clibinarii* and *Cataphracts*, the latter being composed of elite noblemen trained since youth for military service. The backbone of the spah was its heavy cavalry in which all the nobles and "men of rank" underwent hard training and became professional soldiers "through military training and discipline, through constant exercise in warfare and military manoeuvres." The archery equipment of these elite warriors, also called "the Immortals", consisted of a bowcase with two bows and two extra bowstrings, and a quiver with 30 arrows (note the back-up bow concept that was the same for Scythians and archaic Turks). They had nearly all the close fighting weapons and a full body armor. Their horses were armored too. The Sassanians did not form light-armed cavalry but extensively employed troops of allied warriors or mercenaries from warlike tribes who fought under their own chiefs.

Islamic era in Iran

In 637 the Arab forces occupied the Sassanid capital and in 641-42 they defeated the Sassanid army at Nahavand. Islamic culture dominated Iranian land and all Middle Eastern culture for the next centuries. But the horseback fighting techniques, the composite bow and the thumb draw had been adopted by Arabs who were known to have used a four-finger release on their simple selfbows. Among the most important of these overlapping dynasties of Arabic origin in the following centuries were the *Tahirids* in Khorasan (820-872); the *Saffarids* in Sistan (867-903); and the *Samanids* (875-1005), originally at Bokhara. The Samanids eventually ruled an area from central Iran to India. In 962 a Turkish slave governor of the Samanids, *Alptigin*, conquered Ghazna and established the *Ghaznavid Dynasty* that lasted to 1186. Several Samanid cities had been lost to another Turkish group, the Seljuk, as explained above.

Iran's next ruling dynasties descended from nomadic, Turkic-speaking warriors who had been moving out of Central Asia for more than a millennium. They were enlisted as slave warriors in the armies of *Abbasid* khaliphs as early as the ninth century. Shortly thereafter the real power of the Abbasid khaliphs began to diminish; eventually they became religious figureheads while the warrior slaves ruled.

The tradition of archery underwent some major tactical changes during the Sassanian period. The majority of Sassanian archers were infantry. It may be accepted that Sassanian archery was a shift away from the Central Asian horse archery. Archery, specifically horse archery, retained its importance until the *Saffavid* period (1502-1736

AD). Treatises written in this time period shows that systematic teaching of archery was thought to be important. They quoted that "the most important thing for a bowman is that he has to learn the art from a master, since without a master, no one can really learn and master this art no matter how much he practises on his own". It is certain that archery was systematically trained in different eras. Saffavid Iran was an important center for bowshooting where the skill of the archers was demonstrated and tested. Archery training consisted of bending very heavy bows in various positions, even while jumping or running, pulling weaker bows to develop form, and finally target shooting and flight shooting.

Military and Cultural Relations

An historical record about an early Turkish attack on Iran shows how well-developed the Iranian archers were in the 6th century. *Young Souh*, the younger son of Turkish Khagan *Kara Churin,* invaded the eastern part of Iran in August 589. *Behram Chubin,* who was the provincial governor of Armenistan and Azerbaijan had been charged with stopping the Turks. A select army of 12,000 experienced warriors whose ages were between 40 and 50, confronted Turks in the Herat valley. The reason that Behram preferred older warriors instead of young ones was their skill in archery. It was thought that "acquiring the highest skill in archery required 20 years of training." Iranian archers reached their peak in the 6th century and had the reputation of "hitting the enemy not on the chest but in their ears". Persian archers were renowned for their storm of arrows they could unleash on opposing forces. The range of their bows was 700 metres and the arrow was capable of easily piercing the armor of highest quality. The outcome of a fight was determined by the dominant component in both armies — the archers. All Turkish warriors were mounted and the composite bow was their main weapon.

In this battle, in which Turks used elephants, Iranian archers shot the elephants in their eyes and caused a big chaos that brought the victory to Sassanids. Turks were defeated and their leader was killed by an arrow shot by Behram himself.

Iranian land was ruled by Seljuk Turks between 1037-1194, as mentioned before. The *Ilkhanates* (1256-1353) and *Timuride Empire*

(1370-1506) brought a late Central Asian nomadic touch to the Iranian plateau. In Ottoman times, political and religious conflicts were the reasons of war between Turks and Iranians.

After adopting Islam, Turks' culture, especially the language, was severely influenced by Arabian and Persian cultures. Although it is a fact that mutual interactions between these two cultures started thousands of years ago, many changes in archery terminology seem to have happened later. The thumb-ring is called *zihgîr* (zeh-geer; literally "string holder") or *şast* (literally, "sixty", referring to the form of the hand by locking) by Ottomans, both Persian words. For many other terms like "arrow", "archer", and "quiver" Turkish archers have used Persian vocabulary, although etymologically Turkish synonyms were available and also in use.

The hunting and war scenes in Iranian and Turkish miniatures are so similar that the only way to tell them apart is to examine the style of the artist. The clothing, weapons and accessories like quivers and bowcases are almost the same in shape and style. Even the experts sometimes fail to distinguish the military tackle like the helmets and chain mail of Ottomans and Iranians. The hunting techniques of shooting at running or flying game at full gallop indicate another common past, back to their ancestors in the steppes of Central Asia.

The bows are also similar. In Iran there were various types of bows, even bamboo bows as a result of cultural interaction with India. Indian bows were not able to shoot far but they caused severe injuries in short distances. The Indian arrows were often poisonous, a feature which increased their fatality. Despite the variety of bows it is clear that the bows used in the 11th century AD were of a composite nature. The all-wooden rigid tips of earlier Asian composite bows had disappeared and the thickened extension of the limb ("kasan" in Turkish), together with the tips ("bash" in Turkish) form the unbendable extremities –the so-called "siyahs"— as the common feature of both bows. But there are some certain distinctions between them. The Iranian bow has a smaller grip and the limbs in "sal" and "kasan" sections are wider. This design does not allow the use of one single horn laminate on the belly, so the Iranian bowyers glue several narrower horn strips which negatively affect the durability of the bow. Because of these features the Persian bows (*Ajem yayi*) are known to have displeased the Turkish archers, although the high quality of their decorations were highly appreciated.

Horseback archers of both nations used the thumb-release but the Sassanians used a distinctive draw of their own. The so-called "Persian draw", as reported by Byzantian sources, consisted of holding the bowstring with the lower three or middle two fingers, possibly locked by the thumb and laying the index finger along the arrow, as if pointing the flight direction. When using a "Turco-Mongolian" style thumb draw, some twist is applied to the arrow, causing the large knuckle of the forefinger to apply side pressure to the arrow shaft, holding it in place on the string. The Persians probably used their forefingers to achieve the same result, securing the arrow from falling off the bow while riding. Sassanian archers wore fingertip guards as shown by archaeological evidence. The fingertip guards were fastened via a small chain to the wrist to prevent them from falling in the chaos of battle. In a medieval object from Kashan in Iran, there are depictions of warriors holding two arrows in the drawing hand while shooting another. This is somewhat similar to the depiction of the Seljuk mounted archer on a coin, as mentioned before in this chapter. Holding the extra arrows in the drawing hand would make it impossible to use the lower three fingers to draw the string. We certainly know that Ottoman archers used the "conventional" version of thumb draw: The lock or "*mandal*" (mund-ull) was typically made by curling the thumb around the string, pressing the tip of it to the middle finger that is firmly closed together with the ring and little finger. The index finger was pressed on the nail of the thumb to reinforce the lock.

The thumb-rings were not much different either. They are of the typical teardrop shape, a common feature that many Asian thumb-rings share, but Persian and Turkish thumb-rings can easily be discriminated with their shorter thumb-pad from Mongolian and Korean types. The thumb-rings were made of ivory, various metals, semi-precious stones, bone or horn. Although it was mentioned that leather rings were common in the Turkish army there is no single sample left to these days.

There were common mounted games played in both countries. Other than the cirit game, as mentioned above, games like *guy-ı çevgân* ("gooy-i chevgan", a game similar to polo) and kabak game were played in both countries. The Kabak game was known as *kabak bâzî* (qabak-ba-zee) or *kabak endâzî* (qabak an-da-zee) in Iran and was very popular in 16th-17th centuries. These games were played for both entertainment and for practising the martial skills.

www.lrgaf.org

References:

De Busbecq O.G., Türk Mektupları, Doğan Kitapçılık A.Ş., İstanbul, 2005.
Divitçioğlu S., Oğuz'dan Selçuklu'ya Boy, Konat, Devlet, İmge Kitabevi, Ankara, 2005.
Gumilöv L.N., Eski Türkler, Birleşik Yayıncılık, İstanbul, 1999.
İrtem, S.K., Sultan II. Mahmud Devri ve Türk Kemankeşleri, Temel Yayınları, İstanbul, 2005.
Karaalioğlu S.K., Dede Korkut Hikayeleri, İnkilap Kitabevi A.Ş., İstanbul, 1994.
Karasulas A., Mounted Archers of the Steppe 600 BC-AD1300, Osprey Publishing Ltd., Oxford, 2004.
Karpowicz A, unpublished data.
Khorasani M.M., Arms and Armor from Iran, Legat-Verlag GmbH & Co. , 2006
Koppedrayer, Kay's Thumbring Book, Blue Vase Press, Milverton, Ontario, 2002.
Miller B., The Palace School of Muhammad the Conqueror, Cambridge Harvard Unversity Press, Cambridge, Massachusettes, 1941.
Nicole D., McBride A., Atilla and the Nomad Hordes, Osprey Publishing Ltd., Oxford, 2000.
Oman C.W.C., Ok, Balta, Mancınık Ortaçağ'da Savaş Sanatı 378-1515, Kitap Yayınevi, Istanbul, 2002.
Özveri M., Okçuluk Hakkında Merak Ettiğiniz Her Şey, Umut Matbaacılık, İstanbul, 2005.
Uzunçarşılı I.H., Osmanlı Devlet Teşkilatından Kapıkulu Ocakları, Cilt. II, Türk Tarih Kurumu Yayınları, Ankara, 1943.
Yücel Ü., Türk Okçuluğu, T.C. Atatürk Kültür Merkezi Yayınları, Ankara, 1999.

Internet sources:
www.iranchamber.com (History of Iran)
www.steppenreiter.de

The author would like to specially acknowledge the invaluable support of Dr. Mustafa Kacar and Mr. Adam Karpowicz.

Chapter 3

Japanese Traditional Horseback Archery — *Kyūbadō*

By Misa Tsuyoshi

Prologue

I wouldn't have been able to approach the essence and truth of the history of Japanese traditional horseback archery without the book *Hizume no Oto (The Sound of Hoofbeats)* 1962, Tokyo Shobō (only in Japanese, discontinued). This book was written by the 34th Takedaryu Tsukasa-ke (Headmaster), the late Master Yurin Kaneko. Master Yurin Kaneko made tremendous efforts to maintain and promote the traditional Japanese horseback martial arts exactly as it was originally created in the early 6th century. I have also been guided and encouraged by Master Ietaka Kaneko, who maintains the tradition and shows great passion for promoting it both within and beyond Japan. I feel blessed and am deeply grateful to have been allowed to follow and learn from the great masters. Also, I deeply appreciate the dedicated people of the International Horse Archery Festival, who allowed me the opportunity to introduce our tradition to the United States. I wish to give my deepest gratitude to Mr. David Gray and Mr. Lukas Novotny, who made it possible to introduce our tradition in this book. I also wish to thank those who have helped me with this writing project.

The brief history of the Japanese Traditional Horseback Archery and how it evolved

Yabusame

The most ceremonial and formal style of Japanese horseback archery is called *Yabusame*; it first emerged in Japanese history during the middle of the 6th century (about 550 AD). During this period, the country experienced political chaos, and also was under threat from overseas. The Emperor Kinmei, who wished to bring peace back to his country, decided to enshrine the former Emperor and Empress who had successfully suppressed foreign threats. It was the prayer for the peace and the people's health as well as for a good harvest throughout the country. The prayer was transformed into a ceremony centered on horseback archery named *ya-basa-me*, which means "arrow-run-horse". Currently it is pronounced *ya-bu-sa-me*.

The first recorded *yabusame* event took place in Southern Japan on the isle of Kyushu. Three targets on the course represented three enemies. It was the Emperor, not his warriors, who first performed the horseback shooting. The Emperor of Japan at the time was not only a political leader but also revered as a god, so *yabusame* is considered a formal form of the prayer.

You may wonder why horseback archery was singled out as the basis for such an important ceremony. According to *Hizume no oto*, skill at archery was regarded as far more important than sword skill due to the poor quality of swords in the early years in Japan. Long distance shooting was the most effective battle technique. Also, the Japanese bow was considered to have sacred power to invite a good harvest and to prevent evil spirits such as war and epidemic diseases from being around. Thus, skill at archery combined with horseback riding (which was also a highly important skill for warriors) was recognized as the highest and the purest expression of *bushidō* (the way of the samurai). Therefore *yabusame* was thought to be the best way to please and console God and the spirits. *Yabusame* became established as a very important ceremony, and several Emperors are recorded to have performed *yabusame* demonstrations.

Since those very early years, *yabusame* was demonstrated at the ruler's command. The 59th Emperor Uda (reign 887-897AD) commissioned the Minister of the Right Minamoto no Yoshiari to compile the rule on ceremonial forms and horseback archery technique. The rule and the manner became known as *Kyūba no reihō*. This had been handed down from generation to generation within the Genji (Minamoto) family, who were the direct descendants of the Imperial family. Later Genji descendants, the Geishu Takeda family and the Bizen Ogasawara family, maintained and performed the tradition of horseback archery that follows *Kyūba no reihō*. The two families were called "Tsukasa-ke"(Headmaster Family).

Horseback archery was considered and demonstrated as a ceremony to protect the emperor and his domain from war and epidemic diseases. Both bureaucrats as well as *bushi* (warriors) were eager to practice *kyūbajutsu* (horseback archery technique). Enthusiasm peaked when *bushi* came to occupy the top level of the society. In 1195, Yoritomo Minamoto united the Kantō region of Japan, and became the first great *bushi* leader. He gathered the best horseback archers and ordered them to write a formal *yabusame* ceremony regulation book. The book was called "*Yabusame shahou*", and kept by the Geishū Takeda family and the Bizen Ogasawara family.

After fifteen centuries, horseback archery became one of the eigheen Samurai martial arts that were considered to be the most important skills. Eventually firearms took the place of bows and arrows. Then horseback archery gradually lost its value as an efficient and powerful instrument of war. However, as a ceremony, *yabusame* continued to be maintained and performed by the two Tsukasa-ke.

In the 16th century, Japan again underwent a period of political chaos. After Nobunaga Oda became the leader of Bushi society, each of the Tsukasa-ke, who belonged to the defeated former governor's alliance, were invited to Kyushu as guests of the Higo Hosokawa family, whose domain occupied the current area of Kumamoto prefecture in Kyushu. At that time the Higo domain was ruled by Yūsai Hosokawa, who was famous for his preservation of culture and tradition. He must have wanted to preserve traditional horseback archery. This meant that the *Kyūba no reihō* as well as the two families who could perform original *yabusame* and horseback archery were no longer in central Japan. However, as a result, this helped maintain the old tradition in its original form for a long time.

It is said that the *yabusame* ceremony was not performed during the Oda and Toyotomi eras (ca 1560-1603), which continued to be the time of political conflict. Then in the 17th century, the Tokugawa family, relatively newcomers in central *samurai* society, established a new centralized government in Edo(Tokyo). They desired to have the symbolic and traditional ceremony and tried to rebuild horseback archery as well as *samurai* manners. The first Tokugawa Shogun (general, the top governor of Japan at that time) Ieyasu sent a representative to Hosokawa Yūsai and was given records about annual events in *bushi* society and solemn *samurai* ritual. However *Kyūba no reihō* was excluded for some reason.

The third Shogun Iemitsu wanted to hold *inu-oumono* (the other form of horseback archery that involved chasing and shooting dogs) but there were no clear instructions available. So he referred to old pictures in order to recreate *inu-oumono*. The eighth Shogun Yoshimune also wanted to re-establish traditional horseback archery. He ordered his counselors to research the old records available and managed to compile this information into a form. He then had his men practice and demonstrate his re-creation. Yoshimune ordered to call this newly established horseback archery *"kasha hasami mono"* to differentiate it from *yabusame* . However *kisha hasami mono* changed its name as *shinsei (new) yabusame* or *Edo yabusame* later. Many horseback archery instructors and schools emerged in this period. The Ogasawara School was established by the Akazawa Ogasawara family, who were assigned as the instructor of *kasha hasami mono*. They continue this practice and demonstrate *new yabusame* at shrines.

Since the Meiji era (1868), *new yabusame* has been demonstrated in central Japan. At the same time in Kyushu (where the very traditional *yabusame* continued to be maintained by the two families mentioned earlier), the Higo clan continued to perform *yabusame shinji* (sacred ceremonies performed at shrines).

In 1871, the Meiji government decided to abolish the feudal clans (which occupied various regions in Japan with their own governor and regulations) and turned them into prefectures under rule of the central government. During this transitional period between feudal and centralized government, *yabusame* ceremonies came to a halt for a while. Then, in Meiji 13 (1881) the *yabusame* ceremony was conducted at Izumi Shrine by direct descendants of the Geishū Takeda family and the Bizen Ogasawara family, who had kept *kyūba no reihō*. Later, the Bizen Ogasawara family had no heir, so the Geishū Takeda was the only family to continue to practice traditional horseback archery.

In the early 1900s there came the opportunity for traditional horseback archery to return to central Japan. Koremichi Takebara, who had kept *Kyūba no reihō* from the Geishū Takeda family, did not have an heir so they decided to choose their most skilled disciple, Heita Inoue, who was a famous warrior, as the 33rd Master. Then Yurin

Kaneko was chosen to be the 34th Master of the Takedaryu school (the school which is responsible for maintaining the traditional horseback martial arts kept by the Geishū Takeda family). He decided to bring true horseback archery back to Kamakura, once the capital of the Minamoto *bakufu* (military government) and began working vigorously to re-establish the school in central Japan. His effort was so great that he founded an organization to maintain the tradition and train archers, as well as to introduce it to the public. The organization was recognized and certified by the government. He conducted many *yabusame shinji* demonstrations at shrines year after year.

During WWII, all *shinji* demonstrations ceased. Master Yurin Kaneko had a difficult time even feeding his horse. After the war, his riding club was taken over by the US army. The Japanese government at that time restricted all Japanese traditional martial arts. The government did not want to discomfort the occupying forces. However, American commanders who rode at Yurin Kaneko's stable became very interested in and awed by Japanese horseback archery, and they actively supported the reactivation of practice and demonstrations. Some Americans even learned Japanese horseback archery techniques, and they used to join the demonstrations together with Japanese practitioners.

The Americans were not the only people to be fascinated by traditional horseback archery. In 1954, the renowned film maker, Akira Kurosawa, made *The Seven Samurai.* He asked then-Headmaster Yurin Kaneko, Ietaka Kaneko Sensei (the Headmaster's son and the 35th Master to be) and their students to instruct and demonstrate horseback archery in his film. Thus the famous battle scenes were made true to life. The movie was a great success both in Japan and overseas. Thereafter, Takedaryu performance became a necessity in Kurosawa's *samurai* movies.

Mr. Kurosawa contributed a foreword to Headmaster Yurin Kaneko's *Hizume no oto* as follows. "I always wanted to find an actor who could ride in the Japanese saddle but with no luck. I wondered why there were no actors who could keep a good posture on horseback. Then I came to know Headmaster Yurin Kaneko, the only one who maintains and teaches traditional Japanese horseback archery skill. I asked his teaching and found out that this was just the horseback riding I had been looking for." The late Toshiro Mifune , one of Japan's most renowned actors, became a Takedaryu student. He learned how to perform traditional horseback archery. He also participated in several demonstrations with other students.

In 1958 a performance of *yabusame* was included in the Hollywood movie *The Barbarian and the Geisha*. The master Ietaka Kaneko did the performance. One of his fondest memories during the making of the movie was that of John Wayne holding the master's horse, and they had a wonderful time as two horsemen. Of course every Takedaryu student enjoys this story.

The solemn, ceremonious presentation, the archer's beautiful clothing and gear, and the way they handle their extra long bow on the thunderously galloping horses, fascinate people on any occasion. Since 1991, *yabusame* demonstrations have been presented overseas with positive results. It is the effective way to introduce live Japanese tradition to audiences that may not have previously known anything about Japan.

In some places, these demonstrations help seed interest in learning about Japanese traditions. As the 34th and 35th Tsukasa-ke have been open-minded to overseas exchange, many countries have invited Takedaryu for demonstrations. In the past several years, the following countries have requested, and had Takedaryu horseback archery performances: France (1991 and 1997), Brazil (1995), Mongolia (1998), Germany (1992 and 2004), Bahrain (2002), Oman (2006). Some visits were made as national guests while others were to exchange culture and/or horsemanship skills. Some of the countries have asked Takedaryu to give training in their countries. This might possibly be the beginning of Japanese traditional horseback archery school in other countries. The peaceful meaning of *yabusame* is an excellent way to welcome foreign ministers who visit Japan. Two United States presidents have enjoyed *yabusame* demonstrations in Japan.

In the North America, the first Japanese horseback archery demonstration occurred at IHAF (International Horseback Archery Festival) in 2003, and has been continuing since then. A small seed has been looking for good soil and a direction to grow. I will mention more about this later in this chapter.

Three forms of horseback archery

Japanese horseback archery originally had three forms and together they are called *kisha-no-mitsumono*. *Yabusame* is just one of the three forms.

Yabusame course and targets

Most people think *yabusame* encompasses all forms of Japanese horseback archery. This is because *yabusame* is the most frequently presented, since it is the most ceremonial of the three and usually demonstrated at shrines to pray for peace, a good harvest and good health for the people. The course is 218 meters long and 2.1 meters wide. Three targets (the center of each target is 1.9 meters high from the ground) are spaced 65 meters apart from each other along the course. Each target is set parallel to the course fence. The distance from the horse path fence is 2.6 meters. All targets are to the archer's left.

Three different types of targets are used in the demonstration. For the first part of the demonstration, *shiki no mato* are used. In old times, this type of target was made from rattan strips woven into a square shape which is 41 square centimeters (16 inches) in size. Currently we use cardboard. This is covered with paper on which five different colored concentric circles are drawn. Each target is set on bamboo pole. Right above the target is a flower bouquet. Even if an arrow misses the board but hits the flower, it is recorded as a hit. This rule was made in ancient times to prevent an archer from feeling ashamed for missing the target and killing himself. In older days, becoming an archer to perform *yabusame* was considered to be a great honor for the family of the archer. The second type is the shingle target, called *ita mato*. Their size and the way they are set up is the same as with the *shiki no mato*. The third type is a small clay target, and this type is used in the competition component of the ceremony.

Although *yabusame* is a ceremony, the last part includes a competition. After eight to ten archers shoot the *shiki no mato* and the *ita mato*, the best three to five archers will be chosen to participate in *kyōsha*, or a competitive shoot. The round target is 17 centimeters in diameter (about 7 inches), and is called *ko mato* (small target). Two clay

www.lrgaf.org

bowls are glued together. Inside the bowls, the space is filled with small pieces of colorful paper. When the target is hit, the clay breaks into tiny pieces, and the multicolored pieces of paper that are inside the target give an explosive effect. Hitting these small targets which are suspended on strings requires very high skill, especially if the target is moving in the wind.

Inuoumono and *Kasagake*

While *yabusame* is categorized as a ceremony, there are two other forms of horseback archery. During the 9th century, when warriors fought on horseback with bow and arrow, two forms of Japanese horseback archery emerged, *kasagake* and *inuoumono*. Both of these forms were used to sharpen horseback archery skills.

Inuoumono is not practiced anymore, since actual dogs were used. In a circular fenced course, archers chased dogs and shot at them using ball-headed arrows so that the dogs would not get hurt.

Kasagake is still in practice now. According to *Hizume no oto*, *Kasagake* emerged around 896 AD. The author, the late master Yurin Kaneko wrote that anything, such as hats, fan, shoes or small piece of wood could be used as targets. We use different course settings depending on the occasion. The course from the ancient time is 109 meters long, 2.1 meters wide. The course has 5 targets in total. On the way down the course, there is one target, which is 15 meters away from the course. This is called *tōkasagake*. Returning back down the course, the archer shoots two of four small shingle targets on each side. The small targets are about 10 centimeters square, and each is set on a pole which is 70 centimeters long, and angled from the ground. This is called kogasagake.

The other course is 150 meters long, 2.1 meters wide. The course has six targets in total. On the way down the course, the archer shoots two shingle targets which are set 65 meters apart. Returning back down the course, the archer shoots two of four small shingle targets on each side. The small targets are 26 centimeters square (about 10 inches), and each is set on a pole which is 70 centimeters long (27 ½ inches), and angled from the ground.

Shooting a target close to the ground requires more skill. Why did *samurai* need this practice? In ancient times, the enemy leader was

www.lrgaf.org

the most desired target. However, since they usually wore *oyoroi* (armor) which covered most of the body including the head and the throat, the only place exposed was the face. So there emerged the need for accurate shooting skills. In *kasagake*, an archer needs to shoot to the left, right, high, and low. This challenging practice helps to improve archer's skill.

Important elements of horse archery

The horse

Next to the archer's skill, the horse is the important element in horseback archery. The temperament required of horses in older times, when horses were the warriors' companions, was completely different from the current requirements. In *Hizume no oto* it is written that the old Japanese horse breeds could run over anything in front of them without jumping or avoiding, which is different from Western horses. The horses that could crash onto the enemy warriors and horses were the best horses in the battlefield. *Bushi* in the Kanto region developed fighting tactics using large groups of warriors and horses to bulldoze over the enemy's field.

At that time a stallion that required six to eight people to hold was called a *kanba* (a very spirited horse), and the *samurai* who could tame and ride it had great pride in it. This spirit still exists in *Take-daryu*. Students never choose to ride dangerous horses. However, they have great pride in being able to accomplish horseback archery on difficult horses or fast horses if necessary.

In the 17th century, during the 300 peaceful years of the Tokugawa era, *bushi* had changed. Horses were expected to be trained into calm, gentle creatures. Modern massed cavalry tactics demanded obedient horses. Huge, spirited horses were avoided because they were not suitable for group action and they were easier targets for a firearm. When bows and arrows were the main weapons, the rider was protected by armor and everybody wanted to ride on a huge, flashy and spirited horse. But times had changed. Equestrian people in the Tokugawa era disliked *kanba* or spirited horses, and discontinued their breeding.

Currently in Japan, very few pure Japanese horses remain and these are protected in a few reserves. The horses used in horseback archery are mostly Thoroughbred, Quarter horse, Arabian and Japanese mixed breed. Compared with the US and other horse-rich countries, Japan is very limited in horse resources. It is very challenging both financially as well as physically to own a horse. In Takedaryu everyone shares the few horses owned by the school.

When we do demonstrations overseas, local horses are used. We have to train horses in a very short time. Since a full demonstration requires eight to twelve archers, never does everyone get a calm and obedient horse, which is appropriate for horseback archery. Also, not all the horses run nice and easy like the well-trained horses I admire in the U.S.A. We always wish we would get the best horses for everyone, but it is always the most skilled and experienced archer who get the faster and more challenging horse.

Costume

Yoroi hitatare is the costume originally worn under *yoroi* armor. The sleeves have drawstrings to gather excess fabric, so that the sleeves would not get in the way. They are made from colorful silk.

Igasa is the hat that archers wear in traditional *yabusame*. It is also called *ayahigasa*, or *ayaigasa*. The surface of the hat is black, the inside is gold and the rim is curved up like a tulip lampshade. On the top, there is a wooden *kimen* (scary spirit's face), which originated from the *kabuto* (helmet) the Jinko Empress wore when she suppressed invaders. The *kimen* must be taken off when the competition portion of *yabusame* begins, as the *kimen* is only for the sacred ceremonial portion of *yabusame*. Another type of hat used for *kasagake* is called *Eboshi*.

The big floppy hat which is used in *new-yabusame* is called *ayaigasa*, which had the same pronunciation as the traditional *igasa*. It is made of rush and used to be called *hiderigasa*(sun hat), since it used to be a sun hat or a rain hat used by *bushi* and ordinary people. This hat started to be used when Yoshimune Tokugawa established *kasha hasami mono*.

Mukabaki are very similar to western chaps. Samurai used them when they hunted or traveled on horse. For ceremonial *yabusame* they have to be summer fawn deer hides. The gloves, *Tebukuro*, are made from smoked deer skin. In *kyūdō*, gloves are called *yugake* while gloves for horseback archery are called *tebukuro*. *Yugake* is only for the right hand, with the thumb enlarged and lined with a stiff material. *Tebukuro* are for both hands and have soft thumbs. A cover wrap around the left shoulder and the left chest is called *Igote*. It is made with black velvet and each archer's family crest is embroidered on the shoulder.

The bow and arrow

Yumi. The Japanese bow, or *Yumi*, is the longest bow in the world. It is 210 centimeters long (1 inch shy of 7 feet) and with an asymmetrical curves. It is made from bamboo. Bows used in the ancient times were painted with Japan lacquer and wrapped with rattan to protect them from rain and from damage. Later, rattan patterns were determined by hierarchy. Currently carbon fiber bows as well as glass fiber bows are used in addition to bamboo bows.

Ya. The arrows used in traditional Japanese horseback archery have round wooded heads, or *jindō* and *hikime* . Especially for ceremonies at shrines, arrows which could draw blood must be avoided, so arrows which have sharp points would never be used. An archer carries four arrows, three of which are held at the waist in the *mukabaki* sash and one in the left hand with the bow. There is a description in *Yabusame no maki* (1417) by Mochinaga Ogasawara, that states"…in modern days (horseback archers) hold nine or twelve arrows in the *ebira* (quiver on the back)". So the practice in *new-yabusame* of using the *ebira* can be said to have started back in the 15th century.

Tack

Kura (saddle). The saddle consists of four pieces of wood that are tied together with string. Most saddles are coated with Japan lacquer. Since there is no soft padded part like an English or Western saddle, it has pads that are tied to the saddle with string. The saddle uses a cloth or woven girth, which is tied with manila rope, as well as a cloth-ribbon-like *munagai* (breast collar) and *shirigai* (crupper).

Abumi (stirrups). These are very important in Japanese horseback riding. Archers do not "sit" on the saddle, so the stirrups support the body weight. They are made of iron and are very heavy. They have a slipper-like shape, which has changed four times in the past. In the beginning, they used to be similar to Western (or Mongolian) stirrups. Then they changed into a slipper-like shape (with enough space for the most part of sole of the foot), varying the length of the foot-rest, which followed the change in weight of the rider's armor. Currently a mid-length *abumi* is used, which came into use as armor began to become lighter.

Kutsuwa (bit). The bit is a type of a snaffle bit, made of the same Japanese iron as was used in ancient swords. The bit is tied to a cloth bridle, which is called *tenjō*. Unlike the belt-type western bridle, it is infinitely adjustable. The reins are also made of cloth.

How to become a horseback archer

Process and mentality

Western equestrian sports are practiced in Japan. However, unlike most Western equine sports, Japanese horseback archery *kyūbadō* is a martial art. Those who take part in the ceremony of prayer for peace, good harvest and health for the people are expected to have a certain mentality. Let us look into the environment and requirements for those who are called *ite* (archer) or *monjin* (disciple). Since there is no Takedaryu school in the U.S., the description below applies to current practices in Japan.

Can anyone become a disciple? Yes, anyone who has a desire to learn is allowed to participate. Applicants are asked to hand in a resume and will be interviewed. The first year is considered a "trial year". Each student is supposed to have a love for the horse, respect for others and an ability to be in harmony with others. In addition, contributing one's time and work to the *Ryuha* (school), such as being present at each practice and helping with demonstrations and preparation, is required. In other words, willingness for commitment is necessary, in addition to learning technique. Self-centeredness is not acceptable.

Being humble is a virtue. Even an experienced archer regards oneself as "not enough". If a person shows an unacceptable attitude or behavior, the person will be asked to leave, regardless of the rank. In rare cases, a person would not be allowed to present himself/herself as having "formerly belonging to Takedaryu". Some students routinely practice *Zazen* (meditation) each time before joining the practice. There is no one who makes a living at horseback archery. Everyone including the Master has a job, so practice is set up once a week for all to join.

Many applicants have no experience in riding or archery. Some have riding and/or archery experience. How long does it take for one to be approved as an archer to participate in demonstrations? It takes from at least two years for the quickest students to several years to be qualified.

As mentioned in the section on horses, it never happens that everyone will get a horse suitable for horseback archery. In any demonstration, the first priority goes to the safety and the best possible presentation as a whole. Thus, the more skilled and experienced archer(s) tends to take more challenging and faster horse(s). As a result, in spite of having high skill, some archers hit fewer targets because of the difficult horses. However, those who step up to take challenging horses are highly respected. To keep oneself quiet and still on the galloping horse and try to do one's best shooting takes a lot of mental concentration. Our Master Ietaka Kaneko teaches that "the more you want to hit a target, the less successful you will be. Practice well, and keep your mind empty."

Practice

The horseback riding portion and the archery portion are practiced separately, especially for the beginners.

Beginners practice their riding in an arena. The most important skill to learn is *sukashi nori*. This riding skill supports the upper body by putting the rider's entire weight on both stirrups in order to be able to hold the upper body still for a fast and secure nocking on the galloping horse. It depends on individual ability, but it usually takes more than two years or more to be able to appear as if "sitting on a still horse" while galloping. When one becomes able to do *sukashi nori,* he or she might be allowed to do *subase* (galloping through the course without shooting). *Subase* is practice riding without a rein, which requires not relying on one's hands to support the body. This also prepares the rider to get used to the sudden acceleration and sustained speed of the horse.

The archery portion on mounted archery at first is practiced both standing on the ground and mounted on a horse-sized wooden rocking horse. Three arrows are held at the waist sash and one will be nocked. Four arrows are shot quickly at the practice target. This practice is to help in nocking arrows quickly and securely. The first arrow is not as difficult since it is already nocked. The next three arrows have to be quickly drawn from the waist, one at a time, nocked, aimed at the target, and then released. The archer is considered to be proficient if he/she can hit the target within three to four seconds for each arrow. This practice is required before one can proceed to mounted shooting. Through all of this, the student must maintain correct form even in fast nocking and shooting. The huge rocking horse allows the rider to learn to keep the upper body still on an unstable platform so that he or she can nock, aim, and shoot quickly with the correct form.

Finally one gets to practice shooting from horseback. It takes three to four years before one is allowed to shoot from horseback. Without learning *sukashi nori* and the correct shooting form, mounted archery could be dangerous and one can easily fall into an incorrect shooting form. Those who are allowed to participate in demonstrations keep on practicing shooting on the ground as well as riding without shooting.

A Japanese archer's journey and the International Horse Archery Festival

When I encountered Takedaryu

I have always loved horses and as a child dreamt of riding horses. My dream came true when I became a member of my university equestrian team. I learned jumping and dressage as well as how to take care of the horses. I never wanted to miss any opportunity to be around horses.

Several years after I graduated from university, I encountered Takedaryu, the group which is responsible for maintaining the Japanese traditional horseback martial arts from fifteen centuries ago. When I saw the archers shooting arrows from the thundering horses, I felt the partnership between horses and human where the horse works to help attain the human goal. I realized at the very moment that this is what I wanted to do. Right away I asked the Headmaster Ietaka Kaneko for permission to join the school, and was accepted. It was not easy to learn totally different way of riding, but I made my way slowly. One of my best memories during those days was participating in our demonstration in Mongolia. It was a horseperson's delight to ride their spirited horses.

In 2000, I had the opportunity to move to Wisconsin in the United States. I arrived at the Milwaukee airport holding my bow and arrows, hoping to introduce our traditional horseback archery to the United States. Headmaster Ietaka Kaneko has supported my ambition. He generously sent me a complete set of traditional horse equipment. He said "Do your best to introduce Japanese traditional horseback archery in the U.S." His words continue to be my driving force.

International Horse Archery Festival

In 2002, I had the opportunity to meet horse archers in the United States. I read an article about the International Horse Archery Festival (IHAF) in *Primitive Archer*. In September of that same year, I visited Fort Dodge and saw an amazing Hungarian horse archery demonstration by Mr. Kassai Lajos. At the moment I thought IHAF was the place to make my dream come true.

I met a man wearing a *kyūdō* uniform and selling his own *yumi* and *ya*. I greeted him and showed him my pictures of doing *yabusame*. His eyes widened and he took me to the President of the festival. This man was the very famous "human glue", Mr. Jaap Koppedrayer, who helped to make the Japanese horseback archery demonstration happen at IHAF, for the first time in the North America. The lady I was introduced to was Mrs. Meg Beshey, who at the time was the President of the IHAF. She and her family have given me unchanging support.

I was asked to come back the following year to do demonstrations. I felt fortunate to be invited, and wanted to return my gratitude to the master. One who belongs to Japanese martial art school has to get permission from the master to do a demonstration under the name of the school. I asked and he was very happy to give his permission.

At that time, I was riding my dear friend Diana Troyk's quarter horse, Magic. Without Diana and Magic, it would not be possible for me to prepare for the upcoming festival. Magic did not mind when I shot arrows on the ground in front of him. However, when I started shooting at the target from his back, he showed off his wonderful accelerating ability, and we had to work at keeping a steady gallop. It took a long time and much patience before Magic was able to gallop at an even speed before and after the arrow was released.

The preparation for the IHAF was as follows. I needed to plan what and how to demonstrate, and obtain accurate information on course measurements as well as the size and the numbers of the course materials. We had to ask to recruit volunteers who would help build the course and assist in the demonstration. This part was well taken care by Mr. Koppedrayer. We decided to do *yabusame kasha shiki* (we do not call it *yabusame* if the demonstration is not a ceremony performed at a shrine).

The purpose of the demonstration at the IHAF was to introduce the traditional Japanese horseback archery, exactly as it has been for more than 1400 years. Also it was to be the first demonstration of Japanese traditional horseback archery in North America. I thought it was very important to replicate an actual performance in Japan as much as possible. However, the IHAF schedule conflicted with an important demonstration in Japan. I needed to limit borrowing and transporting materials from Japan. Therefore, most of the needed materials had to be prepared in the US.

Demonstration helpers who did things like retrieve the arrows and take care of the targets were performed by disciples of Kanjuro Shibata Sensei, a greatly revered senior Kyudo Master. These *kyūdō* practitioners knew how to treat *yumi* and *ya*, and had their own *kyūdō* uniforms. I decided to make their hats and paint the huge fans (held by the starter). The wooden shingle targets as well as target backdrops were made by Mr. David Beshey, who was the Festival Manager in cooperation with Mr. Jaap Koppedrayer. Hundreds of e-mails went to and fro between Wisconsin, Japan, Iowa, and Canada.

Other than IHAF's help, Ms. Naoko Oshida was a huge help. She is my junior in Takedaryu. She helped me obtain new arrows and other materials which were hard to find in this country. She also helped with getting information on building the regulation course. In addition, she came to Iowa and helped oversee the course building as well as leading the demonstration helpers. It was indeed a tremendous help for me while organizing the first big project.

Early morning on Aug.26th, 2003, I headed out to Iowa for the eight hour drive. When I arrived, Mr. Lukas Novotny and Mr. Dana

Hotoko were already there and in the process of choosing and preparing the horses for their training sessions. Two horses were available for me to choose. I tried both, then decided to use Amigo, a grey Peruvian Paso with pale blue eyes. It was my first time to ride a gaited horse. He was eager to run and did not mind when the arrows were shot in front of his eyes. Mr. Novotny and Mr. Hotko advised me to ride at least two hours to make him tired before shooting from the horseback. So I set up my schedule to ride two hours in the morning then start shooting in the afternoon. Still, he was pretty fast, but his gallop was very smooth, which was nice as long as I could nock my arrows quickly.

After the horse was chosen, the next step was to build the course. Under Ms. Oshida's leadership, Mr. Koppedrayer, Mr. Beshey and volunteers worked to build the course. It's length was 150 meters, which was shorter than the regulation course in Japan (we could not make it longer due to the available length), and it had two targets, which is one less than the regulation course. It was parallel to the Hungarian-type course used by Mr. Kassai and Mr. Novotny, so we took turns using the two courses.

The five days of preparation passed quickly. The first day of the festival, Amigo was very fast. I was overwhelmed by the speed, however, I managed to hit several targets. On the second day, Amigo started to get excited when he saw the course. He tried to take off without my cue, and sometimes he reared. Whenever I needed to adjust the girth or nock the arrow, he tried to take off in different directions, which made it very challenging for me to concentrate on my shooting. On the third day, the human and the horse started to get along better, and the result was satisfactory.

There was not much free time since we were busy with practice and preparation, but we were able to meet other horseback archers. There was also a small lecture to introduce Japanese traditional horse archery. It was a great honor to be there and it gave me a wonderful memory that I will never forget. I deeply appreciate the warm support and patience from the IHAF people for understanding and respecting our tradition. I appreciate their patience in understanding our customs, such as the importance of needing permission from the Takedaryu headmaster. I also appreciate the volunteer helpers, especially those kyudo practioners who generously gave us their help.

www.lrgaf.org

It was such an honor again to be able to do *yabusame kisha shiki* and *kasagake* at IHAF in 2004 and 2006. In 2004, we planned to do demonstrations with three archers. However, it turned out to be a challenge. With IHAF committee's support, head archer, Mr. Yoshsiaki Koike, came along with Ms. Naoko Oshida , but the horses, other than Amigo, did not turn out as expected. However, it was a huge accomplishment to be able to introduce *kasagake*—shooting at a lower right ground target, by the archer twisting his body on horseback, moving the long Japanese bow from the left side to the right side, or visa versa at each shot, crossing the horse's neck, at each passing target.

In 2004, we had the good fortune of having Mr. Koike as an instructor so that we could have training. Due to the limited preparation time and material, we decided to invite those who had already learned *kyūdō* and who could help our demonstration in their own *kyūdō* uniforms.

One unexpected surprise was the need to have each student sign a "Liability Release Form". In other words, we had to learn to be aware of the possibility of being sued by a student. Fortunately, it seemed there was no student who had such thoughts. In Japanese martial art schools, students never even think about suing an instructor. Unless there is an obvious intention to harm, accidents in martial art activities are considered personal responsibility. It was a significant cultural difference, which we could understand in theory. However it still gave us pause.

In spite of our inner concerns, the training turned out to be satisfactory for every participant. Those who are skilled in *kyūdō*, found it meaningful to learn a different style and speed of nocking as well as the history and the equipment of Japanese traditional horseback archery. They said it was a great honor to participate in the actual demonstration. We felt rewarded. First we planned to continue the training every year at IHAF, but the festival was scheduled on alternative years. There have been quite a few inquiries about future training. However where, when , and whether to invite an instructor from Japan, as well as finding the horse(suitable for beginners) and the place all remain a challenge.

In 2006, the IHAF Festival was held in June. Since there was no budget for inviting person(s) from Japan, I was the only one available to do a demonstration. This year, far fewer volunteers were available, but again, Kanjuro Shibata Sensei's disciples kindly gave their helping hands. Special thanks go to Mr. Phil Ortiz, who helped every demonstration since 2003, and who brought Ms.Haruko, a wonderful organizer. Ms.Trinidad Campbell also came back. New wonderful local helpers were Brian D. Healey Black Belt Club, and Ms. Alayne Beshy, Meg and Dave's daughter. I received truly thoughtful and well-minded support from those martial artists. Although the whole schedule was intense and tiring, all of us had a wonderful time.

In 2006, the training portion was separated from the Festival. Instead there were explanations and mini-lectures just for the helpers about the history, the meaning of the demonstration and the horse archer's mentality. I wanted to be a team with them, not just a demonstrator, with volunteer helpers. I personally believe this is the way to build a foundation for Takedaryu to grow in this country so that everyone who chooses to make a commitment would learn not only the skill but also the history and the meaning of what they do, and the mentality of being a Japanese traditional horseback archer.

The 2006 course was set in the different area. This year, I had to spend more time on preparing the ground, measuring, setting up the fence, etc., than previously. I sorely missed the effective help of the Koppedrayers, because they were away in Spain for another major event. Fortunately Mr. Beshey, who does very precise work and was a trustworthy person as well as Brian D. Healey, Black Belt Club members, who were also the demonstrators, helped me. In addition, Mr. David Weiss helped me enormously. His energy and enthusiasm for the best result was so positive that the demonstration could not have done without him. Throughout the program we experienced inclement weather with thunderstorms and tornado warnings. Targets as well as backdrops to catch arrows were continually being blown away. After the wooden backdrop poles broke down for the second time, Mr. Weiss replaced them with heavy duty metal pipes, which withstood the stormy wind for the rest of the festival. I still remember how the poles looked like weeping willow trees, arched against the strong wind.

That year, the content of the public lecture was greatly deepened. In addition to the talk on the history of *kyūbadō* (the Japanese horseback martial arts), there was horse tack, bow and arrows, costume, as well as targets for the audience to see, touch and ask questions about.

The demonstration horse was Amigo again. I rode him in the past two festivals, so I could imagine how he would be. He was a spirited Peruvian Paso, with great speed. Since it had been two years since Amigo had performed, I wanted to practice with him at least for five days. However he came two days before the festival. Thunderstorms and tornado warnings greatly reduced my available practice time. In 2004, we had two other horses as company so he was much calmer, but this year he kept on trying to take off. He did not want to stand still whenever he saw the course. It was very hard, since the Japanese saddle has a girth which often needs to be tightened. I had to ask Ms. Jenna Matson and Mr. Alex Dencklau, who knew Amigo well, for help to hold the horse when needed. Amigo did wonderfully once he was on the course. Due to the weather, the festival attendance was very small, but those who came to see said that they enjoyed the demonstration.

I have participated in IHAF for three times and recognize that Japanese horseback archery demonstration is different from the other horseback archery demonstration I saw at the IHAF. The Hungarian based Kassai course had been permanently installed but the *yabusame* course had to be re-built each year. It takes much work and human power to prepare the course and demonstrate. Targets, backdrops and fence have to be made, built or set up each time. Targets are not reusable. To give it a uniform and ceremonious look and atmosphere, it requires at least five to seven helpers all wearing appropriate garb. Every demonstration requires the same amount of work. However, it can be done anywhere if there is an appropriate place, financial support volunteers and good horses. The outcome is always worthwhile all the efforts, and the Takedaryu demonstration has drawn so much attention wherever and whenever it takes place.

The future in the United States

I truly hope that the beauty and the tradition of Japanese horseback archery will prosper in the United States and I hope that people will have an opportunity to see a performance. It requires a large budget to bring a full scale demonstration from Japan to the U.S., but it is my hope to be part of one.

Similar to other horseback archers as well as other horseback archery events, the biggest challenges are horses, space and financing. It has taken time to find a stable where shooting from horseback is acceptable. There is no problem finding a horse. However, once I start explaining about what I would like to do and what kind of tack is going to be used with leased or rented horse, there seems to be a hesitation. Most people seem to be uncomfortable about putting unfamiliar equipment (Japanese saddle and stirrups, for example) on their horse, which I understand.

However I hope someday there will be an opportunity to have a permanent Japanese traditional horseback archery school in the United States.

Contact information and references:

For more information about Takedaryu Kyubado , please visit
www.yabusame.or.jp
Or contact misa_tsuyoshi@yahoo.co.jp

"Hizume no oto" ("The Sound of Hoofbeats"), by Yurin Kaneko, 1965,
Tokyo Shobo, discontinued, only in Japanese.
"Nihon no Dentou Bajyutsu:Bajou Bugeihen"("The Japanese
traditional mounted martial arts") by Yurin Kaneko, 1975,
Nichibou Shuppansha, discontinued, only in Japanese.

Chapter 4

Horseback Archery in China and Korea

By Stephen Selby

History in China

In common with much of the rest of Eurasia and North America, there is an on-going argument about when human interaction with horses first appeared in the archaeological record. Were horses eaten? Were they ridden? Were they used to pull chariots? The jury is out.

At the time of the 59-year rule of Wu Ding, (Shang period, around 1300BCE), horses and chariots were well-established and traces of both have been preserved – most spectacularly at the chariot burials near modern-day Anyang in Central China. Shang chariots had two horses yoked at the withers each side of a central bar or tongue, rather than between two shafts.

Most strikingly, though, these early chariots – the first in the Chinese archaeological record – were technically highly developed. The same can be said of the bridles and bit-less tack on the horses. While most Chinese scholars are now in agreement that the chariot must have entered China though Central Asia rather than being a Chinese invention, there were clear improvements in design that were unique to China.

One striking improvement was in weight-reduction: Shang chariots were made with light wooden frames, 16-spoked wheels and rattan flooring. Secondly, they were modular. They could be taken apart and re-assembled easily, with the main joints made from finely-crafted bronze fittings.

Clearly, these chariots were platforms for shooting. Each Shang chariot could carry one charioteer. Some larger models are thought to have been able to carry three. Apart from horses and the chariot itself, Shang chariot burials often included the body of a charioteer, bow fittings, arrowheads as well as a weapon called 'ge' – a sort of primitive Chinese halberd that appears to have developed with chariot warfare and declined together with it. A bronze device attached to the front of the charioteer's belt permitted him to retain the reins and steer the horses while leaving his hands free to shoot. (A similar system is also evident from Egyptian wall paintings.)

Those familiar with horse husbandry find it inconceivable that horses could have been trained and horse herds maintained in ancient China without people being able to ride horseback. The literary and archaeological records, however, contain no trace of horseback riding until around 600BCE. This riddle remains to be solved.

In the Zhou period (about 1100BCE – 221BCE), the Chinese Classics relate that members of the Chinese ruling classes started to learn charioteering and archery at about the age of seven, and were required to 'graduate' in the skill when they reached the age of about 14 years. The chariots were low platforms with spoked wheels. Each was normally manned by a complement of three warriors: a driver in the middle, an archer on his right and a halberdeer on his left. Two horses were yoked to the chariot, left and right of a central bar. Two more 'spare' horses were tethered on the outside of the draw-horses.

The archer on the chariot was armed with two bows (one in-hand and the spare one tied to the chariot rail) and a supply of arrows in a quiver at his waist. It is sufficient to look at the ancient pictorial characters in which Shang period Chinese was written to see that the bow that they used was a composite reflex bow (probably horn, bamboo and sinew), with the string permanently attached to one tip and wound on the other tip when the bow was strung. The size and appearance may have been similar to that of a Korean traditional horn bow.

Some commentators have suggested that these low-platform war chariots with their wooden wheels could never have been of practical use in warfare: they were surely just used for command or for show. I myself have never made any experiments; but all the archaeological evidence and abundant written historical records suggest that they were actually used in the thick of battle, as well as for pursuing prey in the hunt.

The defeat of the Shang royal household in about 1100BCE by the Zhou (who invaded from the West of China) coincided with climatic changes. Some 400 years later, similar severe climate drove nomadic tribes (such as the Saka) from the West to attack the Zhou and the latter were forced to move their capital eastwards in 722BCE. From that time until 221BCE, China was ruled by competing centres of power dominated by feudal dukedoms. The northernmost of these dukedoms – Zhao and Yan – were subject to repeated attacks from nomad tribes from the grasslands (Saka, proto-Xiongnu and proto-Korean) who had adopted horseback warfare in which the bow was the main weapon. Chariots were no match for these warriors.

King Wuling of the State of Zhao (325—298BCE) realized that traditional battle formations, involving nobles in long Chinese gowns riding on horse-drawn chariots, could no longer provide a defense against horseback archers. After a long debate with his courtiers, he decided that the Chinese must adopt the leather britches and short tunics of the nomads and learn to shoot on horseback. The Chinese cavalry was born.

From the time of King Wuling, horseback archery became universally accepted in military tactics and the war chariot rapidly disappeared from the battlefield. From Han Dynasty (206BCE – 220CE) tomb paintings, we can see that chariots continued to be used in hunting. Han chariots had horses between shafts; yoked chariots disappeared from the scene. By the end of the Han Dynasty, chariots had completely disappeared.

It seems that the Chinese did not invent any horseback archery tactics of their own: they continued to learn from their neighbors to the North. Intermarriage and strategic alliances were common in the Han Dynasty and the following periods, and nomad allies were an important element of Chinese cavalry battle formations. In the 500 years from the end of the Han to the Sui Dynasty (581CE), the ruling houses of China were predominantly of nomad origin.

From the Ming Dynasty (1368-1644), a number of teaching manuals for horseback archery have survived. There was a ready market for such manuals because horseback archery was a compulsory event in the Imperial Military Examinations starting from the Tang Dynasty in 702CE. I have translated below the whole of a section of horseback archery from a Qing Dynasty work which reflects the Manchu technique of archery, written by Liu Qi in 1722. Only one copy of this book remains worldwide.

The archery examination had two tests: in the first, the candidate entered a walled circle where he could get his horse into a canter on the correct lead; then he galloped out into a walled runway and shot three arrows into three evenly-spaced targets at shoulder height. In the second test, he had to shoot with a blunt arrow at a football-sized leather ball filled with rice placed on the ground and knock it out of a cup like an eggcup.

The disappearance of horseback archery in China is a recent phenomenon. Before the Imperial Examinations were abolished in 1901 it was common. Heinrich Harrer filmed a horseback archery competetion outside the Potala Palace in Tibet in the 1950s.

In the People's Republic of China five years ago, you could hardly find a performance of horseback archery. Occasionally, you can see performances by police and army patrols which can shoot a rifle from on horseback.

History in Korea

In Korea, the development of horseback archery closely mirrored that in China. Korea archeology has to-date not yielded any chariot burials. Horse harness-fittings are in evidence from around 500BCE. From then on, pottery figures and paintings from the Korean Peninsula frequently depict horseback archery scenes, with both hunting and warfare as the context.

A note of caution is necessary though: the people depicted in these paintings are those peoples who have migrated or settled the Korean Peninsula in the past 2,000 years. They may have included Chinese, Ska, Xiongnu, Xianbi, apart from the proto-Korean people themselves.

Following the Mongolian invasion of Korea under Khublai Khan and the retreat of Mongol forces towards the end of the Chinese Yuan Dynasty (1367), the Korean Peninsula was frequently invaded by the Japanese forces under Hideyoshi during the 15th Century. The Korean military establishment was recovering with great difficulty from the successive losses under the Mongols and then the Japanese. To prevent the peninsula from becoming a base from which the Japanese could launch attacks on Northern China, the Chinese Ming court sent General Qi Jiguang (1528-1587) to assist with military training.

Ming Chinese military horseback archery was widely adopted, subject to adaptation, by the revived Korean forces. Illustrated Chinese military manuals were circulated in Korea (the Chinese language was still commonly understood by literate Koreans at that time.)

Many of the Korean horseback archery pursuits shown in Korean manuals mirror those of the Chinese. One innovation was a sport called 'Mogu', in which mounted archers chased a large ball (wool covering a light wooden frame about 1 metre in diameter) dragged behind a leading horse. Blunt arrows with their arrowheads dipped in colored ink showed whose shots had scored on the target.

The horseback archery revival

At the end of the 20th century, horseback archery in East Asia was limited to Yabusame in Japan, occasional displays at the Lijiang Horse Festival in Tibet and some equestrian acrobatic troupes in Inner Mongolia and a performing group in South Korea. Performers from these events provided the stunt-men to perform in Chinese historical movies.

My researches into Asian traditional archery started around the early 1990s. Having no horse riding skills, I had originally hoped to study the history and technique of Chinese archery based solely on foot archery. That, however, was a mistake. It became clear in the course of my research that, with the exception of ritual archery (which had its roots in the charioteering era), all traditional Chinese archery training was a journey which ended on horseback at full gallop. Like it or not, I had to learn to ride.

I was able to take part in the second International Horseback Archery Festival in Fort Dodge, Iowa in September 2001. I went there having no intention of getting up on horseback; but gentle cajoling by Kassai Lajos and extreme patience by Lukas Novotny persuaded me to try. Kassai was patient, courteous and accommodating to me (something he is not always known for) and Lukas found time in his busy schedule to let me learn on the lunge.

I was hooked.

From that time on, I became determined to learn both classical European riding as well as traditional Asian riding. Learning from local instructors and the Ming and Qing manuals (such as the one translated below), I developed sufficient skills to start shooting on horseback. My son, Tim, learned with me and subsequently went to Fort Dodge to learn more formally from Lukas Novotny.

In 2003, I became acquainted with Master Kim Yong-sap, who formed the Korean Equestrian Martial Arts Association (KEMA). Master Kim was a self-taught horseback archer who had never encountered the western developments led by Kassai (though he was aware of them). Dedicated to re-establishing native Korean horseback martial skills, Master Kim and his associates developed a performance-based routine that was rooted directly in the military manuals circulating in Korea in the sixteenth century.

Master Kim was another extremely generous master. Not only did he welcome me to train with his troupe on their excellent Cheju ponies (said to be the direct descendants of those used for Khublai Khan's ill-fated invasion of Japan,) he subsequently trained me in horseback spear and sword skills.

In 2004, KEMA hosted the First Korean Horseback Archery Championship, and in 2005, Master Kim generously invited Hong Kong to send a team to take part in the First International Horseback Archery Competition at Sokcho.

The Korean competition rules are a bit different from Kassai's standard: there are three competition rounds, each divided into child, youth and adult classes. The course is 100 metres for single and double shot, and 130 metres for five shots.

The single shot is taken at the gallop at a target set at a distance of six metres from the course. The double shot is taken at two targets, set 30 and 60 metres along the course at a distance of 6 metres. The first target is angled forward 45 degrees and the second is angled back 45 degrees, so that the archer takes one forward and one rearward shot. The final competition requires shooting at five targets evenly spaced along a 130 metre course.

For all the competitions the archer's gallop is timed. His or her actual run time is deducted from 19 seconds (25 seconds for the five-target competition) and the difference is added to the archer's score on the target face (a standard 130cm FITA target).

On the basis of my own studies and instruction from Kassai, Lukas and Master Kim, I had started teaching horseback archery courses in Hong Kong. My courses are 12-hour courses taught over a

www.lrgaf.org

single weekend. I held three courses, two in 2004 and one in 2005. Many of the students were children and teenagers.

Despite the limitations of training in Hong Kong (lack of space, expense and having to use retired thoroughbred racehorses), we have developed a small team. We were delighted when in 2005, the Hong Kong team came away from the first International Competition in Korea with three gold medals, one silver and two bronzes. Since that time, we have maintained our training and at the second International competition in 2006, we gained one Gold medal, one silver and three bronze. Teams from Korea, Hong Kong, Germany and the USA took part.

In 2006, an association of Tibetan archers in Qinghai province in China asked us to help organize a horseback archery competition. We sought technical assistance from Master Kim and his colleagues (who also sent a team to compete.) Again, we were able to come away with a gold medal, a silver medal and two bronze medals.

Korea has now established a World Horseback Archery Federation as well as a national one. (This development somewhat duplicates the role of IHAF.) Hong Kong will soon establish its own Horseback Archery Association with the aim of gaining government recognition and assistance, as well as formalizing our participation in international competitions.

Spurred mainly by the development of international and intercultural competitions, horseback archery teams now exist in Tibet, Inner Mongolia, Outer Mongolia, Korea and Hong Kong. It remains to be seen whether Yabusame practitioners in Japan would be prepared to join in. Mongolia hopes to organize an international competition starting from 2007. Korea will continue with its annual competitions. Hong Kong will certainly stage a competition when we are able to supply competitors with some suitable horses.

There is no doubt that horseback archery in Asia is back!

From the 'Illustrated Guide to Archery Method' by Liu Qi
(Translated by Stephen Selby and incorporating comments from Bede Dwyer.)

Instructions for Horseback Archery

Since ancient times, horseback archery has lacked any supporting literature. All that is said is that "the rider and his horse must practice together." Even if you survey the literature on general horsemanship, all you find is "six reins in the hand", "like a troupe dancing together" and so on.

"The rider and his horse must practice together" means just this: the rider must know the habits of the horse, and the horse must understand the intentions of the rider. The two should not be [in a relationship of] one driving and the other resisting.

"Like a troupe dancing together" just means that the rider must make all his actions fluid and harmonious; fast and slow pace should proceed appropriately, not in fits and starts.

These two phrases sum the whole thing up and you can use them as a basis to follow on from.

Is it not true that the heart of the matter is in skill in galloping? Those who have such skills are 'in the know' while those who haven't are 'outsiders.' Isn't it true that those who can't shoot on horseback are just those who lack skill in galloping? Those who are afraid panic and get flustered into making errors. People who are frightened do not dare to gallop. Then how can they practice together with their horse? People who are panicked are not in control, then how can they make their actions fluid and harmonious?

Who has ever heard of a capable horseback archer who suffered from these two disabilities?

There is a saying: "The people of the South go about on boats; the people of the North go on horseback." Now Manchu and Han people are called upon to become close to one-another; yet the Han people cannot reach the standard of the Manchus. Why is that? Because the latter practice their own method right from childhood. Starting from childhood, horse and man naturally become as one. How can they but be alone in extending their natural abilities?

Moreover, they are in the habit of making regular visits to the camps of their princes. They travel over very wide areas. As they interact with their peers, they absorb their traditional knowledge more and more deeply. This is in fact nothing more than what is expressed in the two terms "practicing together" and "like a troupe dancing together", and is a completely different kettle of fish from "fear and fluster." It has almost become an immutable rule.

So I shall describe horseback archery so that our generation can rid themselves of this weakness. If we can rid ourselves of this weakness, everyone will receive enormous encouragement and apply themselves assiduously to the task. Furthermore, who will fear that their horseback archery skills are imperfect? I am therefore setting out the following twelve explanations so that my exposition of horseback and infantry archery will be complete.

There is nothing difficult about riding a horse: it's just a matter of becoming accustomed to it. Naturally, there are some special skills involved. In this volume, I reckon nervousness to be the main source of faults. There are centuries' worth of ironclad evidence to support this.

The organization of this work

There are twelve sections to this work. The main premise is that the horse must be well-trained. If the horse is well-trained, the movements of the body will be fluid. Practicing horseback archery is not difficult! So I have set out riding method first, followed by shooting method. This approximates to the idea of 'proceeding from the more difficult subject to the easier one'.

Selecting your horse

A horse must possess inherent quality before it can be ridden. A stubborn or inadequate horse has no place in a battle: even less should you want such a horse to display your prowess [in the Examination]? Any horse that possesses inherent quality doesn't necessarily have to be a champion. It just has to respond correctly to the rider's intention to start and stop, go fast or slow. Of course, there's no harm in champion qualities if you can get them. (Some horse-owners may learn something new here!)

www.lrgaf.org

Training your horse

There are more good horses in the world than bad ones. But how can people just care for them when it suits them? The key to everything is avoiding irregular feeding and watering. Even more important is systematic training and practice. Whatever sights the horse has not seen before, it must be exposed to regularly; whatever sounds the horse has not heard before, it must be exposed to regularly. It must be brought into close contact with the things that will normally be around it and kept away from the things that will normally not be present. The best training starts with training in its nature, and then training its strength. Like this, every horse will be good. (Everyone who owns a horse must realize this!)

Riding a Horse

Once you get up on a horse, your attention must never wander away from the horse. (Not letting your mind wander away from the horse is a trade secret of horsemanship.) You must co-ordinate the use of reins and the crop. Whether going fast or slow, you must keep at ease without using force. When you make the horse gallop, apply equal pressure with both knees. If you relax pressure on one side, the horse will veer towards that side. If you have the reins in your hands, you use them to steer the horse; and if you have to let go the reins, you use your knees for the job. That is the general approach. With an unfamiliar horse, you need to estimate how hard his mouth is before you start to ride it.

Mounting

Mount your horse quickly and lightly. Try always to mount from a block. If none is available, then hold the reins and the mane with your left hand and gripping the pommel with your right, get your left foot into the stirrup close up to the saddle. The special skill is in finding the right stirrup when you are on the saddle. With plenty of practice you will be light on your feet and quick, and look good. Moreover, this looks orderly and dignified.

www.lrgaf.org

Body position

The rider's main aim in his body position should be to maximize the strength in his hips. Secondly, you want to get your crotch firmly settled into the saddle. If your crotch is firmly settled into the saddle, your waist will naturally be straight and firm. The most important remaining skill is to avoid flopping about. For example, you need to get both knees firmly gripping the front of the saddle, both calves gripping the horse's flanks and pressing into the stirrups with the feet. But you should not insert your feet too far into the stirrups. Your grip on the reins should be lively - not insensitive. Your bottom should not be pressing down on the horse's spine and your heels shouldn't be clamped around the horse's belly. In this way, you body position will be correct. It's not difficult once you have practiced it.

Getting the horse into a gallop

Don't try getting the horse into a gallop while you are still in the starting circle. You should hold back on the reins and the bridle and get the horse into the runway first. Move your horse on a few paces to get the movement of the hooves even, then gently give the horse the bit. How many people know 'The rider at ease, the horse going smoothly, and from within this the bow and arrow are controlled.' (Actually, only the old hands know this.)

Reining in the horse

How you rein in the horse depends on the horse's mouth; but it mustn't be done in too much of a rush. Don't force the horse's head up. You need to make sure the reins and bridle are controlled evenly: hold the reins firmly on each side of the mane. Pull both arms in to your side and apply even pressure through your arms, waist, knees, hands and feet. Don't keep your limbs loose or move them around. Don't lean forward or backward. Be natural, firm and without unnecessary movement. (This is really the expert's method.)

www.lrgaf.org

Dismounting

You should dismount effectively and conveniently. 'Effectively' means you should get your feet out of the stirrups quickly. 'Conveniently' means being able to twist your body around quickly. The former should be achieved without getting stuck and the latter without getting encumbered. Every element of horsemanship, from mounting to dismounting, has its own things you should get accustomed to; then shooting will present no problem.

Normal riding and riding off-centre

Normal riding and riding off-centre are two different things. In normal riding, the main force is taken on the crotch. This method is used for shooting level. When riding off-centre, you have your bottom slightly off-centre. This method is used for shooting at the ground. You use level shooting for shooting at a target set up on the wall of the runway. You use shooting at the ground for shooting at the ball on the ground.

Shooting at a target set up on the wall of the runway

When shooting at a target set up on the wall of the runway, the left side of your ribcage should be sideways on [to the target]. Extend your left upper arm outward slightly. That means you can draw the bow easily from the chest. This should be achieved with a heroic action.

As regards aiming, every archer has his own instincts. On the one hand, you don't want to be inflexible; on the other, you don't want to put an arrow through your horse's leg!

(Attain stability.)

Shooting at the ball on the ground.

Shooting at the ball on the ground, you should lean forward onto your left knee, and let your left upper arm extend down slightly. Then your back will be stretched and you will be firm in the saddle. The arrow should go out with sufficient force.

www.lrgaf.org

As regards aiming, you should take account of the horse's speed. You should mainly rely on your instinct, but you want to avoid shooting straight down onto the top of the ball [which would fail to dislodge it from its holder.]

(Attain stability.)

Some things to avoid

With the horse at the gallop, when you let go of the reins, don't use the crop too much. Don't use your feet in the stirrups to slap the horse's flanks.

Don't stand up in the stirrups as you attempt to keep facing the target.

Don't feel around or look at the string or the nock when nocking your arrow.

When drawing the bow and looking back at the target, don't let your chest or knee get in the way of the string.

When shooting level at the target, don't release too soon or too late.

When reining in your horse after shooting, don't hang your bow over your shoulder.

Don't cant your bow as you draw.

Don't yank on the string as you release.

(All of this is good advice.)

The previous twelve sections are all things you need to pay attention to during practice sessions. Internally, you can gain power, while externally you will look better. You can't avoid making yourself completely familiar with all of them.

Once you are on your horse and at the examination ground, drawing the bow and releasing the arrow should be like a flash of lightning; quick as a sudden storm. Moreover, you should take these words from the 'flying general' as the spirit of horseback archery: "A nerve of iron, a cautious heart, easy in your breathing, flexible in your strength, quick of eye and skilled of hand."

Although the eighteen characters above are something the horseback archer cannot afford to overlook, I have left them until last so that if I have left anything out, they can make up for it.

Liu Qi of Luan Jiang (Zhejiang)

References:

Selby. S. 2000. Chinese Archery. Hong Kong: Hong Kong University Press.
Selby, S. 2003. Archery Traditions of Asia. Hong Kong: Hong Kong Museum of Coastal Defence.
Selby, S. Summer 2005. Asian Archery. Primitive Archer.
Website: atarn.org

Chapter 5

Lakota Sioux

by Jay Red Hawk

The Lakota Sioux chapter is in two parts. My personal experience of moving into re-enactments and horseback archery will come first, then the more historical material will follow.

Personal experience

It all started in June almost six years ago. The bow, the horse, the motion, the form and the bio-kinetic energy all came together for my first shot from off horseback.

My first shot from horseback

I had no master, no instructor or teacher to guide me. I made the mistake of holding the reins in my teeth, which felt awkward only because I was holding a bow and three arrows. I quickly figured out how to drop the reins. I was going to finally do it. I'll never forget the horse's name in that 90-degree heat. Her name was *Waci win* (wah-CHEE wee), which means "Dance Woman" in the Lakota (Sioux) language.

That summer, the sun felt good on my skin and baked me a dark brown. I painted my forehead with red earth paint down to just beneath my eyes. This helped to deflect the sun's glare so I could better focus on my target.

She was a small bay quarter horse. Dance was probably about 14.3 hands. She was smooth and "bomb-proof." (A term we like to use for a well-broke horse in South Dakota.) I had confidence that she would do well and put a lot of trust in her. Why wouldn't she do well? After all, just an hour before we had come charging straight down off a hill above Ft. Meade, full blast and I had stood up in the stirrups and

Mounted Archery in the Americas

unloaded both barrels of a 20 gauge shotgun within close proximity of a wagon load of gold thieves.

I had killed two of the five, knocking one man off the wagon firing straight ahead. I knew the other warriors would take out the other man and woman in the wagon.

So as I swerved around the wagon, I fired to our left flank and dropped the other man just as he was drawing his pistol to fire. I pulled up on the reins, brought Dance Woman to a dead stop, jumped down and proceeded to count coups and scalp both of my adversaries. It felt good. They were gold thieves anyway. They were pulling their wagon too close to our sacred mountain known as Bear Butte, with what looked to be an ugly, hairless, retarded buffalo with misshapen horns. These were oxen, and as I said before these people were trespassing and were stealing gold out of our Black Hills.

We started to go into a canter, my hips in tandem motion with hers. The sweat was beading on my face and running down over my cheekbones. My focus was on a small, blue patch of wool just to the right of a shiny brass U.S. cavalry button. I had to make this shot good because there were only eight of us and at least two detachments of the 4th and 7th cavalry all around us.

Everything almost disappeared in my vision but that small patch of blue…almost.

I drew back as we were closing on my target. A second that seemed to last a long time; like being in slow motion. From the short, purple-heartwood, sinew-backed 40 lb. bow I let loose the chokecherry shaft, turkey feather-fletched, raised nock, an arrow I had made by hand with sinew wrappings. The iron trade point that I had acquired from a blacksmith and sharpened myself, sank deep into the breast of my cavalry target. It was a heart shot. I turned Dance around to our left, circled back and put another one dead center into my targets crotch.

Then I heard the applause from the crowd, the re-enactors, the mayor of Sturgis and the Army Colonel and some of his National Guard Unit instructors who had asked me earlier what kind of accuracy I had and how many arrows could be fired from a "little bow like that." I was satisfied and so were they, apparently.

It was unlike any other feeling I've ever had. I've ridden horses in blizzards in the winter on 350 mile rides, in the summer in over 100 degree heat. I've ridden across South Dakota, Minnesota, Montana, and

North Dakota. I've even ridden 550 miles up to Canada in 1993. You mean all this time I could have been shooting a bow off of a horse?

It felt so liquid and natural. I quickly figured out how to drop the reins and shoot. I think I spent another two hours like a little kid who has just discovered something cool, shooting at that life-size dummy of Lt. Colonel George Armstrong Custer. My demonstration was long over, now I was doing it for me. I was just enjoying it!

Of course, the Army Colonel had to come back. He watched, amazed, yet somehow skeptical. I told him that I was not even a shadow of the Lakota/Dakota/Nakota ancestors and that their horse archery skills were light years beyond mine. He asked how many arrows three Sioux Indians could fire in 30 seconds from 20 yards at the Custer target. I dismounted.

I lined up with two other friends and the Colonel got out his stopwatch. He said "Go." We started firing. I am a rhythm shooter and I shoot instinctively at a 45 degree angle and I anchor to my heart or chin. So did the other guys. "Stop." he said. We had unleashed 36 arrows in half a minute at the life-size man target, 32 arrows hit, 26 were in the "kill zone" and the Colonel still didn't get it. "Pretty good...but whaddaya do when you run outta arrows?" he asked in his southern drawl with a semi-smirky, semi-curious grin.

It was at that point that something primal made me snap. From standing there with a blank stare in disbelief that he still wasn't completely satisfied... to bolting towards the Custer target, pulling a tomahawk from my belt and sticking it into the collar bone area from a ten yard throw, pulling out my knife and sticking it into the targets soft cloth and Styrofoam neck, and smashing it in the head with my stone war club. I proceeded to kick the target over and smash it to pieces in a thirty-second tirade of destruction with my club and my moccasin clad feet. I broke a few arrows but it was worth it for educational community outreach and a matter of pride.

I said, "That's what I personally do when I run out of arrows, sir."

"Well that's just damn outstanding!" exclaimed the Colonel, finally appeased.

Now keep in mind, from the time I was a child, my cousins and I and our friends were always grabbing some willow or some flexible stick and tying kite string or whatever we could find and shooting any

www.lrgaf.org

other stick from it… straight, bent, skinny, thick it didn't matter. I had a re-curve bow when I was six which was taken away from me when I was eight because I missed a rattlesnake and hit my cousin Vincent in the foot… or should I say through the foot, with a target arrow. At least I thought it was a rattlesnake; it's bull snakes that hiss like an aerosol can through a small p.a. system. Anyway, traditional punishment with a bow hurts when you get hit across the back with it after it is unstrung.

But a few years later I got another bow and shot at mostly stumps, squirrels, birds and cardboard boxes. I stopped shooting in the direction of any of my cousins or friends and I left snakes alone.

But it wasn't until I was in my thirties that I started shooting again. I started trying to make my own bows, knap my own arrowheads, and make my own fletchings. I started shooting three to four times a week, a minimum of two to three hours a day with a 70 pound sinew backed bow. I started hunting again, rabbits, prairie dogs, deer, antelope and elk.

Another Cavalry Days demonstration

Keep in mind, I had no idea there was anyone in the world still doing horse archery. One year later, I gave another demonstration of horse archery at the same Cavalry Days event. I borrowed a different horse. It was a Paso Fino with a comfortable gait. I got on the horse cold, no practice runs and there was a round bulls-eye target that I had set on two square hay bales stacked and then a 3-D deer target after it. When I gave the gelding a gentle kick it opened up. You see, I borrowed this horse from one of my cowboy friends who competed in mounted shooting with pistols.

This horse was used to running a 12-target course in 14 seconds. Geez! This horse had the bumpiest, most god-awful and uneven gait I'd ever experienced and it had one speed, *too* fast. I shot anyway. My arrows were hitting the targets sloppily and along the edge. The crowd of 100 or so people applauded with sincere "golf claps." I was frustrated. I made 12 passes and I put nine in the round target and three in the deer target, but not a single bulls-eye or kill shot. What a crappy demonstration, I thought. I was kind of embarrassed,

www.lrgaf.org

until when it was over people really started applauding and whistling. I rode off and returned my friend's horse.

I walked back to the demo area to pull my arrows from the target. People were still walking away from it when I noticed they were all kind of looking at me strangely. I thought very frankly to myself, "Man... you really screwed this one up." Two ladies walked by and I overheard one say, "Oh my God! I've never seen anything like that before!"

Some little guy about seven or so said, "That was *cool* man!" "Thanks, buddy," I said. Just then a man about 65 or so came up and grabbed my hand and shaking it with both of his said, "Young man, that sure was somethin! I ain't *never* seen nobody shoot a bow n'arrow off a bucking horse!"

Then Larry the photographer came up with his digital camera in hand and said, "I got some great shots! Check this out." Larry then proceeded to click through the photos one by one. Apparently this horse *was* bucking the whole time. I realized in that moment that one of the most important mental aspects of the art form and discipline of horse archery is **focus**. I had been focusing on hitting the target so much that I hadn't even noticed the horse bucking underneath me.

It was at this point I started to do some serious research about traditional Lakota horse archery. I also checked the Internet and found the website for the International Horse Archery Festival. I was so excited to see that I wasn't alone! There were people from all over the world doing this. Well, at least 25-30 from different countries were showing up at...Ft. Dodge, Iowa? I knew as soon as I saw the website I would wind up there, but it wouldn't be for another two years.

I saw the names of some of the other people involved in horse archery demonstrations and clinics. Meg and Dave Beshey, David Gray, Lukas Novotny, Kassai Lajos, Barb Leeson, Misa and the Takedaryu School of Japanese Yabasume and Jaap and Kay Koppedrayer.

Then I saw Mike One Star's name. Cool, I thought. When I go back to Rosebud Reservation next time I'll visit with him about it.

www.lrgaf.org

Lots of practice, the Tatanka story

An opportunity came up in 2002 when I was offered a job at Kevin Costner's new venture called "Tatanka: Story of the Bison." It was to be located on 1,500 acres he owns in Deadwood, South Dakota. Basically, there would be three main aspects to Tatanka: the largest bronze buffalo sculpture in the world, containing 14 larger than life buffalo and three Lakota on horseback sculpted by local artist Peggy Detmer.

Tatanka would also have a restaurant headed up by five star caterer and chef, Jill McGuire. The third part of Tatanka would be a circa 1840 Lakota encampment. Luckily, my sister Nita Bald Eagle, my brother-in-law Chris Ravenshead, my three nieces, Brenna, Emmy and Carrie, and our friends Jacques and Jim were hired along with myself and my oldest son. Their practical and extensive knowledge on Lakota culture and history would teach me a lot. We worked hard and had fun together, living as if we were actually in that time period. We were hired with a dozen or so other Lakota employees as a close-knit Tiyospaye (tee-YOH-shpah-yay) or extended family.

We had three horses we worked with and I started practicing bareback horse archery and giving demonstrations daily. So, for about 5 months I shot off horseback. This helped me to get the basics figured out. My brother-in-law, Chris, had played *hanpakutepi* (hah-PAH-koo-tay-pee) back in the late 70's on the Cheyenne River reservation. That is the old game of shooting a moccasin off of a stick in the ground from horseback. He shared a lot of research with me about horses, Lakota horse archery and bows and arrows.

In 2003 we received a national award as the best Native American Interpretive Site in the U.S., something we as a family accomplished together and are still very proud of. Now, Jill McGuire whom I mentioned earlier was a partner with Dan O'Brien, an accomplished author of western novels and a conservationist buffalo rancher. Dan O'Brien would be a key person later on that year, however I didn't know that at the time. I couldn't make it to the International Horse Archery Festival that year due to a serious bareback injury, where the horse I was riding, Winterhawk, had stumbled when I was doing an archery demonstration. I tore the ligament in my left knee.

www.lrgaf.org

In front of a crowd of 60 or so people, as Winterhawk went down while I was at a full draw with my bow, I knew it was going to be an ugly wreck. Remember earlier how I talked about focus? Well, as I flipped end over end, I never took my eyes off the target and upside down I let my arrow fly from about ten yards. I hit two inches left of center from the bulls eye...then I hit the ground.

I hit hard on my left leg and the impact separated and tore my ligaments. So, what else could I do? I pulled myself up, dusted myself off, grabbed up Winterhawk and limped over to the crowd. Because there were over a dozen scared children in the crowd, I simply said, "Kids, please don't try that at home, I'm a trained professional." I smiled and waved, they applauded and left.

I immediately called my wife and said, "I'm going to be home a little late."

I was on horseback three days later, doing demonstrations, but for six months I could not walk fast or run. I rehabilitated myself by continuing to ride horses, bicycles, stretch, use cold packs and attempt to run short distances. It was a slow and painful recovery, but I tried to keep it to myself. I got paid an extra $ 25.00 a day for riding horses at Tatanka and I had a wife and two small boys. I've always said that rodeo cowboys make better money than horse archery professionals... but we get to shoot at stuff.

However, my knee still wasn't completely healed in October of 2003 when our family would bring back the traditional Lakota buffalo hunt off horseback, with a sinew backed bow and stone pointed arrows.

The buffalo hunt, Wanasapi

Wanasapi (wah-NAH-sah-pee) is the Lakota word for buffalo hunt. Without going into all the specific details, I will try and summarize. Our family started to discuss the possibilities of bringing back the traditional buffalo ceremonies, songs and dances. If we were going to do this at all, we were going to do it with the most effort and the best intentions we possibly could.

It was obvious to us that we would need to go to a legitimate interpreter, what most people would call a medicine man. We would have to put up a ceremony and ask the spirits if this was a good thing to do and if they approved, to ask for their help and intervention in a good way. We did this and the spirits said it was a good thing to bring back this "good way of life." They said they would help us and told us how it would go. One would mark itself out from the rest of the herd and would give itself to the people.

If it were not for the fact that Chris Ravenshead and Jacques knew those old buffalo songs, we could not "send our voice out" in the proper way to our buffalo relatives, the Pte Oyate (ptay oh-YAH-tay). There are very few people that know these songs anymore, most notably, respected singer Wilmer Mesteth from Pine Ridge. They have been singing these old songs since the seventies and learned from some of the best singers around the Cheyenne River, many of whom have now gone on to the Spirit World. Their years of practice and research would be a key element in our family hunt.

The next time I saw Dan O'Brien I brought up the idea to him. Dan wanted to see me shoot a bow. We went to the encampment area at Tatanka, where the targets were set up. On a fairly windy day from about 25 yards, I let an arrow fly and nailed a bulls-eye. Dan was satisfied. I felt that it was a very lucky shot, myself.

Rule number one

If you can't handle yourself on horseback with a competent level of intermediate skill, do not attempt to shoot a bow off a horse in an uncontrolled environment alone and without an accomplished horse archery trainer. There are no exceptions to this rule.

I've been riding horses all my life and I train 75% of the time dismounted. To me, a wonderful aspect of horse archery is ground training.

One of the best things, in my opinion, that you can do is in the "horse stance" position. To train for this buffalo hunt, when I wasn't riding and shooting in the afternoon, I was getting up at 6:00 am, getting out back and bouncing up and down in place, just slightly to emulate the bounce of a canter.

I had the target, a small 3D deer at 12 yards. One thing for certain I can tell you about Lakota archery technique and form, is that when you shoot dismounted or on horseback, you are always holding arrows in your bow hand as well... always. In this chapter, you will see

www.lrgaf.org

some historical photos that give documentation of this. And I will go into further detail.

Training on the ground pays off later on when you learn to nock your arrows without looking and when you can finally shoot three arrows at a target in a single pass.

On the morning of Oct. 23rd, 2006 it was about 16 degrees Fahrenheit and my wife and two little boys, then ages four and one and a half years were still sleeping when I left the house.

The hunt is on!

It was about a 45 minute drive to Dan O'Brien's 20,000 acre buffalo ranch. Sixteen miles of it on gravel roads. Upon arrival I immediately started saddling up "Buffalo Boy", the only horse around with an impressive resume of buffalo history. Owned and trained by my sister Nita's father, Chief Dave Bald Eagle, Buffalo Boy is a one-of-a-kind horse.

Buffalo Boy had been raised in the buffalo pasture up in the Cheyenne River area with a few other horses and about a thousand head of buffalo. He had "buffalo sense." He had been in a documentary where he ran in among almost 2,000 buffalo. Buffalo boy was a short, stocky Overo paint, with some of the thickest canon bones I'd ever seen on a horse that size. Buffalo Boy and I opened up a few times side by side with a Chevy Blazer and we got clocked at 29.5 miles per hour for 1/5 of a mile. That was not his top speed. Like many people talk about thoroughbred horses having a "fifth gear", he had definitely had a short burst for the chase that maybe put us 2-3 miles an hour faster. Buffalo can run 35 miles per hour and have the fastest, sharpest turning radius of any animal on the planet, for their size.

After the proper songs, dance and ceremony were completed I finally headed out towards the herd. Dan had separated about 16 head on 80 hectares. Besides the cows and young heifers, I remember from 300 yards looking at three very old and large buffalo bulls between myself, and the young buffalo cows.

It was at that point that I thought to myself, "My wife is seven and a half months pregnant with our third boy. I hope I get to see them again. Today might be my day to leave this world." My brother-in-law Chris and my good friend Jacques at that precise moment started to

www.lrgaf.org

sing a Kit Fox Society song. The rough translation of the song is, " I am the kit fox. Whatever is difficult is mine to do." I don't know if I ever really expressed to either of them how much courage and strength they gave me by singing that particular song in a moment when I most needed it. But that is to me, the definition of a "real singer." Someone who when called upon, or upon seeing a need of the people can sing just the right and appropriate song.

I got to within 75 yards of the buffalo at a very slow walk with Buffalo Boy. We stopped. I sat on Buffalo Boy for about 10 minutes and just waited. The bulls turned to face us and their tails went up into the air and they started pissing and shitting, pawing the ground with their hooves and snorting. It wasn't a very good feeling. I thought back to the ceremony we had and I remembered that I am not a strong man, but my faith in these ways is very strong. When riding bareback into or alongside a herd of buffalo, the only safety harness a man had was a length of buffalo hide, fastened like a rope around the waist and slipped over the horses neck. If you fell off of your horse in or around a herd of buffalo, this would be the only way to not get left on the prairie and hopefully be able to pull yourself back up onto your horse.

Anytime you want to find out how tough you're ***not***, get within 100 yards of three old buffalo bulls when there are cows and calves around. Anytime you want to find out how stupid you are, get closer. Observing buffalo and working in buffalo herds on horseback for at least several years is a pre-requisite, in my opinion, to being able to hunt one from horseback.

On the right side of the herd, a two-year old heifer ran out to the south, alone, so I told Buffalo Boy, "Wanayelo!" (Now). He headed towards her at a slow lope. Now, we did have to pay for this buffalo, so there was something that threw me off unexpectedly. Dan had ridden out with me and then turned back, saying with the utmost politeness and respect, "This is your hunt." I remembered discussing with him that the heifer I was supposed to take had a green tag in her ear. By the time I was within 15 yards of her, the heifer presented herself with a broadside shot and just stood still. So did Buffalo boy. I looked back to Dan who was quite a distance away and finally I could hear him scream and wave to go ahead and take her.

She started to run. To his credit, Buffalo Boy was amazing! We couldn't catch up to her for a shot for about the first half hour. I missed with the first three shots. It was at this point that the human side of me was at the point of giving up. I had to remind myself that our family was making history and trying to do something good. We were trying to encourage young Lakota children to relearn this way of life and keep it alive.

I hit my "wall" and pushed through it with my faith. Wowicala (wo-WEE-cha-la). The word 'faith' kept going through my mind. At times, it was just me, Buffalo Boy and the 750 pound two-year old heifer. But giving credit where credit is due, Gervase Hittle, my friend and Dan's ranch foreman, was driving up in his blue pick-up and flanking her every few minutes and trying to push her towards me. The whole time he was doing this, he had a truckload of three photographers including Jim Richardson from National Geographic, award winning photographers Mike Wolforth and Robert Wong and friend and journalist Jim Kent. These guys had a rougher ride than me!

I remember being at a full gallop with Buffalo Boy and at about 45 minutes of chasing this buffalo, she was starting to tire. It is an amazing feeling to be galloping on horseback in cold weather, which was at first cloudy, then turned to sleet, then snowed and then turned grey again.

It is an incredible feeling to be doing that with a sinew backed bow in your left hand and five arrows with flint points. Actually, they were purple chert. Jim Deluca, an accomplished bowyer and flint-knapper had made three of the points for me. They were so sharp at the serrated edges and so well knapped that you could hold them up to the sun and see light through an eighth of an inch of the arrowhead all the way around the edge.

I started to focus and I started thinking about meat and feeding my family. I knew I needed to compensate for the bounce of the horse and the bounce of the buffalo. I was aiming too high. From about 12 yards, as Buffalo Boy opened up and got me close enough, I aimed a little lower and let my fourth arrow fly. I could hear it hit. The shaft flew off almost immediately. My arrow hit high, between the shoulder and the hump on the left side. This shot slowed her down. What I didn't know was what the arrowhead had done under the buffalo's skin. It had penetrated the hide, hit a rib and traveled 11 inches through meat and nerves and hit a hump bone.

www.lrgaf.org

My last shot, I went far right of her and started to close in fast. Buffalo Boy was pouring it on, but I could tell he was getting tired. She cut hard to the right, slowing down and I knew this was my best opportunity. I remember pulling my bow back an inch past it's full draw. I wanted to make sure this arrow would get good penetration. I hit just behind the right shoulder, nicking the shoulder blade. The stone point broke off at the tip and shards exploded into the buffalo's lung. It instantly started filling with blood and she stopped running. She just stood there, wobbling. You could hear the blood in her lung. Gervase took aim with his 30-30 and put a bullet behind her right ear, dropping her instantly. To have waited another 5-15 minutes to see her topple over would have been a merciless kill.

I've never felt like such a real human being or so alive as I did on that day. I have had five, major near-death experiences in my life, but this was different. Meeting my wife Anne and being at the birth of all three of my boys are the only experiences that top that buffalo hunt on horseback. You see, even though I was the one on horseback with the bow, my whole family was with me on Buffalo Boy that day. I couldn't have done it without them.

My wife's Grandmother, Marie Randall who is now 87 was there. She said a beautiful prayer. There were other elders there as well, including Elaine Quiver. I was glad they got to witness a hunt being done the old way. It made me try harder to know they were there. I wouldn't give up no matter how hard it got.

One of the things I do not discuss often with anyone is the fact that I had three identical dreams of hunting buffalo while riding on Buffalo Boy. I've never had a vision. I have had a few very powerful dreams that seemed real.

I also believe there were spirits that were there, helping all of us. If you do not have all that in place and you don't understand that a buffalo is a close relative and that it is like another human being, if your family doesn't know the buffalo songs, if they don't know how to butcher correctly, if you don't know how to pray for the buffalo's spirit to be reborn again, if you do not use every part of it to feed your family and make items that you will actually use… then you are nothing more than a murderer. You are not a buffalo hunter.

I consider myself privileged and lucky in this life to have the family that I have.

www.lrgaf.org

History of Lakota Archery and Horse Archery

Author's note: I have chosen not to write down the five Lakota stories and one Dakota story I have been told regarding the origin of the bow, the arrow and the horse. I reserve my own personal reasons and beliefs in doing so. One can find sources to research, written forms and other versions of these stories on the web or in written form, however these sources may not be accurate.

In modern times

I do not consider myself an authority or expert horse archer by any means. I consider myself a student. I will share the few things I have learned and hope that it gives some better understanding. In re-learning traditional horse archery, it is like finding pieces to a fragmented puzzle. Some pieces are right there in front of you, and others you have to dig deep for. The minute you think you know everything is the minute you stop learning. Every time I shoot a bow from horseback I learn something. Before I start going into historical research and interviews with elders, it's important to note a few things about contemporary Lakota archery and horse archery. When I started getting into learning how to make Lakota bows and arrows the old way, I ran into Mike One Star in Rapid City and he asked if I wanted to help at the Civic Center where he had about 200 kids signed up for a 3D target shoot.

I went down there and helped out. Most of these kids had never really shot a bow before but seventy five percent of them needed very little coaching for the basics. Of course we went over safety rules and gave a little guidance. It just looked like "genetic memory." A very important lesson I learned from Mike is how to coach. Mike's philosophy is simple. Show the basics, encourage and don't over coach or micro manage every shot. If a young person anchors to their forehead and still manages to shoot with a good degree of accuracy and consistency, leave them alone.

What I didn't know until I started going down to Rosebud to shoot with Mike and my wife's first cousin, Gary Hacker Jr., is that they had both been doing horse archery, they had been to IHAF, and

Gary took down a buffalo from horseback before I did. He used a compound bow, I believe, but he did it. I remember him telling me it took him three arrows. I missed with my first three and it took two hits to accomplish my hunt from horseback. Gary put three in to accomplish his. I think we did pretty well considering that a couple of old photos from around 1900 exist that show as far as anyone knows, the last buffalo hunt from horseback, with three Lakota men about in their sixties, three horses and three arrows in the buffalo.

Both Mike, Gary, and myself have also done hunts on foot and it is quite a different experience. The last one I did was this last summer in the first week of July 2006 up in the Cheyenne River area. I had three other archers with me and it was a group effort. Bob Brilhart, Bernie Swank, Byron Buffalo and myself all hit a 1,600 pound buffalo bull with an arrow each, with Byron getting a kill shot in the lung. I was asked to finish it off with a 7 ft. spear. The spear was a chokecherry shaft about broom handle thick and the 8 1/2 inch stone point was one of the most finely knapped sharply serrated spear points I've ever seen. It was crafted by expert flint knapper, bowyer, and arrow maker Mike Stocklin of Faith, South Dakota. It went into the thick bull hide and went all the way through in one thrust, "like a hot knife through butter," as they say. It sliced into heart and lung and ended the hunt in a good way. Why all this talk of buffalo hunts? To give you a perspective about the number one reason for Lakota horse archery.

To me it is amazing to think that North American tribes that used the horse only had a few hundred years to accomplish becoming a horse culture. Compare that to the Mongols or the Huns who had hundreds or even thousands of years. According to scholars, horses were re-introduced into North America in the early 1500's. Because the dissemination of the horse in western United States came mainly out of Santa Fe, the southwestern tribes got the horse first, perhaps in the late 1500s. In the late 1600's and early 1700's, northern tribes were still on foot. But by 1750, most tribes had amassed huge herds of horses in the areas west of the Mississippi. There are accounts of many French traders coming down from Canada, who encountered what they described as "Horse Indians" in the 1730's and after. Some of the tribes were of course, the Lakota and Cheyenne. By the 1800's the Lakota and many other tribes such as the Cheyenne, Comanche and Kiowa had become horse archery masters. Since the advent of the horse, I've never heard of other cultures around the world becoming so skilled and efficient in such a relatively short period of time.

Realizing that shooting a bow from horseback was altogether different than shooting on the ground, several modifications occurred for the Lakota. For one, the bows became shorter. Anywhere from 39 – 47 inches, and they averaged between 40 and 60 lbs. Bent handle bows, "D" style bows and sinew-backed bows made of ash and of course the highly prized and rare sheep horn and sinew bow. I have had the pleasure of firing one of these, crafted by master bowyer Ed Scott of Owl Bows out of Grants, New Mexico. There are only a dozen bowyers in the world, that I know of, including one or two natives attempting to make this particular type of bow. The American Indian horn bow had no wooden core; it had Bighorn or Dall sheep horn in the belly and sinew for the back, joined with hide glue. The horn bow that Ed made was 62 lbs of pull and very short, 43 inches I believe. It had a 23 inch draw and had a faster snap back than osage. It didn't stack like other bows. At a full draw, it was easier almost to hold than a wooden or sinew backed, re-curve. It almost felt like a compound.

Both bows and horses became specialized. A "buffalo bow" and a "buffalo runner" (horse) were the most prized above all other bows or horses and were in their own category apart from say bows or horses used for warfare. A good buffalo bow could be 70-80 lbs of pull. A good buffalo runner you would not ride into battle because if he got killed or became lame, it might be the difference between a successful or unsuccessful buffalo hunt for you and your family. The relationship between the Lakota and the horse is an important factor. While it is well documented that by the late 1800's, U.S. government policy was one of extermination not only towards the Lakota, but also against the buffalo and herds of Indian ponies. Nevertheless, on most of the nine reservations in South Dakota, the horse still exists today. Tribal buffalo herds have been brought back and there are several current archery programs to capture the youth. Having such a special relationship with horses and seeing the skill level in some of the youth and adults that has re-emerged today, one can grasp a sense of the accomplished horse archers of 200 years ago.

In order to achieve any competent level of skill in Lakota horse archery, one has to be able to handle a horse and ride with proficiency. Many people have a mental image of Plains Indian Tribes consuming a lot of their time capturing wild horses and breaking them, or stealing them. While these things did occur, it is a romantic, stereotypical assumption. The fact is, once you have a herd of horses and some or most of them are tame or broke, and they become used to traveling with groups of nomadic people, it is not much different than what is natural to the horse, traveling from this pasture to that meadow to the next grass lands, etc. As young horses grow up seeing the older horses being ridden, for example, they see what is "normal" and what is expected of them. When horses are used to a lot of contact and around people constantly, they are easier to work with than wild horses that seldom see people. Both the Lakota and the horse are very intelligent. In utilitarian cultures, you do what makes sense and that always seems to be the best and sometimes the simplest way.

From childhood, growing up on horseback is a totally different perspective than learning to ride a horse later on in life. Let me give you an insight. There are still communities on the reservations that have herds wandering in them. There are still young people that for fun, jump on this horse or that horse, ride them around and then turn them out. There are still organized rides that occur that cover hundreds of miles in all four seasons of the year. If you've ever spent enough time on horseback, you might know what it is like to sleep and ride at the same time. To catch a couple of hours sleep on horseback and wake up feeling refreshed and keep on riding is a totally different experience than someone who keeps a horse at a stable and rides on the weekends. To ride through blizzards, rain and temperatures exceeding 40 below or 100 and above is different than pleasure riding on trails in good weather. Many things happen when you ride for long distances, with your horse, your tack, yourself; the more experience you have, the more knowledge and confidence you have. I believe this level of skill makes for a different kind of horse archer.

The horse is considered an equal and a relative in Lakota/Dakota/Nakota culture, not just an animal, livestock or a "pet." The attitude towards a horse is very different than in American culture. Perhaps the only non-native subculture in America that truly understands this is the real cowboy or rancher.

www.lrgaf.org

Lakota Archery technique

- Step 1: When holding your bow in hand, upright, with for example, 4 arrows points up, stick your index finger into your "stack of arrows" separating the top arrow from the others.
- Step 2: Reach over your wrist with your draw hand and grab the top arrow at the nock or the shaft by the fletchings.
- Step 3: Quickly lift your three fingers (pinky, 4th and middle) up and taking the arrow out place your same three fingers down around arrows and handle back down while lifting your index finger up. (Your thumb stays in place, always.)
- Step 4: Pull the nock onto the string, draw and fire.

Although in modern times, most Lakota do not shoot "the old way," nonetheless they are still Lakota archers. Some European and Asian techniques have been adopted in modern shooters. I myself am guilty of using four fingers instead of five; I do not use a "pinch grab" (which is the major reasoning for having a "raised nock") and I do not start with my bow above my head, pulling back the string with my "drawing arm" and pushing the bow out with my "bow arm" as I come down for a shot. In almost every old photograph where a Lakota is drawing back to shoot, not only is the pinch grab evident, but placing the index finger on the shaft is also a Lakota archery trait. The finger is quickly taken off during release. I started my oldest son, *Cetan Okinyan*, (chay-TAH oh-KEE-yah) shooting a bow at the age of two. He is now seven. When I first observed him shooting this way, I felt it was a "natural" instinctive trait for Lakota Archers learned from childhood. Most Lakota archers shoot with their bows tilted slightly, even going as far as a forty-five degree angle. This eliminates the bow impairing your vision and gives a clearer view of your target. From this style of shooting you can anchor anywhere between the heart and the eye.

After great and lengthy discussions with my brother-in-law, Chris, the only conclusion one can come to about traditional Lakota archery is that it is uniquely different from any other culture. In doing research one can read the Frances Densmore interview with Grey Hawk, or Laubin's interviews with One Bull. In my opinion, it's good to read those because they were accounts from Lakota that still had first hand knowledge of horse archery and buffalo hunts. Still, you must visit with elders who have a great many oral stories and family histories handed down to them from their grandparents. Many times, their wisdom is priceless. So when you put those pieces of the puzzle together, then you must make it practical by trying it yourself. It is in this way that you truly start to understand all the reasons for why Lakota horse archery is the way it is. For certain, as far as I'm concerned, the center, the very matrix of it all is the *Wanasapi,* the buffalo hunt.

In digging up and hunting down historical photos in museums, private collections and historical archives, there is one notable characteristic that gives you an answer to a particular aspect of Lakota archery as it applies to both mounted and ground shooting. In your bow hand, you will always hold two or three extra arrows, with the points up and the nocks down. This important visual information from the mid 1800's to the early 1900's supports the statements of the Lakota who were interviewed by Laubin and Densmore.

One thing to be wary of, though, it takes a few years at least, and some cultural knowledge of hair styles, clothing styles and distinct cultural features to know a posed photo with historical inaccuracies. For example, you may see a photo that may look old, but is perhaps from the 1930's. If the man in it is from a Southwest Tribe, wearing a Lakota style war bonnet, sitting on a paint horse with a Mexican blanket and Ute style moccasins in a loincloth with a Crow-style beaded vest holding a child's bow and arrows, well it's a posed picture. Many photographers were guilty of this. Many of them had trunks full of items that they would dress people up in, including the famous Edward Curtis. The oldest photograph I've personally ever seen was of a few buffalo hide tipis from 1847 and a portrait of Keokuk from around the same time period. So, remember, good photographic evidence has existed since the mid 1800's.

Before photos, we must turn to painters such as Karl Bodmer and George Catlin and who also wrote accounts of the tribes they painted and buffalo hunts they witnessed. In looking at the bows and arrows and horse archery, again one must have a discerning eye for detail and scrutinize the accuracy. Catlin was more of a portrait artist and when painting large scenes or scenes from a distance, sometimes his proportions are off.

Bodmer was probably a lot more accurate. The proof is in the items from that time period which exist mostly in Europe, from the late 1700's on. The Lewis & Clark collection is in the Peabody Museum and those items are from the early 1800's. Many of the really old items relating to archery or horse archery wound up in Europe because the French were trading, and living among and intermarrying with Lakota when Lewis and Clark were still in cloth or moss diapers.

The bow and shield, Itazipa nahan wahacanka

Let's examine the advantages of the shorter bow. On horseback, the shorter bow is much more practical because it is much more maneuverable and lightweight. A shorter bow is less likely to bump, tap or hit your horse. A shorter bow often has a shorter draw length and when you draw to fire an arrow it is a much more efficient use of your energy and muscle groups. Although it is not talked of anymore, the Lakota had the Sacred Bow Society, very similar to the Cheyenne Thunder Bow Society. I will not go into detail about any of these societies, out of respect for them.

The quiver and bow case is also unique among the Lakota. The Cheyenne had very similar ones, however when you study museum pieces enough you can tell the differences and slight variations in the construction as well as the designs. If you are right handed, the *Woju* (who-ZHOO) or quiver should be worn in such a fashion as to have your nocks on your left as it lies fairly low across the small or middle of your back. When riding bareback, the entire quiver is slung around to the side or front. Your arrows are now within easier reach with the nocks closer to your hand.

Shields were usually made from the hump of a bull buffalo. After being fleshed, the hides are stretched out over a pit of coals and heat shrunk. This condenses the piece of hide into an even thicker shield, sometimes an inch to an inch and a half. These shields were then covered with brain-tanned hide and sometimes painted on the outside or on the buffalo rawhide shield itself. Throughout the 1800's, muslin also became a covering material that was easy to draw or paint on.

The shield designs sometimes portrayed a specific vision the maker or individual had and were for spiritual and practical protection as well. An inch and a half thick buffalo shield could definitely stop a metal or stone point arrow from 50 –20 yards, and perhaps even a lead ball from a flintlock musket or even a percussion rifle. Most times, the shields were kept covered and only had the covers taken off before battle to face the enemy with the power of your shield. About 10 years ago, I remember the "Visions of the People" traveling exhibit of many Plains Tribes artifacts going around the country. Elders advised them on not having the covers taken off the shields and if they did, not to have them facing each other because that only happened in warfare. If one looks at Bodmer and Catlin paintings as well as other less noted artists of the time, when portraits were painted of men on foot, their shields appear larger because of the fact that any infantry of any culture will have a larger shield to cover and protect more body area.

When shields, which also were downsized with the advent of the horse, are attached to the quiver and bow case, they would cover your vital organs in your torso from the front as it was turned in that direction. If you were charging through an enemy line or enemy cavalry, when you rode through their line, you would flip your quiver around to your back and thus be protected from behind. It becomes difficult and dangerous to use that technique with a saddle, the reason being that when you flip your quiver around, the shafts of your arrows get bounced around between your stomach and the pommel, or saddle horn. It can be easy to break shafts or have them bounce out of your quiver.

There is painted art from the early 1800's showing battle scenes on horseback when adversaries were using lances against each other and were using saddles. This makes sense when we think of European knights jousting. It was perhaps easier to stay on your horse with a saddle. When Chris and I discussed this evidence, he brought up the fact that when traveling good distances, saddles always come in handy to tie your equipment and provisions on in any culture. When confronted with an enemy, why not strip your saddles and leave them in a pile and fight your enemy with less weight and more mobility? Two hundred years ago, you were either going to post some of the young men to guard your stuff or not really worry about it. Either you're going to make it back to your saddle pile or, if you don't, you are not going to need them anyway. Besides, you're not going to worry too much about someone popping out of nowhere on the prairie to steal your tack and supplies. There are many accounts in the mid to the late

1800's of men stripping off their saddles to go into battle, including ledger art by Bad Heart Bull that shows Lakota and Crows riding against each other bareback with their quivers lying on their sides in front.

Arrows, Wahinkpe

On average, Lakota arrows in museums are from 22" – 26" in length. Fletchings were made primarily from turkey, eagle, hawk and owl feathers. Different societies and individuals had specific uses for these and different colors of earth paint they used for decoration. Some shafts were "barrel shaped", which from nock and point, tapered up into a thicker center. This would make a thicker spined arrow which would retain it's straightness. It was also thought that another way to keep an arrow straight was to press into the shaft, three "lightning grooves."

I have read a few papers and articles from scholars who call these "blood grooves." I completely disagree with that analysis. The grooves go from the end of the fletching (opposite end from nock) in wavy lines down the shaft to the point. In museum arrows, one can see these under the sinew wrappings. These lines represent the *Wakinyan,* (wah-KEE-yahn) or Thunder Beings. The bow, the arrow and the horse in one of the oldest stories I know of, all derive their power and originate from the *Wakinyan.* There is another reason for these grooves. These lines down the length of the shaft help to take pressure off the outer surface. When arrows are burnished using stone, shell or bone and the grooves are added it makes the arrow less likely to warp. When you spend time heat bending your shafts straight, this makes sense.

Fletchings on Lakota arrows are generally from 4"-9" in length, with around 7" in my observations to be about average. Lakota arrows, like the arrows of most tribes in North America were highly ornamented and decorated. This can be seen in many old photographs as well as in museum collections. Fletchings are usually trimmed very short for several reasons. The shorter the fletching, the less drag and noise are produced. Also, more arrows can fit in a quiver. Lakota fletchings are not twisted, they go on straight, therefore, there is no spin to the arrow.

Shafts for arrows were made of a variety of woods that are mostly still readily available on the Great Plains in South Dakota. Chokecherry, ash, and currant were favorites. Plum shafts have a particularly nasty effect on an enemy when used for warfare. I've bow hunted in draws and been stuck in the hand, arm or leg with plum-thorns and the puncture area will swell up and if not cleaned properly can get infected to the degree where one could fall seriously ill or even die. Points on arrows varied throughout the 1800's being made of everything from stone to bone, sharpened hardwood to metal such as iron and mild steel.

Lakota Horse Archery Games

It is important to note that at the height or "golden age" of Lakota/Dakota/Nakota culture, archery skills and technique were taught to young boys primarily through games. There were so many games, it is not hard to imagine 200 years ago, shooting bows would take up much of a young boy's day. There are many ceremonies in which the bow, the horse and the arrow are connected. I will not go into extended detail about any of these because outside of their cultural context they do not need to be known or used, in my opinion. I make mention of this simply for the reader to understand that the significance of these is very deeply rooted in the culture with much spiritual power.

Red arrow ceremony, Wahinkpe Luta

One ceremony I will talk about is more of a social ceremony, and recognition of a young boys first kill. It is the *Wahinkpe Luta,* (wah-HEEN-kpay loo-tah) the Red Arrow ceremony. When a young boy kills his first bird, rabbit, prairie dog or whatever, he takes this to one of his grandmothers. She of course praises him and prepares the meat. A feast is prepared and the family gathers to have a giveaway, including horses, bows, arrows or other valuable items. The boy would be recognized as a provider of food, not a man yet, but a step towards manhood. Gifts were distributed to band members to distribute wealth equally and to help ensure everyone had what they needed. This accomplished tight bonds of family kinship and discouraged jealousy.

It re-enforced the Lakota value of not placing value of material items over each other.

An arrow would be made by a man and then some of the grandmothers might paint it red with ochre (red-earth paint) and it was presented to the boy. A few Grandmothers I talked to from Rosebud said some times this was still done in the 1920's and 30's. For the most part, it became a family thing by the 30's and after, just recognizing the boy with a feast but throughout the reservation period of the twentieth century, the red arrow within the ceremony disappeared.

Oglecekute

Father Eugene Beuchel, who lived among the Lakota in the early twentieth century is famous for writing the Lakota-English Dictionary. Within it, he describes this game: "to play the game of *oglecekutepi*, which consists in shooting arrows so as to come as near as possible to where the first arrow sticks in the ground." Another source, Eastman (1858) describes it as thus:

"No sooner did the boys get together than, as a usual thing, they divided into squads and chose sides; then a leading arrow was shot at random into the air. Before it fell to the ground a volley from the bows of the participants followed. Each player was quick to note the direction and speed of the leading arrow and he tried to send his own at the same speed and at equal height, so that when it fell it would be closer to the first than any of the others. It was considered out of place to shoot by first sighting the object aimed at. This was usually impractical in actual life, because the object was almost always in motion, while the hunter himself was often upon the back of a pony at full gallop. Therefore, it was the off-hand shot that the Indian boy sought to master."

Sungnaksapi

Another game that can be found in Beuchel's Dictionary is described as shooting an arrow through a buffalo bladder. This would be a fun and challenging game to play. If you wanted to play this in modern times just blow up a medium size, pear shaped balloon, and it is about the same size as a bladder. Hang it off a stick, put it on a stick in the ground or tie the balloon to a branch of a tree then ride past it on horseback and shoot at it!

A long list of archery games for Sioux boys is listed in an old source by an ethnologist and linguist by the name of James (1891). We will just describe the horse related games.

Peji yuskila kutepi

In some mounted archery disciplines, the targets are tossed in the air. This game would be good practice for such aerial targets. The players shoot at grass tied tightly in bunches. This is played by older boys. Grass is wrapped around a piece of bark till it assumes an oval shape, both ends of the grass being secured together. The grass ball that is made is thrown into the air, and all shoot at it, trying to hit it before it reaches the ground. The one who sends his arrow near the heart or mark on the grass ball has the right to toss the ball up into the air; but he who hits the very heart on the ball throws the ball on the ground or where ever he pleases and all shoot at it. This game is generally played till dark, and could be played on horseback.

Can-shung akanyankapi

The player sits on a make-believe wooden beam or stick and makes motions imitating the various horse gaits. Sometimes an actual saddle is placed on a fallen tree and the ride takes place. It is fun to incorporate shooting the bow from these positions and imitation gaits.

Hanpakutepi

To shoot a moccasin on a stick in the ground from horseback is by far, in my opinion, the most fun and perhaps historically the last horse archery game to be played into the twentieth century. An old photograph exists of a Lakota in full regalia on a horse at full gallop drawing back to shoot the moccasin. The interesting part of analyzing this photo, is that all four of the horses hooves are off the ground. This would be the ideal moment to fire and in fact is another traditional Lakota trait and technique to horse archery. As described by Eastman earlier, the "off-hand shot" would be the one to master, but the shot, if one has time, is the shot when the horse is completely off the ground as described in Densmore's interview with Grey Hawk. Why? When the horses' hooves are coming up or down, the bumpy motion can affect the shot. However, sometimes a target or opportunity presents itself with all or some of the conditions, not in your favor.

That is why, again, I say focus is an important factor. There was a moment I have personally experienced doing horse archery, while at IHAF 2004 in a practice exercise before my demo. In that moment, it was as if the horse completely disappeared underneath me, and everything around the exact center of the bulls-eye vanished. I hit the center of the white of the bulls-eye at a gallop, shooting to my left side. I tried to do it again consciously and hit the black outer ring. I realized that you cannot *try* and focus in horse archery. You simply **focus** without trying.

On the Rosebud Reservation, Mike One Star, Gary Hacker Jr., some of their children and the youth in their archery program, as well as a few youth from Pine Ridge, are taking steps to re-learn and keep Lakota horse archery alive in the twenty-first century. My eldest son *Cetan Okinyan* (Flying Hawk), has been shooting since he was two years old and at four years he first tried horse archery. He has shot off horseback on seven different occasions since then and he is 7 years old now. My two younger sons, *Mato Wahacanka,* (Bear Shield) four years and *Wani Pte* (Winter Buffalo) three years, each have their own bows. Tahansi Byron Buffalo and Ben Elk Eagle, the elders and the youth we worked with on the Cheyenne River Reservation are to be acknowledged for their traditional wisdom and personal initiatives to re-learn Lakota Archery.

They are to be credited for their cultural knowledge and dedication to the youth in their program. They are humble men and do not step forward to be acknowledged. Kermit Miner and his horse program and youth from Cheyenne River as well participated in Lakota horse archery. They ride horses like they breathe, and shoot naturally.

My *Mase* (mo-SHAY), brother-in-law, Chris Ravenshead, and my good friend Jacques are to be credited for all of their archival research and time they have spent visiting with elders. They have acquired a wealth of knowledge over the past twenty years and are an invaluable resource.

Faith Spotted Eagle (*Tunwin*) and the Brave Heart Society (*Cante Ohitika Okodakiciye*), grandmothers and youth from Yankton Sioux Reservation are to be credited for being just that…brave. A couple of years back they hosted myself and my oldest son, then five at the time, to come down and give a horse archery clinic. There were 26 *Inhaktowan* (Nakota Sioux) that shot bows off horseback. I don't know when the last time was that many Yankton Sioux did horse archery, and neither does anyone else I asked, in living memory. Perhaps it has been seventy-five years or more. Their bravery, enthusiasm and most of all their amount of respect for themselves, each other and their elders is on a different level than any other youth group I've ever worked with.

In May of 2005, an historical Gathering of Lakota Sioux mounted archers was held at Mission on the Rosebud Reservation. Several dozen youth were given arrows with their own names on them and had the thrill of shooting from horseback with an adult leading. The older more experienced youth and adults shot at a 16" cube on the ground at a gallop and hit it quite impressively. It was a beautiful couple of days, especially the stories at night by the Elders.

I am only an author here. I am only one horse archer. It is all these individuals and groups that I mentioned from different reservations, different bands and branches of the same Great Sioux Nation that are making history in reviving Lakota horse archery. It is my goal to get as many youth interested in traditional Lakota Horse Archery as possible. Within the next five years it is my goal for these youth to all have traditional bows, regalia and horse tack, much like the Japanese Yabusame Horse Archers whose traditional dress and horse tack are a part of all of their demonstrations and fully represent the beauty and strength of their culture.

The beauty of Lakota bows, arrows, finely quilled horse masks, war bridles with scalps decorating them, traditional rawhide saddles and quilled, brain tanned pad saddles, even bonnets and feathered decorations and paint for horses, would be a sight to see in a horse archery demonstration. I also want our youth to be able to fully represent Lakota/Dakota/Nakota culture and look their finest, ride and shoot their best. I would like to see smiles on the faces of the Grandmothers and Grandfathers, to see their youth doing something cultural that we can all be proud of.

www.lrgaf.org

Most of all, I want to keep it alive so that our youth, when they grow into the horse archers of tomorrow can say, "My ancestors fought hard with bows and arrows on horseback, so that I could be here. They mastered horse archery skills to use in the buffalo hunt, so that I could be here. I practice horse archery. I am here."

"We are still here!"

****

References:

Allely, S., and Hamm, J. (2002). Encyclopedia of Native American Bow, Arrows, and and Quivers, Volume 1, Northeast, Southeast, and Midwest. Azle, Texas: Bois d'Arc Press. Sioux bows and arrows on pages 134 and 135.

Beuchel, E. Lakota-English Dictionary.

Densmore. Interview with Grey Hawk.

Eastman, C. A. (1859). The Soul of the Indian.

Hamilton, T. M. (1982). Native American Bows. Columbia, Missouri: Missiouri Archeological Society.

James, O. D. (1891). Games of Teton Dakota children www.puffin.creighton.edu/lakota/publications/dorsey/games_of_te ton_dakota_children.htm.

Laubin, R., and G. (1980). American Indian Archery. Norman, Oklahoma: University of Oklahoma Press.

Red Hawk, J. (Spring, 2005). Wanasapi: The buffalo hunt. Primitive Archer.

Red Hawk, J., and Gray, D. (Fall, 2006) Lakota Sioux capture another lost art: The revival of horseback archery. Primitive Archer.

Chapter 6

Native American Roots: The Blackfoot

By Patrick Stoddard (aka Many Dogs)

As I sit pondering this chapter, I find I must go back to the beginning of my horse archery experience. Even though I had grown up with horses, and loved them, I had not ridden in almost 20 years. The iron pony had gotten my fancy and motorcycles became my horsepower. Now, I was living on a ranch in Laramie Wyoming with thousands of acres surrounding me, and riding other people's horses. I discovered I had not lost my love of horses and I could still really ride. I did not own a horse of my own, and did not intend to get one. Then I was actually given a horse without wanting one when I went to a Bureau of Land Management (BLM) wild horse auction with friends. Let me tell you the story.

How I got passionately involved

I was involved with a group of people who got together once a year to live like the Native Americans, mountain men, and cavalry brigades of the 1840's to 1880's. We would set up our teepees and wall tents, put on our replica clothing, hide all signs of the present, and have mock battles with the cavalry and other tribes. Since the horse was such an integral part of Native American lifestyle especially in that time period, we borrowed or rented horses to ride. So my first experience of horse archery was actually re-enacting games and battle tactics used by Native Americans of the 1800s. We shot blunts at each other, used rubber knives and spears, and a few participated in a real buffalo hunt from horseback using bow and arrow. I was hooked; this shooting bow and arrow off of horseback was fun. Thus we ended up at the auction in order that my friends could find horses for themselves. By the end of the day they had horses and so did I. It seems they entered my name without my knowing or approving. You can imagine my surprise when they called my name for a horse.

The BLM mustang that I have because of that auction is my beloved Diablo. He has accompanied me through my journey into horse archery. We started in Wyoming, giving horse archery demonstrations at a local black powder rendezvous and the Wyoming Territorial Prison. I began training my fellow re-enactment friends in the techniques I perfected by riding and shooting daily. One day as we traveled the acreage behind our home, I saw an antelope which had been wounded in one leg by a hunter. I set out on horseback with my bow and arrow to shoot the wounded antelope. Diablo and I chased this three-legged antelope for several miles before I could take a shot and kill the antelope with one arrow. It was an exhilarating experience. I now knew first hand how the Native Americans were able to feed themselves by hunting the buffalo.

Moving from Wyoming to Montana a few years later, Diablo and I continued doing horse archery shows, shooting at targets rolled on the ground, flying targets tossed in the air, and stationary targets, while riding at a gallop. Crowds loved the shows, and would comment on being so thrilled to experience a piece of the past first-hand. I began to add other weapons while riding horseback, like using a spear, sword, and tomahawk. I even practiced using Diablo as my war horse with my trained companion on the ground being pursued by the horse whichever direction he moved. This is similar to the technique used by cowboys and their cutting horses against a moving cow. I have had the honor of performing at the Denver National Western Stock Show in front of 5000 people with the Great American Wild West Show. I won a Buffalo Bill re-enactment audition in Sheridan Wyoming, which was held in conjunction with the 110th anniversary of the Sheridan Inn. This is the exact location where Buffalo Bill actually held auditions for his Wild West Show. Another Wild West Show I performed in was Monty Montana's Buffalo Bill Wild West Show.

Because I was always trying to learn more about other people's interest in this art, I noticed an article about a Hungarian, Lajos Kassai, who was being introduced to the United States. I was unable to afford to go to a venue with him until the second International Horse Archery Festival (IHAF) in Fort Dodge, Iowa in 2001. Diablo and I traveled three days to Iowa. I didn't believe I could do as well without him. I truly believe horse and archer must act as one, and Diablo and I certainly are of the same spirit. I was thrilled to be able to train with others

www.lrgaf.org

who had my interest in horse archery. I also met David Gray and Lukas Novotny at this Festival as well as several other authors contributing to this book. I went to the third IHAF, and also traveled to Hungary to train in Kassai's valley. It was after this that I realized that I was not as interested in the competition aspect being practiced in Hungary and being brought to the United States. I was much more interested in the actual use of the horse by the Native Americans in everyday life.

The plains Indians' way of life

The horse was life to a Native American family. It provided transportation of both people and belongings, better hunting, wealth, and prestige. Prior to 1730 the Blackfoot Nation was a nomadic tribe and hunted buffalo on foot. They used dogs and horses to pull travois loaded with personal items and teepees when they moved from place to place. Life was hard. Then the horse was introduced and life changed.

Imagine shooting a buffalo from the back of a horse with a bow and arrow. What a thought! This means you must be able to ride your horse without using your hands, while at the same time drawing an arrow, pulling the bow and shooting toward a moving and possibly charging animal. Yet this act changed the way the Native American lived. They could now follow the buffalo herds more easily with horses carrying the load, plus the actual hunt was easier than before. Remember, they hunted on foot previously, using several different methods. I remember one story of men standing above the herd, which had been driven into corrals, and shooting down on them. We all have heard of stampeding herds over cliffs, but I heard a story of a young boy trained to run very fast who wore a buffalo hide over him and encouraged the herd to chase him over the cliff. He had a small ledge to land on just under the cliff as the buffalo fell over him. Or a warrior would wear a wolf hide and slowly sneak up on a sleeping herd and kill a buffalo. One well placed arrow can kill a buffalo.

Now with the horse the warrior could run with the buffalo herd. A horse was swift enough to pull along side the prey and the warrior could shoot an arrow at short range. There have been instances where the arrow went all the way through a buffalo. Each brave carried about 20 arrows with him. It is clear that they could shoot arrow after arrow very quickly. There is some disagreement about how they carried the arrows. I have seen several ways thought to have been used: holding an arrow in his mouth while shooting another; pulling from his quiver whether it was carried on his back, his side, or on the horse; or holding more than one arrow in his hand. They were also able to shoot forward, sideways, as well as a backward parting shot. The white man was no match for the warriors they met when first coming west.

A buffalo hunt was under the total control of the chief. When the buffalo herd was spotted, camp was made and preparations were made for a hunt. When the time was right, a call would come from the chief telling everyone what time to meet for the hunt. All the warriors would gather together in the morning and they would ride toward the buffalo herd. Each warrior rode a horse, but towed his buffalo pony behind him to keep him fresh for the hunt. When they arrived at the hunt site, they would mount their buffalo ponies, and an attendant would watch the other horses. Probably one of the older boys, not yet ready for a hunt, would keep the horses. Then on the chief's signal they would all race toward the herd.

After the hunt they would divide the kill. Each warrior had specially marked arrows so they would know which part of a buffalo belonged to which warrior, according to placement of the arrows. Even warriors who did not own their own buffalo pony would rent a pony to use in the hunt, giving half of each kill to the owner of the horse. Wealth in the tribe was measured in how many horses one owned. If you owned several buffalo ponies, you would be very wealthy. A well-trained horse would make the hunt much easier, and everyone in the tribe needed to be fed. The hunt was set this way to give everyone an equal chance at the herd. They started at the same time. If any warrior went earlier and scattered the herd, he was severely punished and everything he owned was destroyed. This was necessary because everyone needed the buffalo to live, and all needed the same chance. Another herd could be hard to find.

Of course they did not kill buffalo just for food. They also obtained the hide for lodges, clothing, blankets, etc. The sinew was used for bow making, sewing, and rope making. Scraping the hide to tan it provided hide glue used for bowmaking, gluing saddletrees, etc. Rawhide (untanned leather) was the iron of the Plains. They used it for backing bows, covering saddle trees, moccasin soles, bow strings, rope, shields, and parflexes (boxes). The bones could be used as various tools such as needles, spoons, weapons, and arrowheads. They even made bows out of the ribs. The horn could be applied to the belly of the bow to make it stronger. Horn was also used for buttons, spoons, drinking cups, and fire holders. Embers were packed in ashes placed inside a horn (called a fireholder) to be carried from one campsite to another to start a new fire. The fire carrier (a person who carries the fire holder) was an important person because he was responsible for keeping the fire going. The ash was used to keep the coals from burning the horn itself so when they arrived at the new campsite a fire could be started quickly.

As you can see, hunting buffalo and using its parts was an integral part of Native Americans' way of life. Having horses made this easier than when hunting on foot. Horse archery for the Native American *was* life, not a game. However they did play games on horseback. It was a way of teaching the young how to ride, hunt, and exist in the future. One of the games they played was shooting at rolling targets. The target was small tree branches bent into a circle, divided with a string into sections, with each section having a different colored bead. A good shooter could call the color of the bead in the section he intended to hit. They would also hang a moccasin from a pole or a tree and ride by and shoot at it. The winner was the one who hit the moccasin with his arrow. Thus they practiced shooting at both moving and stationary targets. The children were also responsible for the everyday care of the horses, learning at an early age how important the animal was to their life.

When the white man started hunting buffalo and destroying the herds, the Native American way of life started dwindling. After the Native Americans were defeated and sent to reservations much of their heritage was outlawed by the government, and the art of horse archery was lost and not thought of for many years. Anyone who remembered the old ways did not share them with the younger ones, and those that did learn from their elders often did not share.

Today it is difficult to find any interest in horse archery among the Blackfoot or Nez Perce. People who see my demonstrations are excited to know that the chance to learn this art is available, and the interest is growing across the United States, not just with Native Americans. I am developing my own style of mounted martial archery, which I teach privately as well as holding periodic clinics for 6-8 people. I am also involved with the Mounted Archery Association of America, and the Warhorse Challenge Association, both organizations promoting the sport of horseback archery.

A martial art as I see it

Mounted martial archery as taught by me involves more than just archery off horseback. I also teach tomahawk throwing, lance spearing, and sword techniques from horseback using both right and left hands. Balance is very important in mounted martial archery. You must have balance on horseback while riding, balance in body using both right and left, and the end result of all this practice is balance in your life in general. Yes, as you may have guessed, this is being taught as a martial art. You can choose to take it to the level you want. I practice every day, shooting 250-500 arrows a day, both from the ground and from horseback. In the past I have shot as many as 1000 arrows a day.

I do not believe a beginner rider can practice horse archery until first learning how to ride a horse. Since shooting a bow off horseback involves letting go of the reins and steering your horse with your legs, this activity becomes dangerous if one cannot ride a horse, and balance well. You must be in good physical shape also, which is why I teach martial arts, along side horse archery. I give riding lessons as well as train horses. If you can ride your horse without a saddle or bridle, your level in mounted archery will rise accordingly, especially when you also practice archery faithfully.

I have a vision of being able to rate horses that have been specially trained in horse archery with Master being the top level. Belts would be awarded to a horse just like they are to humans. I believe my Diablo has reached the Master level because he can perform even with novice riders on his back. Not all horses adapt to this activity well. In the future I hope to be able to sell horses which already have the necessary training. In fact I have recently sold my first horse archery trained horse, who performs well but has not yet reached Master level. I am training three other horses, but they are not accomplished to that level yet. I do truly believe the connection between horse and rider also makes a big difference in how someone can perform mounted archery.

www.lrgaf.org

You must be able to stop your horse immediately when asked, not several feet beyond the initial request to stop. This also takes practice. I also think trail riding is important, not just riding on the track set up for the competition course. My philosophy is all inclusive, but can be broken down into manageable parts; this is where my clinics can be helpful.

Please let one of my students describe his view on my training. This student has also studied in Hungary with Kassai, and in Iowa at IHAF. These are his words:

"<u>Tomahawk</u>. Pat works a course for tomahawk throwing in this manner. Two cottonwood log sections are positioned about 50 feet apart. The game is to walk toward the target, when it feels right, throw, hit and retrieve the hawk, turn around and walk towards the other target, then repeat the cycle. Do this for an hour and you can cancel your gym membership. Great aerobic workout with some serious strength training. Add in another hawk for left hand throwing and you balance it out. Throw the left hawk about a step before the right hawk. Another benefit of Pat's tomahawk regimen is that you get tired, you stop thinking, and just execute the form. The hawks stick, you pull and do it again and again with I must say surprising consistency.

<u>Archery</u>. Then of course, there's archery. Pat's style of shooting differs dramatically from the Hungarian form that I was taught. Pat's form requires a shorter draw, not more than 28-29 inches. Upon the release of the arrow there is no exaggerated follow through as in the Hungarian or Japanese styles. Holding his arrows against the back of the bow at the grip, Pat's technique of arrow management is much like the Hungarian style, however the arrows are indexed from high to low and not separated by various fingers or thumb. This always presents the high arrow for the next shot. Pat's shooting technique is to rotate the bow with the hand as to open it to retrieve the arrow, then to nock the arrow by passing it between the string and the bow from the right to left (at least while shooting right handed), draw and loose the arrow with minimal follow through, then, rotating the bow again and with almost a striking motion, reach forward to grab the next arrow, nock again, draw and loose. Repeat, Repeat, Repeat.

Pat grabs the arrow between the index and middle finger and uses the thumb to stabilize the arrow and to act as a guide to locate the nock on the string. This requires considerable dexterity in the fingers. Correct breathing for Pat's form is to exhale to facilitate the collapse of the chest while reaching for the arrow and then inhaling on the draw to expand the chest and utilize core body muscles to draw to anchor. Not a common breathing technique for archery on the ground, but in mounted martial archery as in battle, it all makes sense as there is no wasted motion. In Pat's opinion, the exaggerated follow through on the loose makes sense only if you are carrying your arrows in a back quiver slung low on the back as in Yabusame and some North American Plains Indian forms. You need to get your drawing hand to the arrows as fast as you can wherever they are located. Pat reprimanded me once when I did an exaggerated follow through, but apologized when he realized that I was going for the arrows in my back pocket.

Pat is a big believer in balance. Part of the training with both the tomahawk and the bow is to throw or shoot left handed. Look at it this way, when you're in battle, you don't know which side your adversary is going to be on. You might find yourself in a position where your primary arm is injured. This is martial mounted archery, not archery performed from horseback.

Working the left (or weak) hand is slow going at first and requires a great amount of dedicated practice to achieve consistency and accuracy. Surprisingly, it comes rather quickly as training the weak hand doesn't involve 'retraining' as it might with the strong hand. In other words, you don't have to 'unlearn' your shooting style to execute Pat's method with the weak hand." — Richard Grossman, *mounted archery student.*

That is a good description of my philosophy. I am still hoping to bring mounted archery to the Blackfoot. Bob Blackbull has been rebuilding the Spanish Mustang breed, which were the original horses used by the Blackfoot. He is also trying to involve children, and I have done one event with him so far. The future is wide open, and exciting. We are still waiting to see where it will take us, but in no way has mounted archery growth slowed. I am proud to be part of this movement.

www.lrgaf.org

References:

Denig, Edwin Thompson. 1930. Indian Tribes of the Upper Missouri. 46th Annual Report of the Bureau of American Ethnology, 1928-1929.
Ewers, John C. Originally 1955, Reprinted 1969. The Horse in Blackfoot Culture. Washington: Smithsonian Institution Press.
Hamilton, T. M. 1982, Second Edition. Native American Bows. Columbia, Missouri: Missouri Archeological Society.

Websites:

en.wikipedia.org
www.buffalohorse.org
www.mountedmartialarchery.org
www.warhorsechallenge.com
http://mountedarchery.pizco.com

Chapter 7

Native American Horse Archery in the Southwest

By Ed Scott

Introduction

The arrival of the horse in Central America in the early sixteenth century (1500's) surely amazed the indigenous peoples. The fact that strange looking men in shiny armor rode their backs must have astounded them! The men were first viewed as "gods" and great efforts were made to appease them. However, it was not long until they were recognized as oppressors by many. Tribes on the periphery of Spanish domination learned to avoid capture and enslavement. Yet there must have been fascination with the way the intruders used animals, especially the horse.

Survival and personal freedom are among man's strongest instincts, superseded only by procreation. Man survives by intelligent use of what he finds in his environment. In this essay I am attempting to tell the story of how Native Americans (Indians) took advantage of the fact of the horse in their world.

The people

The primary purpose of this essay is to tell the story of how horse archery became a part of the life of Indians in what is now the North American southwest region. The land mass we are considering is huge, extending from Nebraska and Idaho to the north, central Texas to the east, the deserts of Arizona and California to the west and into northern Mexico in the south. The occupants of this land did not know any of these borders. They knew where they lived and roamed in their pursuit of survival, freedom and procreation.

There were many tribes and human nature being what it is, there was often contact between them. Sometimes it was guardedly friendly, but often hostile. The notion that all was peaceful co-existence, health, harmony and good will between the tribes until the

Europeans arrived bringing warfare and enslavement is a silly notion, hardly worthy of comment. Only someone sadly misinformed, uninformed or educated far beyond their intelligence could believe such a thing. Sadly, no group, tribe or nation has ever existed for very long without conflict with other groups. Internal disputes arise as well. Christianity, the religion that teaches love of neighbor, peace, harmony and goodwill toward all, has had bitter, bloody disputes and wars. Such is human nature.

When highly disparate cultures clash, bloody conflict always results. Sad, but true. Fortunately, we have matured in our concept of "all men are created equal" to the point that most of us who love archery can put aside the old hurts and memories of the atrocities and injustices of the past and focus our attention on our sport.

Having gotten that bit of philosophy off my chest, I now turn to the subject at hand, the people of the southwest who were most affected by the arrival of the horse. There were many tribes, too many and too varied to discuss in detail and some will not be mentioned at all. However, some stand out in the use of the bow with the horse and these will get the most attention. Throughout history, the land in which one dwells has always had a profound effect in shaping one's way of life. No meaningful discussion of a group of people can take place without considering the land in which they live.

The southwest portion of the North American continent under consideration varies greatly in topography, landscape, fauna, flora, precipitation, climate and altitude. The eastern plains of about 4,000 ft. elevation rise to over 14,000 ft. in the Rockies and drop to near sea level at the Mojave Desert and Salton Sea. The fantastic shapes of the rocks and canyons of southern Utah give way to the tree-clad heights of the Rockies which in turn descend to the rolling plains of Eastern Colorado, New Mexico and West Texas. The "Great River of the North", the Rio Grande, bisects the southwest. Up this fertile valley came the Spaniards with their horses. Far up the river they came to a place suitable to settle for trade and colonization. They called it Santa Fe (Holy Faith). From here springs unprecedented change in the life of the Southwest Indians. In order to understand that historic change, we need to understand what their life (the people of the southwest) was like before the outlanders brought the horse.

When the Conquistadors began their bloody work in the early sixteenth century (1520- 1540), the upper Rio Grande region had long been peopled by what we now know as the pueblo Indians (descendants of the "ancient ones" - the Anasazi). When and how they (Anasazi) arrived is a subject for scholars and anthropologists. Among that crowd there is dispute and they keep changing their minds. Whether they arrived many thousands of years ago or were found under a cabbage leaf or came up from a hole in the ground is a moot point. They were there in 700 AD and gone by 1300 AD, leaving behind the pueblo tribes, who all claim descent from the Anasazi to some extent.

The Pueblos, tight knit communities living in very close quarters, were the ones most easily dominated by the Spaniards. They were primarily farmers with some gathering and hunting. Some of the most eastern Pueblos even made periodic expeditions to the eastern plains for buffalo. The typical pueblo had many chiefs to cover the various aspects of communal life. One of these was the Hunting Chief.

Picture, in your mind's eye, the Hunting Chief with all the young men eager to go, choosing a group of proven hunters and strong dogs for an exciting, dangerous trip. Purification ceremonies have been held, prayers said and bows, arrows, spears and knives made ready. Perhaps some women accompany them for the bard work of skinning, drying meat and sinew, fleshing hides and cooking for the hunters. They will be encroaching on the territory of other tribes such as the fierce Apache, Kiowa or Pawnee. This is a dangerous undertaking, but the pueblo needs all the buffalo products they can bring back. Robes for warmth in winter, dried meat that keeps indefinitely - a supplement to their crops and survival food when crops fail. Sinew, nice long cords from the buffalo's back that can be shredded in the finest threads for sewing or beadwork. Re-enforce a bow with the magic of sinew, and use it to tie fletching and points on arrows. The list goes on and on and in the pueblo Indians' world, nothing makes a better hoe for weeding the crops than the shoulder blade of a buffalo bound to a handle.

Buffalo products were also items for trade with other pueblos. It is a widely held belief among scholars that traders and trade routes crisscrossed the western continent from deep in Mexico to the Pacific Northwest. This is borne out by the existence of small copper bells from Mexico and abalone and cowrie shells from the northern Pacific.

www.lrgaf.org

As our hunters trek onto the plains they are seeking what is of great value to them but they are also going into great danger. Perhaps they may be able to trade something of value such as their exquisitely made pottery for permission to hunt or maybe simply to avoid hostile tribes. When they find a herd they perform more ceremonies to ensure success and begin the process of harvesting the buffalo.

Wolves often followed the herds in order to live off the weak and injured. A grown healthy animal was not afraid of wolves. Taking advantage of this, a hunter could don a wolf skin and crawl in amongst the herd with his short powerful bow and sometimes make several kills before the herd thundered off. His life was in danger from start to finish. Just because the buffalo weren't afraid of wolves, they still didn't like them. A cow defending her calf against perceived danger can be deadly and bulls are always dangerous.

These hunts could be several months long. As kills were made the hides, meat, sinew and selected bones had to be processed and dried to reduce weight so that they could be transported back to the pueblo. Back packs and travois were placed on dogs. Women and some of the men made up packs of all they could carry. If the group owned any slaves they were loaded heavily.

With the best fighters un-encumbered for defense, our group makes the difficult journey back borne with things of great value to their community. *Imagine how horses would change both the journey and the hunt.* These hunts probably only happened every few years for the pueblo dwellers. The purpose was to obtain large amounts of meat and other buffalo products. Hunts held closer to home supplied meat and skins on a much more regular basis. Deer, elk, bighorn sheep, jack rabbits, cotton tails, squirrels, prairie dogs, grouse, quail, etc. formed a regular part of their diet. The bulk of their sustenance came from corn, beans and squash grown in flood irrigated fields. It is worth noting that Native Americans, as intelligent people making the most of the environment in which they found themselves, developed food crops that are now used world-wide: namely corn, beans, squash, pumpkin and potatoes (from South America). Salt preserves and aids in drying meat. One of the trade items available to the pueblos was a plentiful supply of salt from Zuni Salt Lake near the present Arizona - New Mexico border in Zuni territory. Evidence and oral history indicates that it has been collected for centuries. One of the most valuable commodities a trader such as Kokopeffi could carry in his high bumped pack was salt.

Most probably, one of the items our hunters packed with them as they set off on their hunting expedition was a good supply of salt. Lightly salted, air dried lean meat will keep for many years when stored in low humidity. Such dry conditions existed in the food storerooms of the pueblos. They dried corn, squash, beans, meat, pinyon nuts and sometimes pigweed seed and stored them in rooms off their living quarters. The prevailing low humidity kept the food stuffs secure, for regular use and to have as a buffer against famine. Crops fail at times, whether from lack of enough precipitation or raids from hostile tribes such as the Apache. Food that they could accumulate above daily needs enabled them to survive and prosper for centuries.

The buffalo hunt supplied excess meat for such storage. During drought animals often became scarce. Nomadic tribes move to find game and food plant products to gather. Sedentary tribes such as Pueblos must have stored food to survive. Their methods allowed them to survive until now.

Zuni

It is appropriate at this time to mention the unique Zuni tribe. Their life style is somewhat like the Pueblos, but not really. Far enough away from the Spanish settlements of Santa Fe and Albuquerque not to be dominated by them, they have continued to be an isolated tribe to a certain extent. Superb craftsmen with a deeply ceremonial life, they are not very warlike except when attacked. Fierce fighters in defense of their homeland, Apache and Navajo raiders learned to leave them alone. The first Spanish soldiers to visit them were offered hospitality but were soon in retreat leaving their dead behind when some of the soldiers attempted rape.

The Zuni Mountains furnished game in abundance and most probably there were buffalo from the Great Basin herd on Zuni territory at times. Crops were also raised. The story is told of Cabeza de Vaca viewing Zuni from a distant height with the sun gleaming off the adobe walls. When he finally completed his seven year journey of survival from the Texas gulf coast through various tribes back to Mexico, he told of his experience. From this tale arose Coronado's expedition in 1541 searching for the "Seven Cities of Gold".

The Zuni adamantly claim to be descendants of the Anasazi. They take the Navajo word to mean "ancient enemy" rather than "ancient ones". While they get along today, the undercurrent of dislike and distrust still exists. As the Apachean peoples (Apache and Navajo) migrated down from the north they were most likely one of the major causes of the abandonment of the ancient cities at Mesa Verde, Chaco Canyon and other sites. Protection was the object of their style of building. The fortified towns were not built because the people liked a home that was difficult to get into and very crowded.

Climatic changes coupled with increased raids by more and more warlike people would account for their abandonment. In addition, less rainfall and worn out crop land makes for poorly nourished people, prone to disease. All these factors together caused the survivors to look elsewhere for a better life. Many settled in or near the upper Rio Grande Valley, but Zuni came into existence much further to the west in a different sort of land and thus became a different kind of people. Even today, when you travel far enough off the more beaten path and arrive in Zuni you feel that you are in a world apart.

Apachean

When the Athapascan speaking people (Apache and Navajo) migrated down from the north, the migration most likely took several centuries. The fact that they did come from the north can hardly be disputed. Why? Because linguists affirm that the difference between the languages of the Navajo, Apache and the Indians of Alaska and Northwest Canada is about the same as the difference between Portuguese and Spanish. Not a great deal. Whether they started out as raiders or became such when they bumped into other groups is not known. What is known is that both oral history and written history describe them as extremely warlike people who took whatever they could from any outsider. Raiding others was simply their way of life. Of course they hunted and sometimes raised crops if it was convenient. The Apache did not make pottery or do hardly any sort of artwork. Did they like the convenience of a ceramic pot and the beauty of ornaments? Of course. They simply acquired them in raids. Corn and beans were on the menu, but it was easier to get them from the Pueblos than to plant and hope for a harvest. This is not to say that they didn't have favorite places to camp for long periods and that they never raised crops. They did, but they did not depend upon them as did the Pueblo and Zuni.

The Apaches were migrants. They wandered over an enormous expanse of plains, the Rocky Mountains and dry deserts extending from Texas to California, central Colorado down into Old Mexico. Mostly it was wasteland from the view point of others, but to the Apache it was home. They loved the green mountain ranges that rose up, tree clad with clear mountain streams. Sweetened with fruits and berries, abundant game and cool meadows it was a great place to be in warm weather. But a brush arbor or tipi is not a fun place to be in zero weather, so they spent their winters down on the warm desert.

This harsh, enormous land was called *Apacheria* by the Spaniards. The Apache was a child of the desert and mountain fastness. Highly intelligent, tough beyond belief, cunning, and extremely warlike, he was a bane and a constant danger the Spanish could never defeat except in a few skirmishes. Defeat only came near the beginning of the twentieth century by the combined efforts of U.S. Army and Mexican forces with vastly superior numbers and resources. Today our military is fortunate to have many Apache who serve with honor and distinction.

Other tribes

As we set the stage for the arrival of the horse, we must not forget some other players. The Comanche had long dwelt in the Rockies and Great Basin as hunters, gathering what they could in way of plant life. Their transformation into "the best light calvary the world has ever seen" is about to begin. Meanwhile the various tribes out of the plains are following the buffalo as best they can with their dogs. Life is hard, but the abundance of the herds makes it possible. The map on page 158 gives some semblance of the stage our next players are moving onto. The Spaniards brought their wonderful durable horses — the riding horses of Spain mixed with the Barb during the occupation of the Moors resulted in a tough, beautiful horse. The wild mustangs of the west still show some of their characteristics today.

www.lrgaf.org

Spain

The same year Spanish Queen Isabella agreed to finance Columbus on his voyage that resulted in his arrival in what we know as the West Indies, her armies were able to drive the Moors from their last stronghold in Iberia. The fall of Granada was the culmination of 750 years of effort to re-conquer the southern part of Spain from the forces of Islam which had arrived in the 8th and 9th century. Northern Spain remained intact and it was the steadfast policy of the rulers over the centuries to drive them out. Extremadura, the harsh, dry interior highlands of Spain produced both the fighters capable of re-conquering Granada and conquering Central and South America. It also produced the horse to do the job.

As new lands were now available to conquer, the government used this formula as their policy. Having mastered the art of conquest during the years of the re-conquest, they now became adept at imperialism. Aristocratic men were given grants to rule over large tracts of land. They had authority to tax the local people provided they would Christianize, civilize, and protect them. Most laws were left to their discretion and authority.

Now the new world lands came under the same policy. Given authority by the monarch, an aristocrat would raise and finance an army and set out to conquer, tax (enslave) Christianize and defend his holding. In this way Mexico was settled by the Spanish. They called it New Spain. Great wealth accumulated to the successful ones. Their efforts to "Christianize" were most often secondary considerations and carried out only because it was required of them by the monarch. Jesus would not approve of the methods often used.

With the Spaniards came domestic livestock. Cattle, hogs, sheep, goats, burros and horses were shipped from Spain to New Spain. The horses were of the utmost importance to the Spanish aristocrats as they set themselves up as "PATRONES" of large land holdings. They considered themselves horsemen (caballeros) and it was both beneath their dignity and impractical to walk when they could ride. As a consequence, breeding and raising horses was one of the main purposes of many ranches. The Indians who had been enslaved learned to work with horses. It is easy to imagine them stealing some horses and slipping away to find refuge with some remnant of his tribe or perhaps another tribe. In this way horses could have come to southwest tribes much earlier than many believe. As horse herds became larger, keeping track of them became more difficult. I can imagine wild herds developing that could have been captured by energetic young tribesmen on the periphery of Spanish domination. They would have seen how the horses were ridden and being intelligent folks they would have seen how horses could benefit them.

The map indicates the first record of horses among the tribes of Southwest Texas in 1690. However, official Spanish records tell of a raid on Monterey in 1632 by mounted Indians. So we know that some tribes in Old Mexico were well acquainted with the horse before then. Since the Rio Grande is no real barrier to a horse, mounted or running free, horses among the tribes in West Texas and Southern New Mexico could have occurred much earlier than records indicate. For records to exist, the observer must know how to write and think the event worthy of recording. Then the record must be preserved. Therefore most of history has not been recorded. When Coronado and his men made their journey of exploration as far as the plains of Kansas in 1541 we have a record. But if others made forays up into the Southwest no record exists. That doesn't mean that it didn't happen.

We do know that conquistador Don Juan de Onate was given a royal grant to proceed up the Rio Grande claiming all the land drained by the river. This happened in 1598. He was a wealthy Basque born in Mexico's silver mining town of Zacatecas. He not only claimed all the land and adjoining lands, but he claimed jurisdiction over all the people found in the land. Such was the arrogance of Onate and others given grants by the monarch of the Spanish Empire.

When Onate and his colonists arrived in present day Santa Fe they brought priests with them. Empire policy said that they must conquer and Christianize the people. This gave them the right to tax the people in any way they chose. The atrocities perpetuated in the name of Spain and its most Holy Catholic Empire makes me sad and I am most certain that Jesus was not pleased. However, the Spanish came to the lands of the Pueblos and they brought horses with them; fine horses for the "aristocrats" to ride, to awe and overrun the culture they were conquering.

www.lrgaf.org

The Puebloans endured much over the next 80 years. Then they rebelled under the leadership of Pope' (meaning ripe squash), a medicine man. (His name is pronounced Po-pay, not to be confused with the Roman Catholic ruler.) The rebellion was a success, killing many of the colonists and driving the rest south to Mexico, leaving behind their possessions, livestock and many horses. Even as they retreated south some of them were planning the re-conquest of the land and people they considered their own, their property. For the next seven years, until his death, Pope' ruled, unfortunately becoming a despot himself.

In 1692 the Spanish did return in force and were even welcomed by some of the people. The previous oppression had disrupted their lives to such an extent that the communities could not function well. At least the Spanish brought a semblance of order and stability with their rule. The twelve years during which the Spanish were absent left the people unhindered access to horses and undoubtedly many went wild. Without doubt the upper Rio Grande drainage became the primary source for the dispersion of horses throughout the western portion of the continent. During the coming decades any tribe that had not already acquired horses could get them through trade, theft or capture. That they would desire them is a foregone conclusion. People who were primarily nomadic hunter gatherers with only dogs as beasts of burden could readily see the advantage of the "medicine dog", the horse.

Santa Fe became a trading center for many tribes. The colonists' blacksmiths soon learned that steel arrowheads, knives and lance points were very profitable items of trade. A stone point can be very effective, but often breaks, while a steel point can be used over and over again. Within a few decades the tribes had all but abandoned flint knapping. The colonists also desired slaves and the tribes were happy to supply them. For many centuries it had been the practice of most tribes to take captives in raids. Sometimes the captive would be incorporated into the tribe, but often they were used for menial labor. Pre-adolescent boys and girls and young women were most often those spared death and taken into captivity. Adult men were too dangerous to keep and older women were not as desirable.

All the Spanish colonists considered themselves "aristocrats" no matter what their status prior to their arrival and so were not disposed to menial labor. Slaves were considered a necessity. Nomadic warriors found that captives could be traded for horses, cloth, beads, arrow heads, knives, etc. So Santa Fe became the trading center of the Central Southwest. The upper Rio Grande Valley region had already been a trade center for centuries before the Europeans arrived. Now it continued in that tradition. Here a group of warriors could get as many as three horses for a young girl or two for a boy. They were happy to make the exchange.

The ratio of trade varied over time and slave trade was eventually outlawed by Spain. History records an incident that shows the attitude and morals of the times. Some Apache warriors brought about 20 slaves to be traded at Santa Fe. It was now illegal, but the exchange was about to take place anyway. Soldiers intervened to stop the exchange. When the warriors saw that they were thwarted and could not trade, they killed all the prisoners before the eyes of the merchants and soldiers and rode away. Open exchanges were outlawed but the slave trade continued well into the nineteenth century. Of course there was other trade such as buffalo robes and meat, furs and decorated moccasins and clothing. Sometimes even horses were traded to the Spanish merchants for knives, arrow points, beads, hawks bells and other such trinkets. Commerce in native goods is still a large part of life around Santa Fe and the Southwest.

Dogs to horses

The wolfish dogs that the Indians kept were helpful in hunting and used as beasts of burden. They were also a source of food in hard times or as a special feast. A strong dog could carry a pack strapped to his back or pull a small load between the poles of a travois. Imagine how much more a "medicine dog" that was 10 to 20 times larger could do. A clan walking with dog transport could travel 10 - 15 miles a day, maybe. Mounted on horses with pack horses they could do 50 miles a day just as easily, with energy to spare. With horses life became easier, less starvation took place and more leisure time was available and thus population increased. In short, some tribes become affluent. Times were good.

When the Pueblos rebelled in 1680, making a large quantity of horses available, the southern Apache tribes most probably already had a good supply of horses. But now tribes such as the Pawnee, Kiowa, Kiowa-Apache and Comanche had much easier access.

Comanche

The hunter gatherers who lived near the head waters of the Arkansas and Platte rivers are now known as the Comanche. By 1700 they had acquired the horse and became very adept in its use. The tribe grew and expanded out onto the plains because of the horse. With bow and lance they harvested buffalo at will and overcame small groups of Querechos (buffalo eaters). Captured women and children made the tribe grow quickly. The Comanche warrior had as many wives as he desired and could support. The abundance of the buffalo and his expert use of his horses and weapons enabled him to support several. Thus the tribe grew at a rapid rate. They swept southeast across the plains, lords of all they surveyed. A military man later described them as "the best light cavalry the world has ever seen".

Their expansion into Texas was hindered to the west by the Apache. Colonel Don Antonio de Cordero, in his report to the Spanish government in 1796, wrote that the Apaches were in constant conflict with the Comanches. Why? Because the Comanches wanted to expand into the Apaches' ancestral land. Thus their expansion tended to be more to the southeast and covered much of Texas, but not far West Texas.

It is worth noting that while the Spanish were able to expand their New World Empire up the Rio Grande to the north, they were not successful in their attempts to expand onto the southwest plains. Why? They were not able to overcome mounted tribesmen with their soldiers. Swords, lances, armor, cannon and muskets were no match for the superior tactics of the tribesmen. Mounted on fleet ponies and armed with short powerful bows the Apache, Comanche and others effectively stopped Spanish colonization of the southwest plains.

Warfare

Colonel Don Antonio de Cordero spent more than 20 years fighting the Apache. His mission was to subdue and "civilize" them. In 1796 he was ordered to submit an official report to the Spanish government. In the introduction of his report he stated "the Apaches are for Mexico nothing but a constant and disastrous peril." Later in his report he states, "The war with the Comanches is as old as the two nations". Why? The reason, Cordero states "Their hatred arises from the fact that both the Comanches and Apaches wish to have exclusive rights to hunting the bison which are abundant on the borders of the two nations."

The constant conflict with the Comanche wasn't really any different than the Apaches' relationship with other groups. Raids on the Spanish colonists for horses and plunder was a way of life for them. From 1632 onward the record is full of reports about horses stolen, communities decimated and outposts abandoned by the colonists. The weapons favored by the Apaches were the lance and bow. Dawn surprise attacks on foot to steal horses, mules and other items such as metal for arrow and lance heads was their usual practice. No tribe or group was immune from such raids. The Comanches did make alliances with some of their neighbors such as the Cheyenne, Kiowa and others, especially during the later wars with the United States. The Apaches never did, to the best of my knowledge.

The nine tribes of the Apache also fought among themselves. Cordero reports that even though they spoke the same language (with different accents), they often raided each other for horses, women and plunder. He lists the Navajo as one of the nine tribes. The Apache word used to describe them meant "the ones living far North." The warfare among the different Apache tribes was not constant and relentless as it was against the Spanish and Comanche, but rather depended upon circumstances.

The Navajo do not consider themselves Apache. Their lifestyle was influenced by the Spanish and Pueblo people to some extent. They readily took to horses and even began to herd some of their stolen sheep. Over the years they became weavers which was probably brought to them originally by stolen Pueblo women. Much later Navajo men became famous as silversmiths. This craft developed after they were released from Bosque Redondo internment.

It is an understatement when I say that the name Kit Carson is not popular among the Navajo. During the Civil War (1861-65) United States military forces were not able to maintain a strong presence in western New Mexico. As a result Navajo raids on settlers increased to the point that the renowned scout and Indian fighter was given a special

www.lrgaf.org

commission to round up the whole tribe and imprison them on a small area around Bosque Redondo near Fort Sumner in the eastern part of New Mexico. When the War between the States concluded, they were allowed to return to their ancestral lands in northwestern New Mexico and northeastern Arizona. Their horses were taken from them, and bows, lances and firearms confiscated. When the survivors were allowed to walk back to the huge reservation (arid, useless land in the white man's view) they were given two sheep each and made to swear that they would make war no more. During the next century they increased their herds of sheep, perfected their weaving techniques and became artisans in silver work. Today Navajo rugs and silver artwork are much sought after.

Getting back to Indian warfare, it is worth noting that the Comanche used buffalo bull hide not only as a shield for personal protection but also as armor against arrows for their horses. In 1724 an observer wrote: "They have also many dogs, which carry their equipage when they lack horses. When they go to war, they go always on horseback, and they have leather armor which protects the horses against arrows." Other observers describe the armor as a "cuirass of tanned leather." Within a decade or two they had no lack of horses. An observer reported an encampment of about 300 Comanches with a horse herd of over 2000.

The riding skills of the Comanche warriors are legendary. It is reported that toddlers were often placed on the back of a gentle mare to keep them from underfoot around camp. Archery games, both mounted and on foot were favorite pastimes of young boys. By the time they were 8-10 years old groups of boys would race their ponies into camp on mock raids. Striving to be like their fathers and uncles, they would go on hunts for small game, proudly displaying whatever they could bring back. Adults indulged them, letting them "run wild", saying "The work of children is play." Thus the youngsters learned the skills necessary for life. The onset of puberty brought out the daredevil antics that plague the parents of boys the world over. Trick riding feats like standing up at full gallop, bouncing to the ground on one side then the other, etc. You get the picture. Of course the object is always to impress ones peers and the girls.

Boys in their early teens were considered young warriors. They participated in horse stealing raids and the buffalo hunt. By the time he reached manhood the Comanche warrior could ride with extraordinary skill and accurately shoot his bow from any conceivable position from horseback. With leather armor protecting his horse, be could use the body of the horse to protect himself while he shot arrow after arrow. How? A broad band of leather is placed around the barrel of the horse behind the withers to hold down the saddle pad. He places his left toe in a loop attached to the saddle band (girth). Now he can swing his body around the right side and shoot under his horses' neck with a right hand draw. Extra arrows are held in his bow hand and in his quiver across the front of his body or swung around on his back.

Expert horsemanship and such fearless tactics as these helped to make the Comanche lords of the southern plains. I do not know if the Apache had this skill of shooting under the horses' neck. I surmise that they did. The constant conflict between the two tribes means that they at least knew of it. As tough and resourceful as the Apache are I would expect them to develop similar tactics. Raids on missions and ranches by the Apache and Comanche effectively kept the Spanish Empire from expanding onto the Southwest Plains. While claiming the land, they could not hold it. At the time of the Boston Tea Party (1774) the Comanche were raiding San Antonio and vicinity. A few decades later they were raiding as far south as Victoria and Corpus Christi on the Texas Gulf Coast.

Paint Rock, Texas, a small cow town in Central Texas, is located on the Concho River. Sandstone bluffs, about a half mile long and set back about 300 yards on the north bank of the river, are covered with pictographs dating back hundreds of years. One pictograph shows an attack on a Spanish style church building and near it is shown a European woman captive. It is an interesting place to visit if you are ever down that way. Both Apache and Comanche regularly made raids deep into Old Mexico for horses, slaves and anything of value that caught their eye. The Apache raids continued to the end of the nineteenth century. The Comanche were defeated earlier by the Texas Rangers and the U.S. Army.

The mounted Comanche archers were so bold, skilled and fearless that they were not easily defeated. Texas Rangers did not win any mounted battles until equipped with five shot revolvers. The advantage now went to the Rangers, but until then the advantage and the victory belonged to the Comanche. They would charge, loosing arrow after arrow while the Rangers were reloading their single shot weapons. But now a small detachment of Rangers, armed with rifles and revolvers could out-match a larger party of warriors. Until his final defeat and surrender, Quanah Parker was trying to outfit his warriors with revolvers, never succeeding in getting more than a few.

Hunting

An 1852 painting by Charles M. Russell called *Running Buffalo* depicts a brave hunter on horseback in the midst of a thundering herd. He has what appears to be a sheep horn bow at full draw ready to loose an arrow into a buffalo close by his running horse. Mr. Russell's first hand knowledge and skill as an artist makes the painting a classic view of hunting from horseback. Our blood races and we can picture ourselves doing the same thing if we only had the opportunity and courage. An undated rock painting at Meyers Springs in a canyon west of the Pecos River and north of the Rio Grande a few miles shows two Indians on horseback chasing an obviously badly wounded buffalo. The horseman further away is at full gallop while the one nearer the sick bull seems to have his horse standing, waiting for the wounded animal to collapse. The painting is probably much older than the classic one by C. M. Russell.

Paintings of nineteenth century Native American life by Russell and Catlin tend to make us equate hunting from horseback with bow and arrow to hunting the bison, but this surely was not the only animal hunted thus. But it may have been the most common one. An exciting hunt with plenty of meat and other buffalo products as a pay off, providing you didn't lose your life in the process, was both an attraction and a necessity. I will try to tell of the picture in my mind's eye of a typical mounted buffalo hunt on the southwest plains. He is mounted on his best, most fleet and nimble horse, a highly prized *buffalo runner*. The previous night ceremonies and prayers for a successful hunt have been said, the herd having been located the day before. He and the other half dozen hunters are followed by their women and children. Only the old, infirm and very young wait in camp.

He has in his left hand a short, powerful bow (probably about 45 to 60 pounds draw at 23 inches) made of mesquite wood heavily backed with sinew. He also has in his bow hand three arrows. Across his lap is his quiver with a dozen more in easy reach of his right hand. Most of his arrows are tipped with razor sharp steel points, some made from wagon wheel hoop irons, others obtained years ago by his father from the traders from Santa Fe. Two of his arrows have stone points. One of them was knapped by his grandfather and the other he found at an ancient rock shelter. They are small, less than an inch wide and very sharp for deep penetration in large animals. (This type of point would later be classified by archaeologists as "bird points". They were actually big game points.) With the wind in their faces they top a rise; there is the herd of about a hundred animals grazing near where they were spotted the day before. While the women wait with their horses, travois poles and butcher knives, the men approach the herd at a walk. Because of poor eyesight and constant herd noises, buffalo are hard to spook unless they smell danger. The aim of the hunters is to get as close as possible to the herd before they begin to run. They want fat cows and the six month old calves, with bulls as third choice.

Our hunter is able to approach within 20 yards of a cow and calf pair grazing on the edge of the herd before she senses danger and begins to hesitantly trot back into the midst of the herd. He gives his horse free rein, tucking the end under his thigh. His well trained horse quickly moves forward on the right hand side of the cow with his head about even with the cow's shoulder. This gives our hunter an ideal angle for a kill. He nocks an arrow, points his bow hand toward the sky, draws as he brings his bow down, pointing his hand about a foot below the backbone and just behind the short ribs. Thump! The arrow disappears into the animal, penetrating the diaphragm and driving on down at an angle into its vitals (a mammal with a punctured diaphragm doesn't have long to live). Within a few seconds he has driven an arrow into the rib-cage of the calf.

Now the herd thunders away into the wind with our group mixed in with them. For about five miles they run with them, loosing deadly arrows every time that they can bring their faithful horse into position for the fatal diaphragm shot. As they run the plain is dotted with dead and dying buffalo. Some have two or three arrows in them because the hunter wasn't satisfied with the first shot. The only bull killed has six arrows in him. The youngest hunter (14 years old), wanting to show his valor chose one of the slower bulls as his target. His horse became skittish and he had to keep shooting from a distance as he circled the angry bull.

One of our hunters prefers the lance, a 12 foot hardwood shaft with a 20 inch steel tip. His horse has been trained to approach the animal on the left side. The lancer drives his blade behind the ribs, through the diaphragm into the heart lung area and quickly withdraws it. This is a right hand thrust, slowing his pony and he pulls back to remove the lance, keeping it in his hand to ride on for another kill. His method was probably adapted originally from Spanish lancers a century before. (The lance seemed to be a favorite method of the Puebloans who ventured onto the plains to obtain large supplies of meat.) Our lancer has had about the same success as the archers. Because they had a good long open run they have about five animals apiece or about one third of the herd.

Now as they rest their horses, the women and children move forward to begin the happy job of butchering. Skins for tipis from the cows, clothing from the calves are highly valued items. Horns for spoons and drinking cups are needed. All the back sinew is saved for backing bows, sewing, binding arrow heads and fletching and halting lance heads. Tons of meat! Delicious, nourishing, life-giving meat for immediate feasting and drying to see them through the coming winter. This is the buffalo hunt as I imagine it. Today we can't do such a hunt except in our imaginations.

There were other animals in the southwest that could be hunted from horseback with bow and arrows. One of the Apaches' favorite foods was the meat of the burro. Many of them had escaped from the Spanish and still roam wild in parts of the southwest. It is easy to see how one could overtake a burro on horseback to shoot it with a bow. The Spanish Don who was the earliest administrator of northeastern Mexico and southwest Texas recorded a list of animals found in his province of Nuevo Leon. He lists deer, antelope, jackrabbits, coyotes, cottontails, prairie chickens, javelina, armadillos, raccoons, bobcats, "and wild or feral cattle and hogs." Of this sixteenth century list there are some that are good candidates for horse archery. Deer would be very difficult to hunt from horseback, but in special circumstances it did take place. In his official report on the Apaches in 1796 Don Antonio de Cordero describes a hunt conducted on occasion by Apaches he was familiar with. Here is a quote from a translation of his report: "In the big hunts men, women and children take part without distinction, some on foot and others on horseback. The buffalo hunt is called a "carneada": time and offensive preparations are needed to hunt in lands near to hostile nations. It is peculiar to the Mescaleros, Lianeros and Lipanes, who are near this sort of cattle. The present object of description is the hunt which is made usually for deer, burro, antelope, javelina, porcupine, mountain lion *(leopardos),* bear, wolves, coyotes, hare and rabbits. Having reconnoitered the valleys, mountain ranges, plains, and brush which they inhabit, for the traces of these animals, and having decided on the day, the leader of the undertaking determines at dawn the places where the different groups who are to start the hunt should be, the points which are to be occupied by *archers on horseback and on foot,* and those who are to serve at a distance as lookouts in order to guard against attacks of enemies, and in these places those appointed take up their posts. In this way at dawn a piece of terrain is encircled, which frequently is five or six leagues in circumference. The sign to commence the chase, and consequently to close the circle, is given by smoke signals. There are men on horseback assigned to this project, which consists in setting fire to the grass and herbage of the whole circumference; and since for this purpose they are already placed ahead of time in their posts with torches ready which they make from dried bark or dried palmilla, it takes only a moment to see the whole circle flare up. At the same instant the shouts and the noise commence, the animals flee, they find no exit, and finally they fall into the hands of their astute adversaries."

Antelope is another animal that is undoubtedly difficult to hunt from horseback, but Pat Stoddard has proven that it can be done. On the short grass plains of Wyoming he took an antelope at full gallop with his bow. I suspect that the superior stamina of his horse was a strong factor in the chase. Congratulations are in order for such a feat! The feral cattle mentioned in the records of Nuevo Leon developed over time into what we know as the Texas Longhorn. This is another target for the mounted archer and a good source of meat and hides for the Indians of the southwest.

www.lrgaf.org

Wild hogs

As the Spanish were establishing their New World Empire, they brought with them European domestic animals. Hogs were a staple food for them. When they mounted expeditions of exploration they often traveled with a herd of hogs as a ready meat supply. Hernando de Soto had a herd of over 300 with him when be started out in Florida and spent 3 years traveling to the Mississippi. Hogs love to escape and go out on their own. They are very prolific and well adapted to life in the wild anywhere they have a steady supply of drinking water. Florida has had a substantial population of feral hogs for more than 400 years. The same is true for northeastern Mexico and southwest Texas.

I grew up in south central Florida in the 1950's. We lived in the country and our main source of meat was wild hogs, small game and fish. Our most common way of hunting hogs was with dogs. That is a thrilling way to hunt them, especially when you want to capture them alive. We didn't have electricity or refrigeration so it was good to keep them alive for later use. An adult boar has rank smelling meat, but if you castrate him and feed him out for three or four months he makes fine eating. Our home was located about five miles west of the Avon Park Air Force Bombing Range, an area of about 100,000 acres bordering the Kissimee River. In the mid-fifties the Air Force personnel were reduced to the point that the State of Florida began to use some of the facilities to house low-risk state prisoners. Our father was given the contract to haul away the swill (leftover food) from the prison camp mess hall. He was also given permission to catch wild hogs provided we didn't use dogs or guns.

Daddy and us boys worked hard to enlarge our hog pen and bought an improved Chester White boar to cover the wild sows. That summer we caught about 30 sows from horseback, if you caught a pregnant sow in the open you could chase her until she was exhausted, get off, catch her and tie her down. One of my older brothers was real good at roping any of them including large boars with a limber rope. The point of this story is to say that shooting wild hogs from horseback with a bow is quite feasible, which Howard Hill proved. If I remember correctly, it was one of my cousins on my mother's side that furnished both the horse and the opportunity for that feat.

Javelina

The collared peccary (javelina) inhabits much of the southwestern United Sates, Mexico, Central America and much of South America. They travel in packs of up to one hundred animals, but usually ten to twenty. Often you can spot a pack up to a half mile away. With the ever present wind in your face, you can usually walk in amongst them with your bow and choose your target. If you were mounted, there would be some opportunities also. Someone should try it. I believe the Apache did it often. As you can see, there were plenty of animals that the southwest Indians could hunt from horseback with their short, powerful bows.

Bows

Even before the arrival of the horse, Indians of the Southwest preferred shorter bows than those of the Eastern Woodlands. Why? Undoubtedly part of the answer lies in the availability of suitable bow woods. However, as a bowyer who collects his own bow staves, I know that long bow wood can be found in many locations in the Southwest. Yet, despite this availability, the local natives preferred short bows, usually sinew backed.

The hunter or warrior on foot finds it easier to stalk with a shorter bow. Also, a short, reflexed bow will almost always have better cast than most straight or somewhat deflexed long bows, every thing else being equal. It is reported that an Apache could shoot his bow accurately lying under a bush on his belly. Try that with a long bow! The advantage of a short bow from horseback becomes obvious. With the exception of the Japanese, horse archers the world over have preferred shorter bows.

Modern archers advocate always coming to "full draw", bow arm fully extended, consistently "anchoring" to the same point on the cheek. But remarkably consistent accuracy is reported by observers of early Native American archers who followed none of these rules. The draw was often toward the face or chest with the elbow and wrist of the bow arm somewhat bent, thus causing a shorter draw. I grew up shooting like this, loosing the arrow when it felt "right". This method allows the archer to shoot any draw length up to his "full draw."

www.lrgaf.org

Accuracy comes with practice. I enjoy shooting long bows at "full draw" and short bows at whatever the draw is for that bow. In actuality, the draw is the draw length the bow was designed for.

Consider carefully two Apache bows in order to understand the "magic" of sinew. Both bows are 52" long. One is made of superior osage wood, and the second is made from less desirable oak, but turns out to be better, The recommended maximum draw length of the Osage bow is 23", the Oak bow, 26". Let us examine the shooting characteristics and durability of these two bows. The Osage bow is an adequate bow for hunting or warfare. The fact that it is mostly sapwood gives it slightly more elasticity than it would have if it was all heartwood. Being a well-made bow it should be good for many thousands of shots. As it is shot over and over it will very gradually lose cast (arrow speed) and eventually break from stress. For the sake of this discussion, let us assume both bows have the same draw weight at 23 inches. The oak bow, highly reflexed and re-enforced with sinew will have much greater cast, will not lose arrow speed with long use, nor break from stress if it is not drawn beyond its' recommended draw length. Why? Because the elasticity of sinew is many times greater than that of the most elastic wood. Most, if not all, of the tension work is being done by the sinew and the wood only needs to supply compressive strength. Thus the heavily sinew backed bow, tillered properly, becomes virtually impossible to break under normal use.

Sinew allows us to use woods that have good compressive strength and poor tensile strength to make wonderful bows. Two of my favorite such woods are Juniper and Mesquite. Without backing, they easily break, but properly re-enforced with sinew they make fast, very durable bows. For centuries bowyers have been using hide glue to apply sinew backing. It has performed very well and I have no quarrel with those who want to use it. For several years I have been applying sinew using weatherproof wood glue. The same company has also come out with a waterproof wood glue that also works well. The use of this glue is easier and makes a superior bond. As a self bowyer who makes all of his living from bow making, easier and better are important to me. This is not to say that I use a lot of power tools. I do use a chainsaw for cutting staves and an electric drill on occasion. I do not use a band-saw or power sander. My tools of choice are a hatchet, draw knife, rasp, hunting knife, pocket knife and sandpaper. It is very important to follow the fibers of the wood as much as possible and these hand tools allow me to do that.

The use of sinew on the back of bows undoubtedly began in Asia. This use has allowed some amazing developments to take place over the centuries. You can see the Asiatic influence in Eskimo design in their use of siyahs. Instead of gluing the sinew to the back, they used an elevated, adjustable, sinew cord. This same method was used by the Anasazi on some of their bows. Once the principle was understood, the ingenious bowyers of various tribes used sinew to make bows of sheep horn, elk horn, buffalo ribs and of course, wood, here in western North America.

The horn bows of Asia use a wood core sandwiched between the horn belly and the sinew back. Laplanders do essentially the same, while American Indians developed the method of applying sinew directly to the horn or bone to make some amazing little bows. At present there is no archaeological evidence that shows the existence of these bows prior to the advent of the horse in the American West. However, knowing the advantages of a short, amazingly fast, hard shooting bow of sheep horn or elk horn, it seems reasonable to think that some were made long before they became more widely used as horse bows. The material was available and the principles were known for hundreds of years. *Bowyers are always trying to make a better bow.* Here in the Southwest, only the Utes made sheep horn bows, to the best of my knowledge.

Many thanks to my wife Carolyn for translating my scribbles into a readable document. Thanks to Dave Gray for asking me to write this chapter.

References:

Allely, Steve, and Hamm, Jim. 2002. Encyclopedia of Native American Bows, Arrows & Quivers; Plains and Southwest, Volume II. Azle, Texas: Bois d'Arc Press.

The Buffalo Hunters. 1993. Time-Life Books.

Chapa, Juan Bautista, Original late 1600s, current edition 1999. Texas and northeastern Mexico, 1650-1690 (Historia del Nuevo Reino de Leon 1650 to 1690). Translated by Ned F. Brierley. and edited with an introduction by William C. Foster. Austin: University of Texas Press.

www.lrgaf.org

Davis, Ellis Arthus, (Editor). 1945. The Historical Encyclopedia of New Mexico New Mexico Historical Association.

Encyclopedia of Native American Wars and Warfare. 2005. Book Builders Incorporated.

Kirkland, Forrest, and Newcomb, W. W., Jr. 1967. The Rock Art of Texas Indians. Austin, Texas: University of Texas Press.

Matson, D. S., and Schroeder, A. H. 1949. Cordero's description of the Apache. New Mexico Historical Review, XXIV.

Mayhall, Mildred P. 1962. The Kiowa. Norman, Oklahoma: University of Oklahoma Press.

McNitt, Frank. 1962. The Indian Trader. Norman, Oklahoma: University of Oklahoma Press.

Opler, Morris Edward, and Opler, Catherine H. January 1950. Mescalero Apache history in the southwest. New Mexico Historical Review, XXV.

Roe, Frank Gilbert. 1951. The North American Buffalo: A Critical Study of the Species in its Wild State. Toronto.

Roe, Frank Gilbert. 1955. The Indian and the Horse. Norman, Oklahoma: University of Oklahoma Press.

Sonnichsen, C. L. 1958. The Mescalero Apaches. Norman, Oklahoma: University of Oklahoma Press, 1958.

Worcester, D. E. January 1945. The spread of Spanish horses in the southwest. New Mexico Historical Review, Volume XX.

Above: Erik Hildinger giving a lecture about the mounted archery culture of the Eurasian steppes, holding a Turk horn bow made by Saluki Bow Company. Photograph courtesy Sandy Gomke. (Chapter 1)
Below: Murat Ozveri showing the Turkish/Persian release position. Note the use of the thumb-ring, and the particular manner of holding a second arrow. The bow is a modern wood and fiberglass rendition of the Persian bow by the Hungarian maker Csaba Grozer. Courtesy Murat Ozveri. Chapter 2.

The 35th Takedaryu headmaster Ietaka Kaneko performing Yabusame demonstration at Kamakura Hachimangu shrine. Year unknown. Courtesy of The Takeda School of Horseback Archery, Chapter 3.

Above: Misa Tsuyoshi performing Yabusame demonstration, 2006 IHAF. Courtesy of Masahiro Tsuyoshi, Chapter 3.
Below: Holm Neumann with Korean colleague ready for action at the Second International Competition in Soksho, Korea, 2006. Courtesy of Holm Neumann. Chapter 4.

Above: Jay Red Hawk on Buffalo Boy and in hunting regalia, ready for a buffalo hunt. Jay also appears on the book cover. This photo and the one on the cover courtesy of Guy de Galard. Chapter 5.
Below: Pat Stoddard on his faithful Mustang, Diablo. Courtesy of Trinidad Campbell. Chapter 6

Above: Ed Scott shooting one of his typical five-curve horse bows made of wood and sinew. The bow is 46 inches long with a 23-inch draw. Courtesy of Ed Scott. Chapter 7.
Below: Old Lakota style archery. Courtesy of Jay Red Hawk.

Mounted Archery in the Americas
Page 158

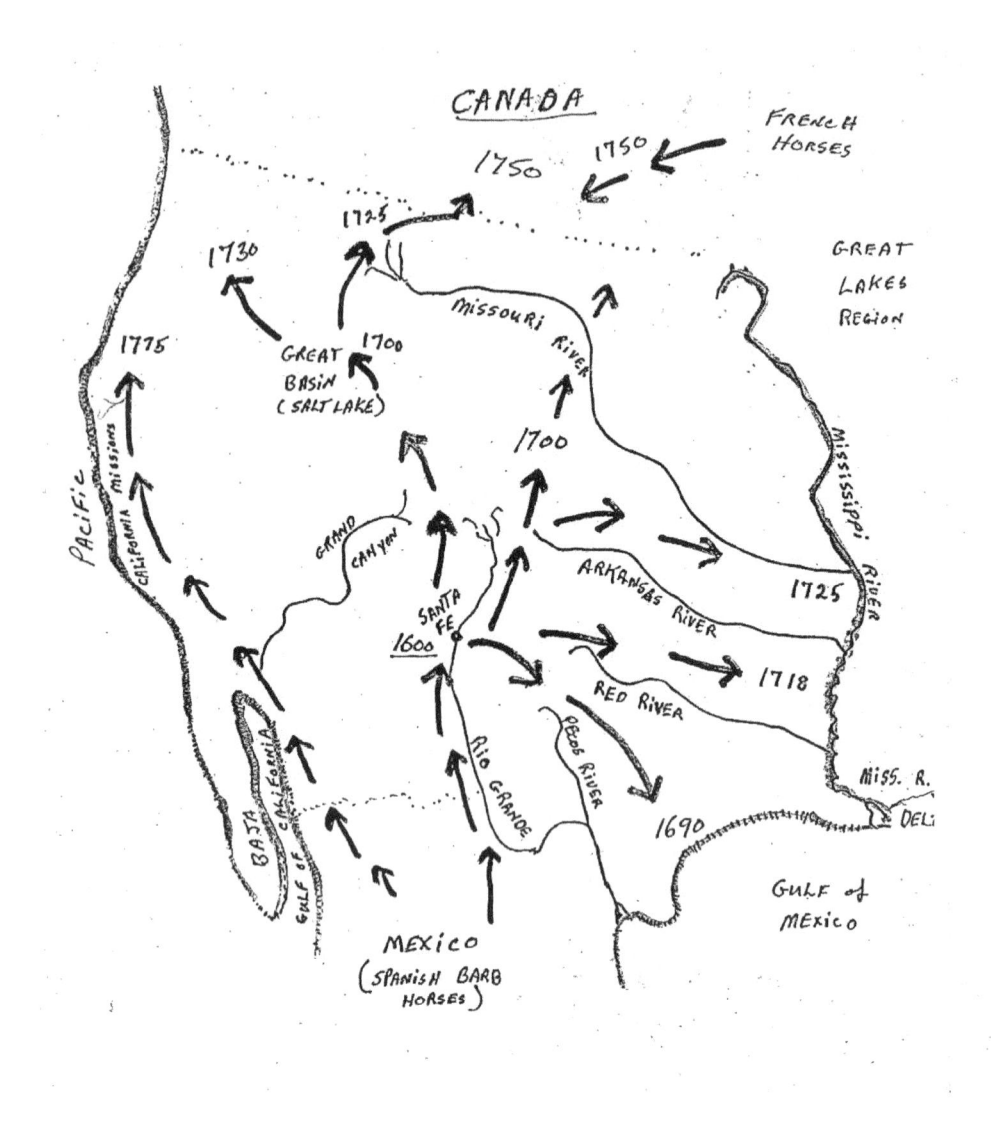

Map reflecting the general consensus of opinion regarding the dispersion of the horse west of the Mississippi. As early as 1624 Spanish records report very effective raids by American Indians mounted on horses. By Ed Scott. Chapter 7.

www.lrgaf.org

Above: Zuni tribesman and bowyer Ernie Mackel shooting a rare sheep horn bow made by Ed Scott. These rare bows were made of horn or elk antler on the belly and sinew on the back without a wood core. Courtesy of Ed Scott. Chapter 7. *Below:* 41" sheep horn and sinew bow. 53# @ 23" made by Ed Scott.

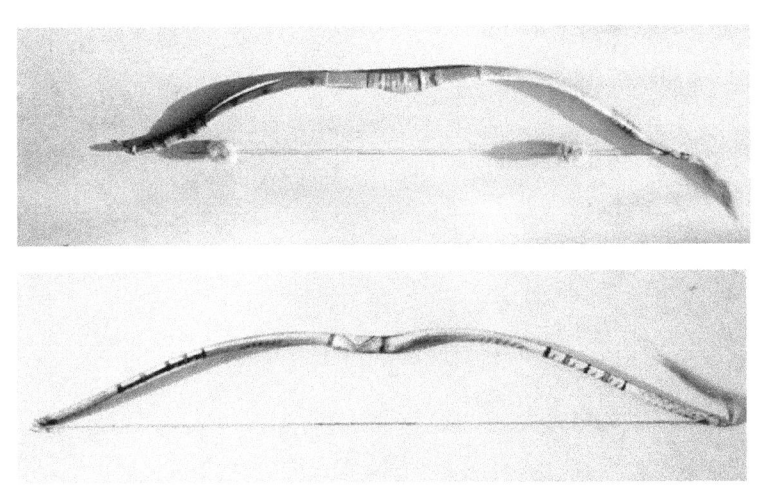

Above: One of Ed Scott's typical horse bows made from wood and sinew.

www.lrgaf.org

Above: The Pennsylvania roots of the first formal mounted modern archery demonstration in the United States, from left to right, Kassai Lajos, Mary and Tom McKinley, owners of Little Neshannock Stables and providers of the horse, and Phyllis and David Gray. Chapter 8.
Below: Kassai Lajos at full draw with a carefully loaded bow hand of arrows for speedy nocking and rapid shooting. Kassai can shoot and hit releasing nine arrows in a 16-second run down the 90-meter course. The bow is the asymmetrical Hun style made by Kassai. Courtesy of Kassai Lajos. Chapter 8.

Above: David Beshey showing a high level of skill. David and Meg Beshey were the on-site leaders of the International Horse Archery Festivals, 2000-2004. Courtesy of Sandy Gomke. Chapter 8.

Below: Jaap Koppedrayer along with his wife Kay provided the international vision and program of the International Horse Archery Festival, 2000-2004. Jaap here is drawing an all-bamboo bow designed first around 1945 and inspired by the great long Yumi bow. Courtesy Kay Koppedrayer. Chapter 8.

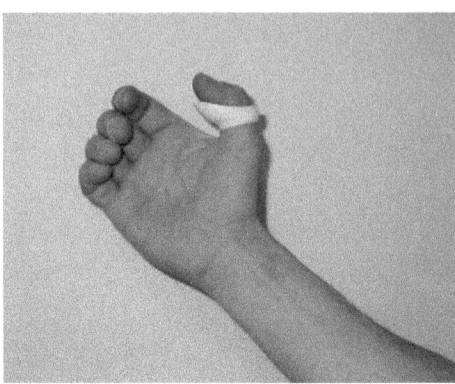

Above Lukas Novotny training students, not mounted, at the International Archery Festival, Fort Dodge, Iowa, 2004. Courtesy of Sandy Gomke. Chapter 9.
Left: Proper placement of shooting ring on thumb. Courtesy of Lukas Novotny. Chapter 9.

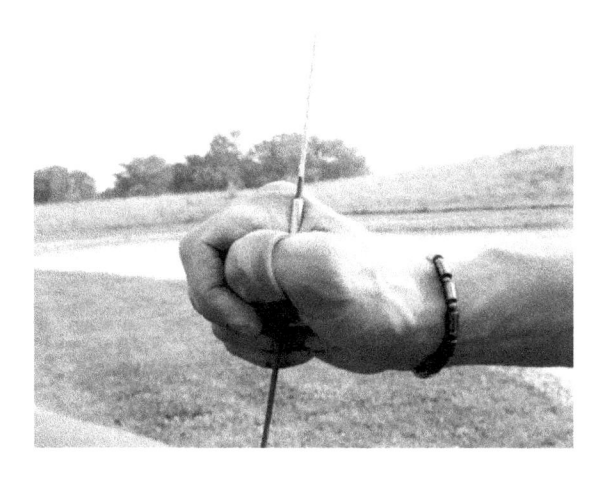

Above: Close-up of the thumb ring on the bowstring. Chapter 9.
Below: Lukas Novotny demonstrating in Chambord, France, in 2005. Courtesy of Lukas Novotny. Chapter 9.

Above: The Brazilian mounted archer and emerging instructor, Sathy, at the mounted archery center, Escola Desempenho, Brazil. Courtesy Jet Cowan. Chapter 10.
Below: A marvelous Turk horn bow at full draw made by Lukas Novotny and shown by him. Courtesy Lukas Novotny. Chapter 11.

Exquisite composite display of Asian saddle, ornate quiver of arrows, and modern Asian-type bow on animal skin. Products of Saluki Bow Company. Courtesy Lukas Novotny. Chapter 11.

Above: Dana Hotko on his trusty Arab, Murphy. Courtesy Sandy Gomke. Chapter 12.
Below: Barb Leeson checking out an old style side-saddle for mounted archery. Courtesy Barb Leeson. Chapter 13.

Above: Logo of the Mounted Archery Association of the Americas (MA3), by Lukas Novotny. Chapter 14.
Below: Todd Delle shooting from his roan Mustang at his training ground in Montana. He is shooting the Hun-inspired bow made by Kassai. Courtesy Todd Delle. Chapter 15.

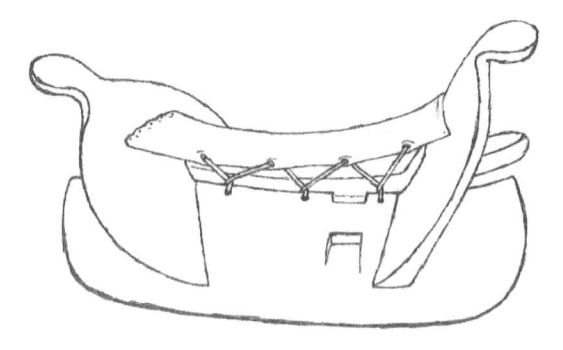

Above: Magyar (Hungarian) type saddle tree which is the basis of the Kassai-type saddles made by his shop in Hungary today. The horns or handles are optional in the design. Courtesy of James Merrilees. Chapter 13.

Below: Japanese saddle tree. Pommel and cantle are lower than the Magyar tree. Courtesy James Merrilees. Chapter 13.

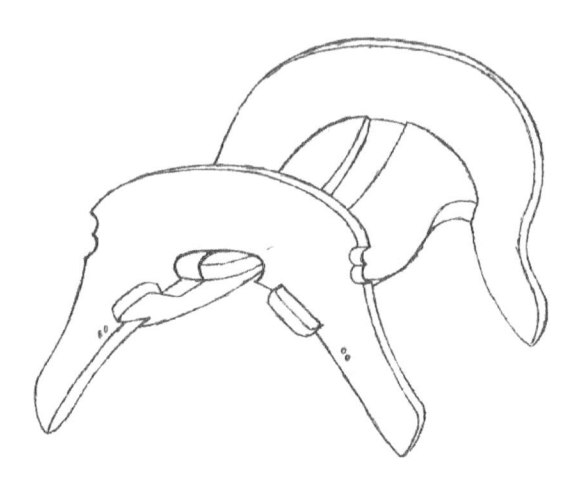

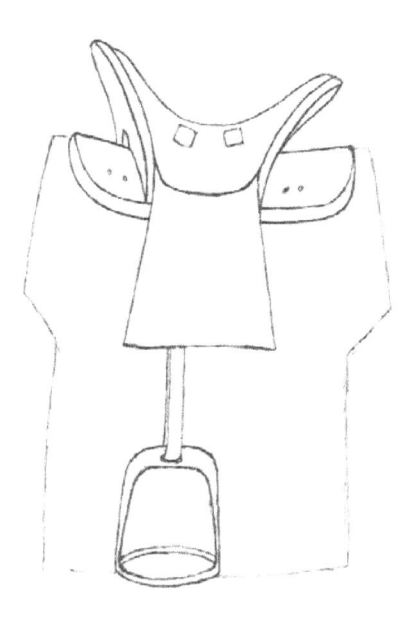

Above: Mongolian saddle. Courtesy of James Merrilees. Chapter 13.
Below: American Plains Indian women's saddle tree. Courtesy of James Merrilees. Chapter 13.

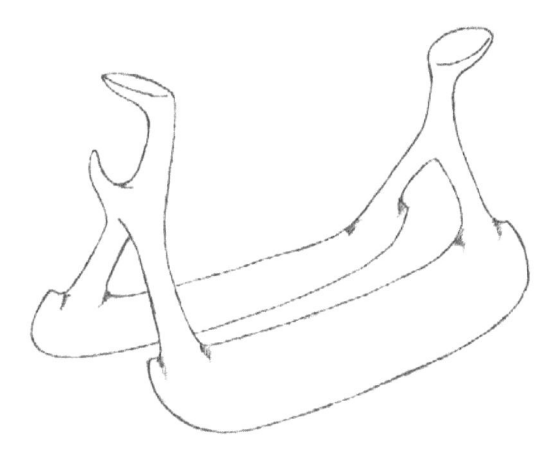

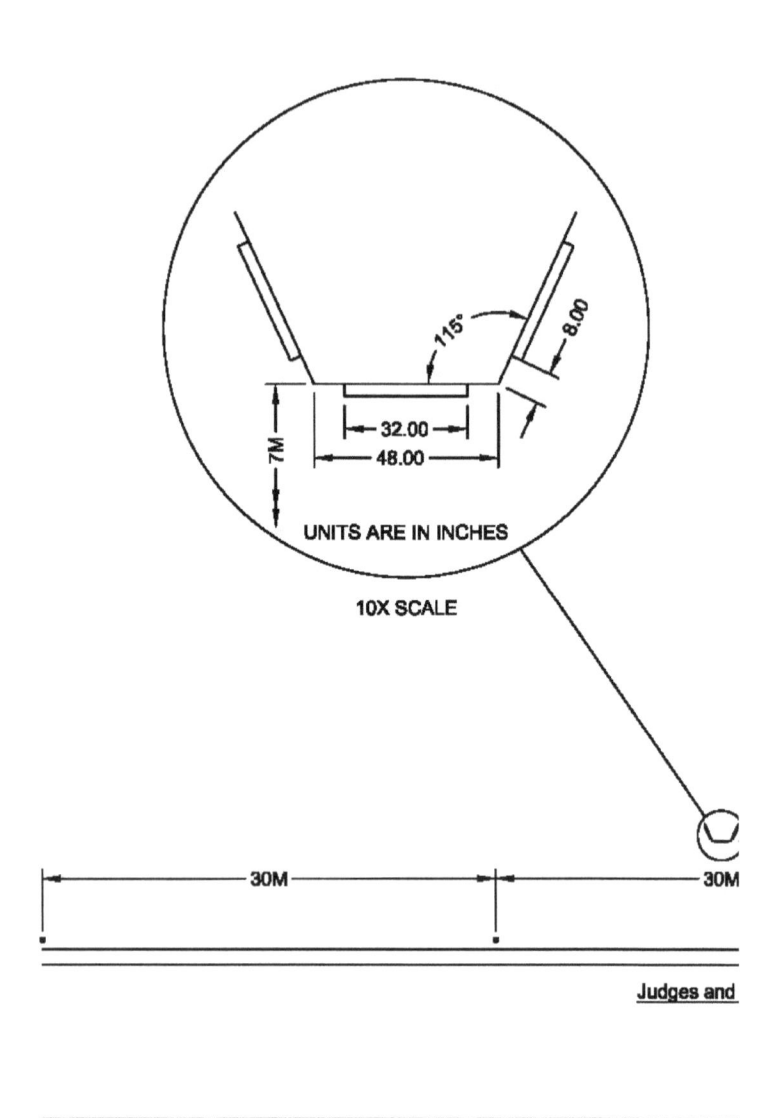

Modified Kassai Hungarian-style standardized horseback archery course.

This and facing page: Diagram of the Hungarian type of course as originated by Kassai Lajos. By Scott Gray. Chapter 14.

Scoring

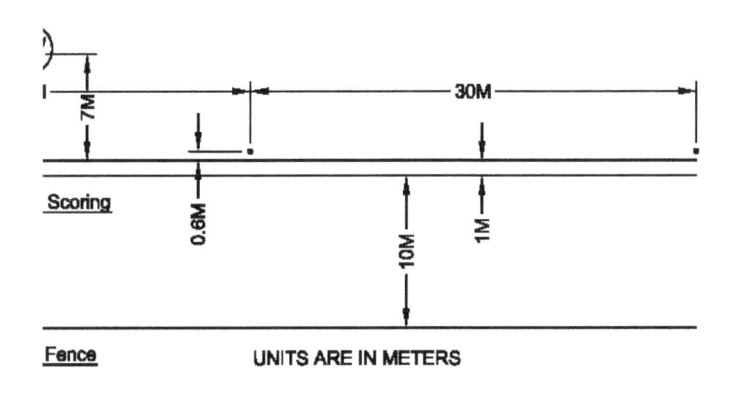

Fence UNITS ARE IN METERS

7M, 0.6M, 30M, 10M, 1M

Mounted Archery in the Americas
Page 172

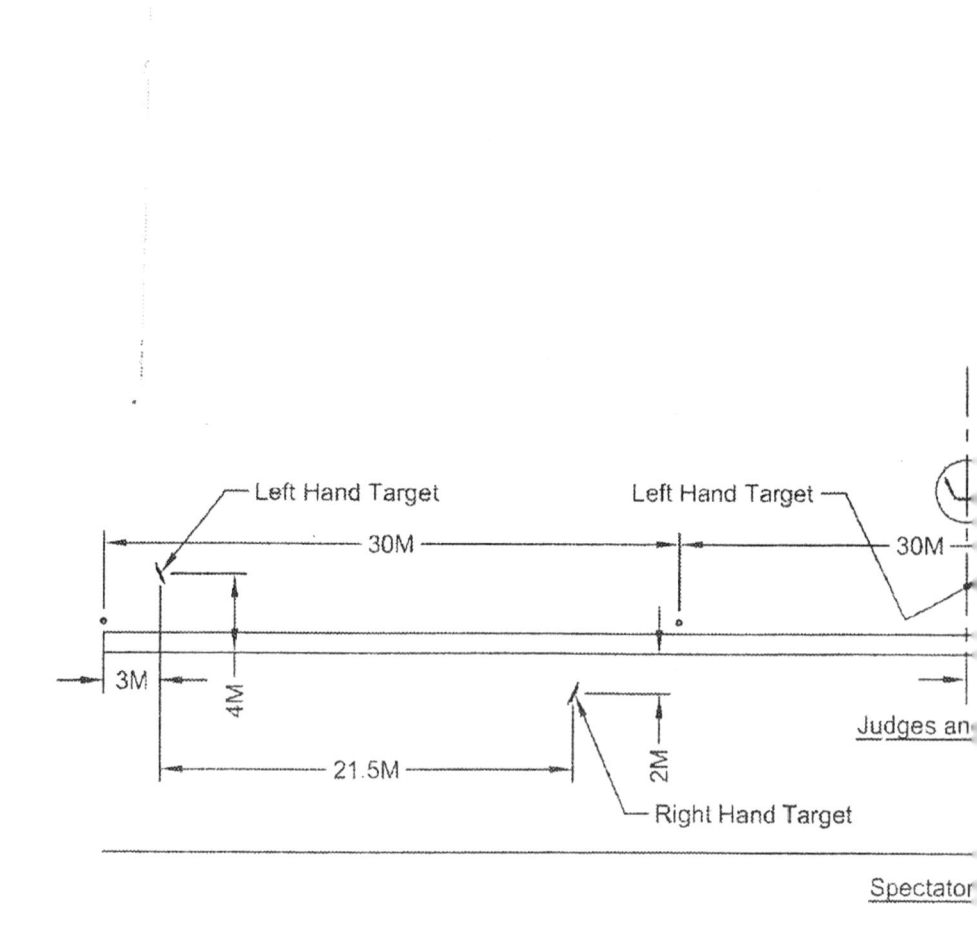

[Diagram showing archery course with labels: Left Hand Target, 30M, Left Hand Target, 30M, 3M, 4M, 21.5M, 2M, Right Hand Target, Judges an[d], Spectator]

Alternate Target Course

This and facing page: Diagram of Discipline Three: alternating sides course. By Scott Gray. Chapter 14.

www.lrgaf.org

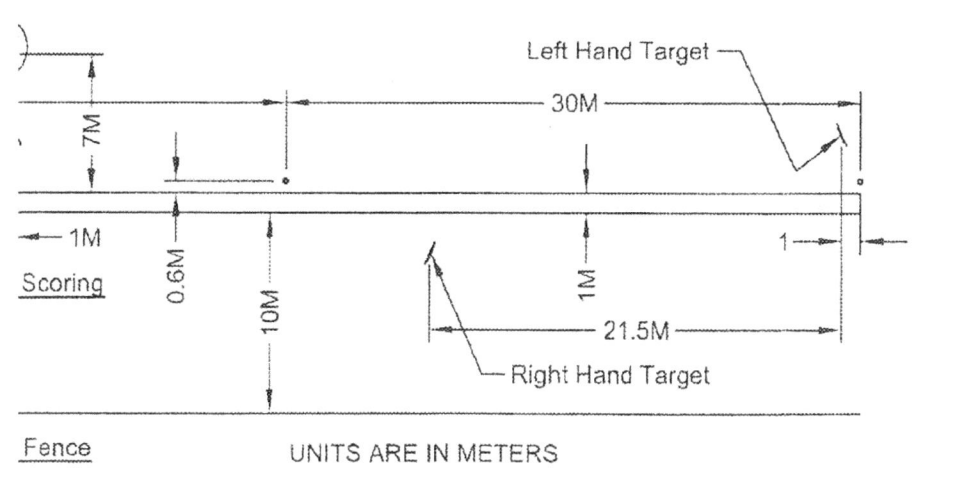

Mounted Archery in the Americas

Page 173

Left Hand Target

30M

7M

1M
Scoring

0.6M

10M

1M

21.5M

Right Hand Target

1

Fence   UNITS ARE IN METERS

Chapter 8

Founding and Growth

By David Gray

The Journal of the Society of Archer-Antiquaries is responsible for the entry of a modern form of standardized mounted archery into the Americas. I am sure this would be news to the editors of that journal; it is indeed a bit tongue-in-cheek. What really happened is this. Back in 1995 when I received that issue of the journal (Volume 38), I turned to the second page and saw a bow I had never seen before. My interest in the universal history of archery was taking root at that time but the whole Asian archery scene was still largely removed and foreign to me. What in the world were those funny looking bows with the ten inch levers on the ends of the limbs? There were two very clear photographs of Dr. Peter and Mrs. Zsuzsanna Walker shooting bows they had purchased while in Hungary.

The beginning

I wrote to the Journal immediately inquiring about how to contact the Hungarian bowyer. Thus the American connection with Kassai Lajos in Kaposmero, Hungary was born. Other Americans may have contacted him sooner but I am not aware of it. In October of 1996 Kassai responded to my letter introducing himself, his bows, and furthermore the modern discipline of mounted archery. Kassai said, "I want to go the States where I could make the mounted archery, and my bows popular. It would be a very good idea for you to come to Hungary. You are welcome here at any time."

Sometime during that winter of 1996-97 I purchased a basic Magyar bow from Kassai and started shooting it in my back yard. It was comfortable, aesthetically pleasing, accurate, and of course steeped in history going back to the founding of Hungary in the very late 800s. The design of the Magyar bow really goes back that far, but of course the bow I bought did not include the old materials of horn and sinew, but rather was made of modern materials with beautiful ash wood and leather coverings.

My first visit to Kassai's valley and archery center was in July 1997. The first stop on that trip was to meet another Hungarian bowyer, Csaba Grozer, in the northwest corner of Hungary. It was nice to meet him in person, see his version of the Magyar bows, shoot a few arrows, and spend the night in a hunting lodge with trophy heads anchoring each of the main walls. It was then on to Kassai's in the southwest corner of the country. There I feasted on the sight of all his Magyar bows, his formal outdoor mounted archery course in a secluded and lovely valley, marveled at a demonstration of mounted archery, slept in his Yurt, and later returned to Budapest. The impression was profound and I knew at that point that we had to get Kassai to come the States.

In January of 1998 I was to present a psychology lecture on leadership at the University of Heidelberg. I just had to get back to Kassai's valley for another visit when I was that close. My son Josh accompanied me on a wonderful cold January visit. The morning drive into the archery valley was a fantasy land of total hoar-frost. Kassai demonstrated mounted archery again in spite of the cold. In the evening we took a long walk over a rough plowed field to a neighboring fish farm to select our dinner fresh from one of the fish tanks. Kassai made dinner for us that night on his new tile stove in his imaginatively styled new archery house overlooking the valley. Kassai agreed to come to the States for a major demonstration; the details were worked out over the next several months.

The launch in the United States

The demonstrations were to be given at the Great Lakes Longbow Invitational XIV at Berrein Springs, Michigan, July 10-12, 1998. The demonstrations were funded and sponsored by the Michigan Longbow Association. John McCullough was the key person in the Michigan Association facilitating the arrangements at the Michigan site. Kassai arrived in the States about a week early in order to acclimate the horses and make sure all the necessary elements were coming together for a successful launch of the discipline in the United States.

www.lrgaf.org

Now that mounted archery in this country is well established it does not seem so exotic, foreign, formidable, and mysterious. However as we approached the launch of the discipline back in 1998, it was an unknown factor and somewhat intimidating. Where would we find horse owners who could be sold on renting a couple of horses? Who would trust a total stranger from Hungary to take their horses three hundred miles away to do an equine sport that they had never witnessed before, except on video? We found the answer two miles from my home. Little Neshannock Stables is the home of the Westminster College Equestrian Team. I had taught at the College for many years and thought the Stables were appropriate to approach. The significance of the positive response of the owners, Tom and Mary McKinley, cannot be overemphasized. Furthermore, the horses had to be appropriately selected to train and adapt in a very few days to a strange rider and a strange event. Tom and Mary took the risk and played a pivotal part in launching this discipline.

Gemeni was to be the prime horse; he was at the time an eight year old bay Appendix (half Thoroughbred and half Quarter horse). He had some experience with roping and was thought to be very level headed which proved to be the case. Two weeks before the event, before Kassai's arrival, we desensitized the horses to the bow and the arrows by shooting on the ground around the horse and then on horseback.

We were hoping that when Kassai arrived, a week before the event, the horses would accept the task of cantering down the 90 meter track and maintain a moderate steady speed with the reins dropped. Gemeni cooperated very well and quickly did exactly what was expected of him. Kassai had three days to finish the horses for the event. Thursday was consumed in shipping the horses the several hundred miles from western Pennsylvania to eastern Michigan for the Friday-Saturday-Sunday demonstrations. Dundee was the second horse taken along as a backup just in case Gemeni would be temporarily injured. Dundee was a very young mixed breed roan. He did not moderate his speed in the canter and would have been a difficult backup, but he was there just in case.

It was a treat and honor to have Kassai stay at our house here in western Pennsylvania while he was training the horses. Much time was spent over good food prepared by my wife Phyllis, with liberal conversation about world events and of course mounted archery. Kassai is a fruit freak. Actually he is a connoisseur of all natural foods including the full array of vegetables and nuts. I can still see him sitting in our kitchen eating directly out of a large half of watermelon. One evening he made what he called a Hun sacrifice; it was a fine beef stew and was enjoyed by all. The only anxiety connected with the stay at our house was that his bows did not arrive from Hungary. We were on the phone to the airport constantly, and made two trips to the airport with final success. It gave us a chance to show him a bit the city we are proud of — Pittsburgh.

A public demonstration was held by Kassai at the Stables on an evening before we left for Michigan. The Pittsburgh Post Gazette had run a full page photo coverage of the discipline the Sunday before the demonstration resulting in about sixty people driving for an hour to the Little Neshannock Stables in New Wilmington for the demo. Our local friends and spectators, along with the Pittsburgh group, made up an expectant and enthusiastic audience. The air was filled with the sense that something unique and historical was about to happen. The launch was on, and the next step was Michigan.

A local horseman, Doug Meyer, transported the horses and did a great job of getting them to the event and back home in good heath and in a good frame of mind. One of the Westminster College Equestrian Team members, Tony Genosco accompanied the horses to help keep them quieted and well tended.

The horses arrived on the site in Michigan one day before the three-day event began in order to allow at least a little time for on-the-site training, building the course, and installing the targets. The mounted archery course which Kassai standardized in Europe is a 90 meter straight run with the target at the 45 meter midpoint and 7 meters off to the left side of the track. The target is three-faced and is designed for three types of prescribed shots — an approach shot which must be taken in the first 30 meters of the course, then a side shot in the middle 30 meters, and finally the archer turns backwards for the last shot during the remaining 30 meters of the course. The three sections are clearly marked off with very tall posts. The horse runs the course without rein control and is somewhat assisted in keeping a straight line either by earth berms on each side of the track, or caution tape on flexible stakes.

www.lrgaf.org

The targets are three feet in diameter consisting of a bulls-eye and two concentric rings. The side shot is the easiest (about 7 meters long) with assigned scores of 3,2,1. The approach and the backwards shots are both quite long, about 30 meters on the average depending on exactly where the archer releases the shot. The approach shot is the second most difficult; the scoring is 4,3,2. The parting or backward shot is the most difficult reflected in the scoring being 5,4,3. The course must be run in 16 seconds for scores to be registered for that particular run. A point is added for each second that the horse beats the 18 second rule. The rationale is that the faster horse makes the task much more difficult.

While the course was being built and Kassai was starting to make some practice passes on Thursday before the official event one could easily sense the buzz among those arriving a day early. "Did you see that guy on horseback shoot yet? I cannot believe it." Kassai gave two demonstrations on each day of the three-day event attracting a good crowd each time and generating great excitement. The Great Lakes Longbow Invitational is an old event with considerable stature. This was indeed an heralded and historic inauguration of the discipline in the United States. The weather was fine, the horses remained sound, Kassai outdid himself, the Great Lakes sponsors gave their full support, and the archers added the culminating ingredient of a memorable beginning. Instead of the minimal three arrows on a pass, Kassai could actually often get off anywhere from six to nine with a good hit rate, roughly two seconds per arrow.

John McCullough and I co-authored an article reporting the demonstrations at the Great Lakes event: "Horse Archers Sighted in the United States," Traditional Bowhunter, February/March 1999, pages 73-80. In that article, John said, "It is hard to describe the trepidation I felt about this whole undertaking until I watched Kassai loose that first practice arrow from horseback." John ticked off a mountain of concerns. What if: the horses went lame, Kassai got sick, the equipment was lost by the airlines (which it was for several days), there was a bad accident, the spectator safety was inadequate, etc. And it is expensive to rent, insure, and transport horses, and to buy international flights and pay expenses (although Kassai charged no fee for the event). John and the Great Lakes Association took a great risk, and we will never forget it and always be grateful for their role in bringing mounted archery to the United States.

At the end of the article, I reflected on what seemed to me was the broader significance of the event. I thought our awareness of our archery legacy was dramatically broadened and enriched. "Kassai helped us connect to the Lakota and Cheyenne, and to the Mongol, the Magyars of course, the Avars, Huns, and clear back to the Scythians before the time of Christ. Kassai helps to link us to a very long line of archers strung out across the great plains of North America and the vast steppe of Europe and Asia. Thank you Kassai." I still think it is a part of what mounted archery does for us. To me this vision is arousing, emotional, and inspirational as well as heady.

Founding of the International Horse Archery Festival

We were unsuccessful the following year, 1999, in getting any organization to meet the financial and other challenges of bringing Kassai back for more demonstrations. Thus 1999 was a quiet year. Some witnesses of the '98 demonstrations went back home and started to emulate a bit of what they had seen at Great Lakes, but nothing very visible happened. The year 2000 was a different story. The International Horse Archery Festival was organized and met for the first time at Fort Dodge, Iowa, in early September. The Festival has become a widely recognized and truly international event. The Festival has attracted several traditions of mounted archery—Eurasian (Hungarian), emerging modern American mounted disciplines, American Indian (Lakota Sioux), and Japanese Yabusame. There is also a rich array of ground archery activities from around the world—Popinjay, Cherokee corn stalk shoots, Iowa "coon hunt," clout shooting, Chinese, Japanese Kyudo, Korean, Mongolian, Bhutanese, English, and Sudanese.

While the Festival has a broader scope than just mounted archery it nevertheless became the nurturing soil for mounted archery in the United States. The vision for an international festival originated primarily with Jaap and Kay Koppedrayer who are international to the very core of their being. They, together, are international travelers, archers, bowyers, scholars, writers, and bridge builders across many archery traditions at home and abroad. The way they first met may be a window into the spirit of who they are. They were both trekking, youth style, across Eurasia, and happened to cross paths at the Kyber Pass in Afghanistan. They joined forces there and have been a marvelous team ever since. They reside in Ontario and will eventually occupy a farm in Georgia to grow bamboo for the great Yumi bows and do all the other things they do. Jaap is a world-recognized bowyer, specializing in all Asiatic types of bows and is a serious practitioner of Kyudo. The breadth, depth, distinctness, and longevity of his bows may be unparalleled. Kay, by profession, is a University Professor of culture and religion, a prolific writer about archery and other topics, and an Associate Editor of Primitive Archer Magazine. Jaap was born and raised in Holland and worked in the tulip and nursery industry before coming to Canada, and Kay was born and raised in Ohio and is of Hungarian descent.

The Koppedrayers initiated many conversations about an international festival with Thomas Duvernay, David and Phyllis Gray, and Lukas Novotny, usually at the big Eastern Traditional Archery Rendezvous at Denton Hill in Pennsylvania. During the fall of 1998 Kay and Jaap did a presentation of Asiatic archery at the Blanden Art Museum in Fort Dodge, Iowa. It was there that they met David and Meg Beshey who were the onsite organizers for the Museum event. Meg is an art teacher in Fort Dodge, and David is an Officer on the police force. Their conversation led to the question of an international archery festival with horses playing a central part plus all other kinds of archery traditions constituting such an event. Fort Dodge is a land of horses, farms, and rodeos. Bingo, Fort Dodge sounded like a real possibility.

The Besheys seemed willing to shoulder the responsibility of being the on-site developers of an international festival. Meg became the President and David the Festival Manager and Treasurer and they served energetically and generously in those offices for five years, through the 2004 Festival. The cooperative efforts of the Besheys and the Koppedrayers led to the successful launch of the first Festival in 2000. The Besheys carried the local fund raising and physical facility tasks and the Koppedrayers guided the building of a program plus providing major financial support. My part was to negotiate with Kassai and to get him to the Festival as a demonstrator and director of training for the mounted archery school.

Demonstrations and a training school were the focus of the mounted activities of the first Festival. Kassai was back in the States again with all expenses paid, plus a small stipend. He was back wowing the crowds by shooting a fistful of arrows while galloping the track in 16 seconds or less. The spectators also saw some of Kassai's beginning students demonstrate. The vast difference in skill between Kassai and his beginners highlighted our appreciation for his accomplishments. Kassai's performances and interaction with all the attendees, and mounted archery students laid the groundwork for a movement which could not be stopped.

A four-day mounted archery training school was conducted by Kassai concurrently with the larger events of Festival; that first year it used a makeshift track and had seven students. The seven became the pioneers of the discipline in the Americas. The "charter members" included Todd Delle from Montana, and Alex Tiberi from California; they would subsequently train with Kassai in Kaposmero, Hungary nearly every year. Victoria White Hawk and Summer Kaline, both Lakota Sioux, helped to resurrect the nearly lost art among the original Americans. Johannes Fischnaller from Austria was the fifth member, and the sixth was Vinson Minor of Bows of Wood from North Carolina. Lukas Novotny was the seventh and final member of this class emerging eventually as the point performer and later became the trainer at the Festival, and more widely in North America and beyond. Actually all members of this first class, except Vinson, have trained more intensely in Hungary and have competed there. The first year was fraught with the unknown and the unexpected challenges of a totally new organization but the excitement ran high and carried us over into the second year with flying colors.

Kassai was contracted to come back to the Festival for the second and third years, 2001 and 2002, as demonstrator and director of mounted archery training. He had a profound influence on the fifteen to twenty trainees registered each of those two years.

The training schools at Fort Dodge started to have a cumulative effect, and the trainees were going home and practicing on their own. Trainees without their own horses can do a lot of shooting while walking or even running on the ground which simulates shooting from a moving horse. Some have gone to Hungary to take the demanding week-long training to speed up their progress.

www.lrgaf.org

The Festival in 2003 had enough of our own indigenous talent developed to take over the demonstrations and the training. This proved to be more economical than bringing Kassai from Hungary. Lukas Novotny from Grand Rapids, Ohio became the head trainer in 2003 and was assisted effectively by another rising horse archer—Dana Hotko of Milan, Indiana. Lukas was born and raised in the former Czechoslovakia, trained as a glass sculptor, and came to the States when he was 21. He worked with his father in California inoptical glass to get a start, and eventually earned his living as an artist. In the very early 2000s he started pursuing his passion for bows. In less than a decade, Lukas has left an indelible mark on modern traditional archery. His research on the ancient roots of, and recreations of Persian-Turkish bows is perhaps unsurpassed anywhere. His creative modern hunting and horsebows, clearly cousins of the ancient Asian horn bows, are sought by archers around the world.

Dana Hotko has been with the Festival every year except the very first. He has been a breeder of the fairly rare Blue Star Line Arab horses for many years, and rides a wonderful gray Arab mare for mounted archery, named Murphy. He and Lukas are only four hours apart so they train together occasionally. They compliment each other extremely well; Lukas is a bit on the fiery side, and Dana is the calm steady puller.

This new home-grown leadership provided a strong shot in the arm for the training program. Lukas and Dana have demonstrated excellent teaching and leadership skills such that without exception the trainees have been very happy with their progress and the whole training experience. With two instructors, it has been possible to separate the raw beginners from the more advanced and tailor the instruction accordingly. The trainer's success is partly due to sensing the needs of each individual trainee and giving individualized feedback and coaching. The training atmosphere hit a happy balance between demanding rigor on the one hand and human understanding and support on the other.

For trainees bringing their own horses, we have also outlined the basic requirements of the horse—being able to canter at a moderate speed on a straight track with the reins dropped, and relating well to the other horses in a clinical setting. Trainees are encouraged to bring their own horses if they are appropriate and if distances are not prohibitive.

www.lrgaf.org

We have had a wide variety of breeds—quite a few fine Arabs, Appendix, Quarter Horses, Tennessee Walkers, and mixed breeds. The Festival provides horses for those who cannot bring their own which presents real challenges. Some of the horses have been fine, but some are too fast and there is not enough time before the Festival to do much training. Lukas and Dana have spent a great deal of time several days before the Training starts just assessing each possible horse for ability to adapt to mounted archery.

The school has always been open to all levels of trainees except that in the last two years we have insisted on the possession of basic equestrian skills for any applicant. Trainees are carefully assessed on the first day and assigned to either a beginner or advanced group. For both beginners and advanced trainees, many ground exercises are used to develop or sharpen basic skills relevant to mounted archery. One must learn to hold several arrows in the bow hand, pull them out one at a time, and nock an arrow on the string without looking. This is something which must be practiced back at home for many, many hours, and it can even be done in the small confines of an apartment by dropping the arrows on the floor after nocking instead of shooting them. By the end of a five-day school, the beginners are usually doing some shooting at the canter in the more controlled environment of an inside arena. The more advanced trainees may spend about a third of the time doing ground work, but most of the time is spent shooting from horseback on the outdoor 90 meter course. In another chapter, Lukas Novotny will present a full treatment on the training of the mounted archer.

Growth and expansion

The yearly schools at the International Festival at Fort Dodge introduced about a dozen new persons to the discipline each year. Returning trainees from prior years filled out the rest of the yearly classes. Forty-four people gained either elementary or advanced mounted archery skills over the five year period. Nine of these people have gone on to build complete or abbreviated tracks on their home turf for themselves and their friends to practice on—in Indiana, Georgia, Michigan, New York, North Carolina, Ohio, Ontario, Oregon, Pennsylvania and two in Montana. There are probably others I do not know about; the discipline is captivating. If one has a bit of time, adequate space, a horse, and has been initiated, there is a good chance of a driving inner compulsion to build a course in order to stick with the discipline.

Expansion dreams started to be realized in 2004 in the form of two satellite training schools. Pat Stoddard held a class for several students in Libby, Montana, and a similar group trained in a satellite school in Ontario, organized by Barb Leeson, and taught by Lukas Novotny. Even though the formal five-day training school will no longer be held in conjunction with the International Horse Archery Festival, the Fort Dodge mounted archery track is one of the best in the country and will continue to provide important training opportunities in more flexible ways.

More expansion ground was broken in 2005 by breaking into the west coast with a training school location. Holm Neumann, an IHAF trainee in 2003, hosted the event at his ranch in beautiful Bend, Oregon. Of the eight students, three had prior training in earlier schools at IHAF, and the other five were new to the discipline but good riders. It is amazing how rapidly the younger students learn. I am thinking of the three college-age students. Lukas Novotny was the instructor and had great success. A delightful bonus was a trail ride up into the mountains toward the Three Sisters mountain peaks, all of which look down on Holm's and Susan's ranch. The significance of this event is that another training outlet is now available to people in the northwest. It will most likely be a stable, yearly opportunity.

An additional training site in the northwest is located near the Flathead lake area of Montana, and is run by one of the original IHAF trainees, Todd Delle. Todd is the representative of what is now Kassai's formal United States division. Todd will explain that activity in a special Chapter. Two areas where we still need training outlets are the southeast and the southwest, but they have not yet materialized.

Also in 2005, the Lakota Sioux took an historical step in holding their first Mounted Archery Gathering. It was not a training school but was devoted to gaining and maintaining the interest of more children and youth in recapturing their old, but lost art of combining the horse and the bow. Lying behind this Gathering were the ongoing training efforts of Mike One Star, Gary Hacker, and Jay Red Hawk. They have been training groups of Lakota youth in ground and mounted archery for several years and continue to do so. They have been successful in helping many of their youth to move toward a constructive future through the avenue of archery. Mike has had an ongoing relationship with IHAF: he has brought his youth there to train, and has even assisted them in going to Hungary to train with Kassai. Jay Red Hawk demonstrated at IHAF 2004 which has helped to build some bridges between these Lakota events and the wider mounted archery movement in the States. He personally encouraged a number of us to come to the Gathering. I attended and thought it was a rare and highly important occasion. The event was open to the public and is becoming an annual affair in Mission, South Dakota.

The author instructed a class of four students in the summer of 2005 at the Little Neshannock Stables in my home town of New Wilmington, PA. It is where I board my horse, Yeremi, and you will recall its important role in the very first mounted archery appearance with Kassai. We had three of the young riders from the Stable and one young school teacher registered for the class. They were all good riders but none had archery experience. We met one full afternoon for five days. By the end of the week, they were all hitting the shortest, right angle shot, at a canter with fair consistency. I was very pleased with their progress, and they all apparently felt that they had accomplished and conquered much. The Little Neshannock Stable horses performed cooperatively and that helped the students immensely. One horse, a thoroughbred, performed well in the inside arena, but needed more time to adapt to the distractions of the outside track. Also at the Stables, throughout the year, there is an open training night every Tuesday evening. Brad, a high school freshman, has been coming now for a year, and is just about ready to compete as a beginner, and Zack, another high school student, has recently been attracted to the discipline.

There are several difficulties in recruiting and maintaining a larger number of trainees, and creating a more brisk pace. In terms of totally new recruits, potential mounted archers face a compounded set of barriers — equine ownership or access, equine skills, archery skills and equipment, a liberal amount of ongoing time to train, access to a course and instruction, and underlying all of this is funds. Among those who have already had some training, there is also bound to be some attrition which slows the pace of expansion.

www.lrgaf.org

When Kassai first came to the States in 1998 there may have been a few scattered and unpublicized persons doing some horseback archery on their own. For example, we know that Pat Stoddard in Libby, Montana, had been doing small demonstrations. However, when he trained at IHAF 2001 it seemed to inspire him to move ahead more quickly and expand on his own. Pat practices daily and tirelessly on the ground and on horseback. I am not sure what his current score would be but it is most certainly very high. He is and will be a high-standing and valuable instructor, promoter, and model for the discipline.

As already mentioned, Lukas Novotny has been the very successful lead instructor at IHAF during the 2003 and 2004 training camps. Lukas is in much demand for instruction and demonstrations internationally. That coupled with his Saluki Bow making business has created a very demanding schedule. Dana Hotko, his assistant, can and will provide capable and much needed instruction. David Beshey at Fort Dodge (and a lead organizer of the Festival) has developed excellent mounted archery skills and is playing an important role in the instruction of others informally at the Fort Dodge track. A number of other archers who may not be quite as far along can nevertheless offer at least introductory mounted archery instruction which will be very significant in the expansion of the discipline.

Books, magazine articles, CDs, and websites are helping to promote and nurture the discipline. Some are documented within the next few paragraphs, and others are listed in the References section. The first article, described earlier, told the story of the very first demonstrations by Kassai in the States in 1998 (Gray and McCullough, Traditional Bowhunter, 1999).

Most of the magazine articles covering the mounted archery story are part and parcel of the more comprehensive story of IHAF. Six great black and white photos highlight the first story of the "First International Horse Archery Festival." The mounted part of the Festival was celebrated but the wider scope of the international ground events were also described with excitement (Koppedrayer, Instinctive Archer, Fall, 2001). Another story depicting the incredibly rich flavor of the international ground events, with some content about the mounted portion, was entitled, "Worldwide Archery Traditions" (Koppedrayer, Primitive Archer, Fall 2001).

www.lrgaf.org

A veterinarian and mother of nine told an unusual story of her entry into the training process at IHAF in 2002. This is a woman who goes with her husband and her family on humanitarian trips to Africa on the one hand, and weaves her archery story around comparisons to the Wizard of Oz on the other hand. We all loved her presence and her several grown children she had with her. Her name and the author of the article is Elizabeth McGee ("Horse Archery and Momma," <u>Primitive Archer</u>, Winter 2003). The Festival has also received mention in the <u>Wall Street Journal, Equus</u>, and other sources.

Two additional articles, while still set in the unfolding IHAF context, had somewhat different emphases. "Mounted Archery from the Ground Up" by Gray and Novotny, <u>Primitive Archer</u>, Fall 2002 highlights the stimulation of adding motion to ground exercises for either horse archers, hunters, or target shooters. Shooting while walking, jogging, or doing squats is a different world from still shooting. It simulates to some small extent the motion of shooting while on horseback. Blind, speed nocking can be incorporated naturally and effectively into these exercises.

An article somewhat more pitched to the hunter appeared in the June/July 2002 issue of <u>Traditional Bowhunter</u> entitled "Training to Hunt or Compete from Horseback," by David Gray. About half of this article recounts the adventures of Howard Hill doing high speed horseback archery in Florida for feral hogs, and for buffalo in Thermopolis, Wyoming, and the very contemporary story of Pat Stoddard taking an antelope in Wyoming at full gallop on his trusty Mustang Diablo. Another theme of the article was the breadth of the trainees that have come through the IHAF school at Fort Dodge, and of course the theme of how closely horseback archery has been tied into hunting from ancient times.

In both 2003 and 2004 IHAF has produced professional CDs covering the full scope of the Festival with generous coverage of mounted archery. See the IHAF website <u>www.intlhorsearchery.org</u>. Until the book you have in your hands appeared, the only other extensive treatment was Kassai's book entitled <u>Horseback Archery</u>. It was dedicated to the Hungarian story, but nevertheless has had a big impact here in the United States and should not be missed by any aspiring horse archer. <u>Bows of the World</u> by Gray has a significant section (Chapter 4 on Asia) on the evolution of the Asian hornbow and the historical uniting of the bow with the horse. Our dear friend, the late Bonnie Anderson, has a nice introductory treatment called The Horse in Horse Archery. There is one other book title that the serious reader should examine. Mounted Archery by Laszlo Torday, 1977, is a scholarly and linguistic journey into the steppes of China to uncover the roots of the Huns, the Sarmatians, and many others.

The Festival and horseback archery has attracted international attention and publicity. The Glade (published in England) promoted the mounted portions of the Festival with two extensive articles, one in the Winter of 2000, and another in Winter 2000/2001. The first was entitled, "Here Comes the Arrow Man," and the second was "Second International Horse Archery Festival." Ted Bradford, the editor, covered both festivals personally with his wife Brenda, and enhanced his stories liberally with great color photographs. A very dramatic ten-page piece in Saudi Aramco World, September/October, 2003 featured David Beshey on the front cover in full action. There is a rich photographic and narrative account of the ancient hornbows of the Arabs and Persians juxtaposed against Lukas Novotny of Saluki Bows making modern versions of these bows while being interviewed for the story. Hilary Greenland and our friends in the Society for the Promotion of Traditional Archery in England have published several informational pieces about the mounted activities in the States. Similar activity is occurring in the UK.

The international exchange of horse archers is growing in the form of explorations, demonstrations, and competitions. Lukas has now demonstrated in Brazil, France, Germany, Italy. He will be going to Ireland to demonstrate. With Holm Neumann, he has helped some of the Brazilians to incorporate mounted archery into their equestrian smorgasboard. Four of our US mounted archers competed in the Korean competition in Korea in the fall of 2005—Dana Hotko, Holm Neumann, Lukas Novotny, and Jett Cowan. I was able to introduce a business intern to the discipline while he was here in Pennsylvania, and he is now able to plant some seeds of the discipline in his home area in France. And of course demonstrations are becoming very widespread here within the United States and Canada. A web of connections is being made here and abroad; the discipline is being noticed.

The discipline of mounted archery has gained considerable name recognition as it now approaches nearly a decade. Hundreds of people know what mounted archery is, what IHAF is, and who some of the major figures are. Now people ask, "What is new; what is happening next year; where can I train; and is there a mounted archer near my home area?" Information about what equipment is needed has become more and more widespread, and people know where it can be gotten easily.

The wonder of our ancient inheritance

There is something about horseback archery that makes one ask about its source or sources. Where are the origins? What happened along the way? There is this almost primordial sense that the roots must be long and deep in antiquity. I enjoy our national spectator sports, but I never ask, how did football, or basketball originate. As one sits on the horse and takes a breather, one has to ask where it all started. I can see the Sioux thundering on his mustang alongside a ferocious buffalo with an arrow pointed for a heart shot. The horse culture in the northern plains only lasted about a hundred years. How and when did the Spanish horses enter the plains and the lives of the Indians? How did they learn it all so quickly and how did it disappear just as quickly? Beyond all those questions, the American Indians have earned worldwide respect for their remarkable equestrian achievements.

Who were the horse archers on the great steppe of Eurasia? Who caught the first horse? Where, when, why, how? Could it really have been over five thousand years ago? Did domestication and breeding occur independently or interdependently on the steppe, in Africa, and in Iberia? What was the earliest equine equipment like? How did the horse change the history of humankind? How did the ancients train their horses and how similar or different was it to the current revolution in horse training? I am always reminded of Joseph Bronowski's (The Ascent of Man) speculations about the first mounted riders. The first galloping rider must have been seen as an alien out of an entirely different realm. The horseback archer was twice as high as the ground archer, three times as fast, and had expanded his long-range mobility in orders of magnitude. In eras of ignorance, superstition, witches, and evil spirits, the appearance of a horse-man creature, a "centaur," must have instilled mystery and terror into the first observers.

www.lrgaf.org

Beyond the physical challenges and excitement of learning and practicing mounted archery, there is the wonderful story of its long social evolution, the history, the art, and the stretching of the human mind. These topics warrant full chapter treatments in this book. But I will pause for a few reflections here. My immersion in horse archery has led me to see how prejudiced I have been in many ways about horses, and these mistaken preconceptions have reminded me of how off-base we have often been about human cultures.

With a brain one-third that of humans to control a bodily mass eight times that of the human, the horse is unlikely to be our complete equal. The horse seems hard wired into hierarchies; he has the need either to dominate or be dominated. This may suggest the rider had better establish who is alpha. Nevertheless the revolutionary training methods all tend to be non-forceful, non-violent, and incorporate a profound sense of having to partner with the horse. For some of the senses, and reactions, the horse is clearly our superior, cognitive abilities are generally a fraction of ours, and on other things like assessing fear or resolve they are probably our equals at least. For example a recent well-known training magazine just featured a training problem of when a horse was resistant to crossing a bridge. Conventional wisdom says urge the horse on even as one approaches the bridge and then be ready with spurs, or whip, strong legs, or a slap of the reins, etc. If he does not go, our conclusion is often that he in obstinate, stubborn, lazy, or dense. The magazine article on the other hand argued for very patient moving of the horse toward the bridge a step at a time, stopping as much as the horse needed to stop, never going backward, but never forcing the horse excessively. The rider may not get across the bridge the first day and may have to return to the same lesson several days. Fear probably motivates the bridge balking more that anything else, and the antidote is to gradually and patiently shape the horse to trust the rider for safety in crossing the bridge.

Underlying all this patient approach is the fact that the horse is an animal of prey with highly developed emotions of fear and flight as his survival mechanisms. Thus a serious question of trust arises; to what degree has trust been built in the horse by the rider, and just as foundational, have basic cooperative behaviors been established and the mutual "language" or cues that control those behaviors. So one either needs to work the horse across the bridge slowly, or take him back home and return to more basic control training. Although smaller, the horse's brain looks like ours; he is intelligent and has somewhat similar emotional responses as well. Horses, like humans, need firmly established boundaries on the one hand, but they do not perform or learn well in an atmosphere of fear. "Show them who is boss" has some important truth but an animal of intelligence needs and deserves much more than that.

Human-horse relationships may be a useful metaphor for human relationships. When we are not getting along well with someone we are prone to think of that person as unreasonable, stubborn, dumb, recalcitrant, and obstinate, just like the "bad" horse. When we force people in a corner, why should we expect benevolent behavior? Our prejudice toward horses may parallel our prejudice toward other people. Ironically, the sources promoting prejudices are not necessarily the uneducated but sometimes the voice of the university as well. Many of us learned in our History of Civilization courses that the waves of horse people who swept into Europe from the great steppes such as the Scythians, Huns, and Mongols were barbarians, the lowest form of human life not yet civilized. They were unlearned, uncouth, heathen savages who drank horse blood. Most of these tribes and nations with significant nomadic patterns also had supporting, stable town and villages which generated lasting art forms. The absolutely exquisite gold vases, pins, combs, and plaques of the Scythians, several centuries before the onset of the Christian era, shows great aesthetic sensitivity. Some of the gold pieces portray skillful realistic renderings, other pieces are stylized, and some utilize abstract forms (Rolle Renate, 1980). Other archeological findings from the Scythians reveal flamboyant yet tasteful tapestry like adornments for their horses in bright gold, red, and blue hues.

The current archeological trail of the Huns contradicts the stereotype of the savage brute. The findings are not as dramatically beautiful as that of the Scythians, but impressive nevertheless largely in the use of bronze, especially nicely ornamented cauldrons and cooking vessels. Impressive gold and silver jewelry, plaques, etc have also been uncovered (Maenchen-Helfen, 1973).

The story of the Mongols warrants ample straightening. The emergence and translation of the Secret History of the Mongols, hidden by the Soviets until the collapse of the U.S.S.R, has greatly aided a more balanced view of the Mongols. Yes, they slaughtered whole towns and burned every stick to the ground. But they normally gave the town the choice to pay monetary tribute, and nothing more. It is true that slaves were taken, craftsmen were conscripted, but they were treated well generally for that time. The town which paid the tax was never belittled and never forced to accept an ideology or foreign religion. The Mongols never tried to annihilate a complete race as the Nazis did, succeeding to the barbarous extent of six million. The Mongols never designated a whole religious group as infidels worthy of destruction. The carnage of the Mongols may have been no greater than that of the Hundred Years War, or the Crusades of the Christian nations.

    The written record of the west will admit that the Genghis Khan, and his sons, had an ingenious method and discipline of warfare, but they contributed much more than that. Because they for the most part did not leave great cathedrals and castles they must not have had civilization. It is the same mistake we made in much of African history. Actually Genghis laid some strong roots of democracy, opportunity, and progress by merit rather than inheritance. He broke up old enclaves of privilege and aristocracy and made all compete for status positions of leadership in his government and military. Even the "enslaved" had the opportunity for social mobility. Remember that Marco Polo was impressed with the Mongols in Cathay, enough to urge Isabella and Ferdinand to fund Columbus on his expensive voyage to learn more about Cathay or China. Genghis' grandson, Kublai Khan, led China into a kind of golden age of achievements. It is strange that the Renaissance scholars were in open adulation about Genghis Khan, but by the time of the Enlightenment in the 1700s, scholars had forgotten the early records about the Khan and painted him as a destroyer and a pre-human inferior. Learned literary people like Voltaire, and later the emerging scientists (forerunners of the pseudo-science of eugenics) apparently needed to puff themselves up and assume global superiority for their supposed great reasoning abilities — the celebrated products of the enlightenment. It was the age-old technique of manufacturing one's own group superiority by diminishing and bad-mouthing another. This kind of narrow-minded prejudice helped set the stage for the age of imperial conquests and colonial domination.

It is interesting that the Huns and the American Indians suffered a common prejudice. The Huns were known for possessing a wealth of artfully designed gold pieces. It is now clearly fatuous to say these pieces were really forged by the "more intelligent" and "civilized" Romans, just as it is embarrassing now to think that our European forefathers thought the dramatic Indian mounds such as Cahokia in St. Louis had to have been built by earlier and more capable Europeans who arrived in the States earlier than usually believed.

I have not had all these thoughts while I was literally sitting on my horse, but it is the horse and all that it entails, and horse archery that has swirled me into an endless journey back into our rich inheritance. But now we return to the current and physical activity of mounted archery and its future.

The future

No one can accurately predict the rate at which a young sport will grow. There are a number of inherent barriers to growth which put it beyond the reach of many people. Nevertheless mounted archery is well planted in the Americas and growth is under way. There are currently about a half dozen training sites spread across the United States, and some opportunities are emerging in Canada, Mexico, and Brazil. Instead of depending on just one training site in Fort Dodge and just one week at that site out of the whole year as had been the case in the early years, there are now multiple sites, at multiple places at varied times of the year and with very different schedules. This decentralization and expansion of training should make it possible for many more interested persons to enter the discipline. The necessity and expense of traveling to a distant site and taking a full week off work is prohibitive to many. Two of the sites have training on one evening each week—a group at Fort Dodge meets each Wednesday evening, and another group in Pennsylvania meets each Tuesday evening. Both of these opportunities are informal and are without fees. Most clinics require a substantial fee and may run for three to five days. Still others may be spread over two or more weekends in a row.

The new flexibility of types of training opportunities should impact the growth rate favorably. The reader may consult the list of websites for leads on trainers and training sites at the end of this

www.lrgaf.org

chapter and watch for up-dated listings on the new mounted archery association website. Aspiring archers may still train with Kassai in Hungary by making arrangements through Todd Delle

Another manifestation of the growing maturity of the discipline is the new Association and website "Mounted Archery Association of the Americas" or MA3 for short, www.mountedarchery.piczo.com. The Association is open to all mounted archery participants, spectators, and supporters anywhere, but it is especially designed to service North and South America. Its purpose will be to promote training schools, demonstrations, competitions, seminars, and pertinent mounted archery information. The Association lists standardized rules for competitions and will publicize and record scores. The rules and events have been inspired by those of Kassai in Hungary, but have unique elements and activities.

Another need of the maturing discipline is to get live exposure at large population centers. Fort Dodge has been a friendly and hospitable place for the early years, but the critical population mass is not there for a large audience exposure. The International Horse Archery Festival (IHAF) may shift in the coming years to large well-developed horse facility in a larger city such as Jacksonville Florida or Indianapolis Indiana. Other expansions opportunities may be connected to ongoing Renaissance events at select sites.

A special tribute to Kassai is certainly in order at this point. Mounted archery in the Americas is indebted to Kassai for his pioneering work in Europe, and for his key role in launching the discipline in North America. We never would have been able to do the start-up without his many trips to the States to inspire us with his demonstrations and generate and train a core of our own mounted archers. We appreciate him not only for the physical performance aspect of his accomplishments but also for the internal and mental dimensions of a mounted martial archer.

Mothers and daughters, fathers and sons, you are invited to take on a new challenge. Our vision is that mounted archery will become so visible and attractive that the video games will be turned off, the foot will go into the stirrup, and the hand will hold the mighty bow. We are convinced that many more will be arrested by the beauty of the horse, the lure of the ancient horsebow, the incredible thrill of integrating it all, and the mental journey of the long inheritance.

www.lrgaf.org

References:

Gray, David. 2002. Bows of the World. Guilford, Connecticut: Pequot Press. Chapter 4 on Asia deals with the appearance of the composite bow, the addition of siyahs, uniting the horse with the bow, and a sampling of horsebows across Asia.

Gray, David, and McCullough, John. February/March, 1999. Horse Archers sighted in the United States. Traditional Bowhunter. A more detailed story of the very first mounted archery demonstrations in the United States by the master Hungarian archer, Kassai Lajos.

Hildinger, Erik. 1997. Warriors of the Steppe, A Military History of Central Asia, 500 B.C. to 1700 A.D. Cambridge, MA, 1997.

Kassai, Lajos. 2002. Horseback Archery. Budapest, Hungary: Puski Kiado kft. This is a fascinating book-length story of creating the modern European discipline of mounted archery. It is factual, inspiring, humorous, and unfolds across nearly two decades.

Koppedrayer, K. Fall 2001. The first International Horse Archery Festival. Instinctive Archer.

Maenchen-Helfen, Otto. 1973. The World of the Huns: Studies of Their History and Culture. Berkely: The University of California Press.

Miller, Robert M, and Lamb, Rick. 2005. The Revolution in Horsemanship. Guilford, Connecticut: Lyons Press, Imprint of Globe Pequot.

Olsen, Sandra (Editor). 1996. Horses through Time. New York: Roberts Rinehart Publishers. An account of the development of the horse by several authorities including twelve years of research on equine domestication beginning 5000+ years ago in Kazakhstan by Olson.

Podhajsky, Alois. 1997, originally 1968. My Horses, My Teachers. North Pomfret, London: Trafalgar Square Publishing. The Director of the Spanish Riding School in Vienna for 26 years tells his biography in terms of learning from his horses that cooperation, understanding, and affection can produce amazing results.

Rolle, Renate. 1980. The World of the Scythians. Berkely: The University of California Press.

Red Hawk, Jay and David Gray. Fall, 2006. Lakota Sioux Capture Another Lost Art. Primitive Archer, The Revival of Horseback

www.lrgaf.org

Archery. The story of the first modern Sioux Mounted Archery Gathering.

Skipper, Lesley. 2001. <u>Inside Your Horse's Mind, A Study of Equine Intelligence and Human Prejudice</u>. London: Clerkenwell House. This work asserts the considerable intelligence and other human-like characteristics of the horse in spite of human prejudices to the contrary. By an author who knows and lives with horses, and draws primarily on European equine literature in a very readable fashion.

Torday, Laszlo. 1977. <u>Mounted Archers: The beginnings of central Asian history</u>. South Church, Bishop Auckland, Durham, England: The Durham Academic Press.

Weatherford, Jack. 2004. <u>Genghis Khan, and the Making of the Modern World</u>. New York: Three Rivers Press, a division of Random House. A more favorable story of the original Khan, his sons and grandsons relying to a large extent on the <u>Secret History of the Mongols.</u>

www.atarn.org
www.horsebows.com
www.intlhorsearchery.org
www.krackow.com
http://mountedarchery.piczo.com
www.mountedmartialarchery.com
www.ponybow.com
www.salukibow.com

Chapter 9

Training the horseback archer

By Lukas Novotny and David Gray

> **Wanted:**
>
> Twenty of the world's top mounted archers to squelch a terrorist band of horse archers in a remote country. Applicants must have the following characteristics and skills developed to the maximum: ....

How would you complete the ad?

Or put yourself in the place of a Magyar commander in the early 900s when European citizens prayed, "Lord deliver us from the arrows of the Magyars." Or go to the 1200s when the Mongols were thundering across the steppe. What were those commanders seeking in their mounted archers? Toughness, courage, self-control, keen senses, horsemanship, timing, flexibility, balance, speed, accuracy...? In antiquity, all of these characteristics and more were hammered into the mounted archer from childhood.

The lines above are directly quoted from an article Lukas and David wrote jointly for <u>Primitive Archer</u>, Fall 2002, entitled "Mounted Archery from the Ground Up." The article invited archers to try a series of ground practices which to some extent simulated shooting while on a running horse. This chapter will build on the suggestions in that article, greatly expand them, and will progress to include actual archery training under canter and/or gallop conditions.

Because this is a chapter on training, the reader may be more interested in the "credentials" of the authors than with some of the other chapters. Lukas has emerged as one of the lead instructors and performers in the Unites States. He trained under Kassai for several years in the States as well as in Hungary. He has conducted many clinics in the United States, Canada, Brazil, and France. David has trained under Kassai and Lukas in several clinics and conducts introductory horseback archery instruction.

Predispositions of a horseback archery trainee

Almost anybody of any age can try this discipline and make some satisfying progress. That open picture needs to be qualified and elaborated. We have worked with people from as young as very early teens to over 70 years old. Age is not a great limitation; it is encouraging to some of us to have a discipline that reaches far into one's life. Some normal physical conditioning and strength is essential in order to make good progress and to help avoid injuries which the less fit are more prone to suffer. One of the many varieties of aerobics and fundamental muscle toning and strengthening will set the person up for multiple long days of vigorous participation at one of the training schools or clinics.

Mentally, fast food, fast track, Type A, bottom line types of persons will probably not gravitate to this sport and would probably not do well or endure if they did try it. Pushing one's self toward incremental goals is critical to progress in any of the great sports, but patience, endurance, and realistic self assessment are also essential. Patience is a fairly empty word for most westerners who are tied to clocks and end-of-the-day deadlines, often squeezed by downsizing and handling double work loads. The world of authentic martial arts is indeed foreign. There, patience is a lifetime task. One is always learning, even the Sensei and Master are always moving toward improvement. How long will it take to become an engineer? Four years of college. How long does it take to memorize a poem? Maybe 30 minutes. How long does it take to learn patience? A lifetime. A lifetime of deeply satisfying inner growth of character, but that slow progress is also very humbling. A friend of mine sent me a card some time ago to cheer me up about my chemo treatments. The front of the card simply displays a quote by Ralph Waldo Emerson. "What lies behind us and what lies before us are tiny matters compared to what lies within us."

Mounted archers will tend to be self-selected to have a more cooperative and supportive attitude toward others and his or her horse, rather that having the nasty dog-eat-dog, versions of competition, strife, and jealousy. Please study the statement on personal growth at the end of the Introduction for an expansion of these desirable characteristics. The trainee who is likely to stick with training is one who wants to develop a much stronger inner character with less need to fall back on the weakness of arrogance, feigning superiority, and lording it over others. I was staying for a week-end with a martial arts Master in Minsk, Belarus, just shortly after the iron curtain came down. From visiting his classes, the images are still totally in focus in my memory. When the students came into the studio, all valuables (wallets, keys, etc.) were laid out in the open on a table showing honesty and trust. Respect for each other, in spite of the hard physical contacts, was obvious, and mutual respect between Master and student was evident in their unhurried and genuine bows to each other to start the session of training. There was no question about who was Master, but the way he bowed to his students was overflowing with his sense of dignity toward them. We also think that the long-term mounted archery trainee will find himself or herself wondering about the long reaches of the past, where this all came from, and having the desire for some sense of sweeping historical connection.

We have found that if a trainee commences with just one of the two major skills—either archery or equestrianism, the equestrian has the advantage by all means. In other words, the horse person can pick up the archery know how much more quickly that the archer can acquire a good seat and an understanding of the horse. If a person is attracted to the discipline, but has neither a horse nor a bow background, then he or she should start riding lessons immediately.

Tuning the equipment

Tuning is simple and makes things a lot easier. Because the nocking of the arrow onto the bow string has to be fast and without looking, the archer needs all the help he or she can get from well-tuned equipment. The serving on the bow string should be of sufficient dimension that the arrow slides easily into the nocking point on the bow string. If the serving is too short, one may slide the arrow on the string only to hit the bump as it were where the serving begins and that may stall the shot or at least be distracting. The serving should extend five or six inches beyond the nocking point. The serving also needs to be very smooth and uniform to facilitate an easy sliding of the arrow on the string.

As in all traditional archery, and especially when one is shooting the arrow directly off the bow hand which is standard for horse bows, the nocking point should be fastened onto the string in order that the arrow is nocked about a half inch above right angles to the bow string. This allows the fletches to pass over the hand more smoothly. For the thumb-ring shooter, the nock point is all one needs on the string, and it should be positioned taking into account that most thumb-ring shooters will pull the arrow up the string; the arrow will be below the nocking indicator on the string. For the three finger release, the arrow is usually pulled down on the string and therefore the arrow rests on top of the nocking point. Kassai is a three-finger shooter at least in part because he has no thumb; he wraps the string with broad adhesive tape which serves both as a nocking point and as a finger protector. The thumb-ring shooter does not need to worry about a finger protector because the thumb ring is the protector and takes the cutting pressure of the narrow string, not the fingers in any direct way.

There are several elements to tuning arrows. The arrow nocks should fit onto the serving snugly so they do not fall off, but not so snug that they are hard to get on the string. Either heat the arrow nocks to get the right fit, or they can be filed if too tight. The other arrow check is the security of the front points of the fletches. Remember that those fletches are sliding directly over your bare bow hand. If there is a loose and sharp tip on the front of the fletching your hand may be painfully sliced. Therefore sand the front tips of the fletches, apply some extra fletching glue at the tips, and for good measure place a wrap of artificial sinew or even scotch tape around that front edge of the fletching for an extra precaution. This should be totally sufficient. But if you are still concerned, there are little leather hand protectors designed for this purpose.

We need to describe a few more things about the arrows. It is a good safety idea to blunt the sharp end of the field tips. A metal file does this easily. Create a blunt surface of one-sixteenth of an inch or more, and then round off the edges. One may need to finish with some coarse sand paper. This will avoid gouging or scratching your bow or your bow hand, especially for the three finger shooter. The blunting will also reduce target penetration and make for easier pulling of arrows. Most horseback archers, although steeped in traditional ways, have forsaken the wood shafts for aluminum or carbon. Wooden shafts break up rapidly in this discipline. The shaft has to be long enough to accommodate your draw, and should be spined about five pounds lighter than your bow. The reduced poundage lessens the extent of the archer's paradox when using bows without shooting windows.

Learning to nock the arrow on the bow string

The location of the arrow supply varies with traditions. In the Kassai style, a fistful of arrows are carried in the bow hand with the fletches up. Start with three. This is similar to photos of American Indians while hunting or in battle. For Korean and Japanese competitions, the arrows must be drawn one at a time from a quiver or sash.

When using the thumb ring style, the arrows are held in a bunch toward the back of the bow (as opposed to belly) and fanned somewhat to the left side of the bow allowing the nocked arrow alone to be against the right side of the bow. For the thumb ring shooter the arrows are firmly gripped by the nock and pulled into position by sliding the arrow nock up the string to the nock point on the string. The nocked arrow will be held in horizontal position momentarily by the thumb and index finger; these fingers are withdrawn just before release.

For three finger shooters, the arrows are bunched toward the right side of the bow. The arrow is pulled down in a similar fashion to the thumb shooter, but there is an additional motion of crossing the arrow to the left side of the bow. This entails threading the arrow tip between the string and the bow. From a purely time and motion point of view, this is a serious disadvantage of the three finger method; it adds an additional step. Once threaded through, the arrow is slid down on the string to the nock point. In either of the two methods some sliding of the arrow to the nock point is necessary because one cannot intuitively hit the exact nocking point of the string directly while on a running horse and without time to look.

All of the above must be practiced over and over and over. This can be done anywhere, even in a small apartment. After an arrow is nocked it can be flipped on the floor, followed by another arrow, etc. The archer must also add nocking without looking to the practice list, and then gradually add speed. But do not put speed into the equation for several weeks. Concentrate on getting all the motions correct and then coordinated. When you do start to go for speed, if things fall apart, drop back on the speed goal until the nocking is very smooth and confident again. In riding the European-type course, one has 16 seconds from entry to exit gate, and if you are on a course that has three targets, the math indicates that you have about three seconds to nock, and about three seconds to shoot. That is not super fast, but it is not slow, and remember you are on an undulating, cantering horse. The archer's riveted attention must be on the targets without interruption or accuracy will never be increased. The upshot is that shooting is relatively fast, on a bouncing horse, with no chance to look at how the nocking is going.

Learning the release of the arrow

When one examines all the elements of shooting— breathing, concentration, nocking, drawing, aiming, and releasing—the release is the most difficult and a pivotal element in success or failure. Most archers have no problem pulling their bow if they are not over bowed, and most can acquire a steady bow hand so that the bow is glued as it were to the heart of the target, but the release is never mastered in some cases. The slightest torque of the releasing hand or fingers will put the arrow off the target significantly. The string should leave the human hand in an absolute straight line to the heart of the target, without the slightest twist. A straight laser-like line of energy should flow from the elbow, through the forearm wrist and hand, through the arrow, and on to the very pinpoint of one's aim.

The thumb ring technique is superior in gaining a smooth release, and superior in a number of other ways as well over the popular three-finger release. In the thumb release, the string is held by a very small area of hard surface and in the actual release only has to slide over this small hard surface. There is less likelihood of twisting or torquing than with three soft gloved or bare flesh finger tips sliding across the string in the release. The release tends to be smoother, crisper and has less room for error.

Some description of the thumb ring itself is in order at this point. As the descriptor implies, the thumb ring goes around the thumb. (See page 162.) One could shoot with the unprotected thumb after developing thick calluses. Thumb rings were as simple as an oval shape piece of leather with a hole cut through it, or as elaborate as ones made of gold set with precious gems. Most commonly, horn, ivory, bone and semi precious stones were used, while today horn and phenolic are most common. Many were also made of bronze and other metals. See [Kay's Thumb Ring](#) book in the Reference section for the many types of rings, and some of the history.

If the reader looks at the picture of the ring, one can see that is has a slight groove cut into it. That groove does not necessarily have to be there and is not featured on all thumb rings. The groove helps to keeps the string where it belongs and keeps it from slipping off the edge of the ring onto the thumb, which can be painful. Often a piece of soft leather was used on the inside of the ring so that if the string slipped off the ring and onto the flesh of the thumb there would be some protection. Leather liners can also be used to help size the rings if they are too large.

The ring needs to fit well. The ring is slipped over the thumb oriented so the oval of the ring and the oval of the cross section of the thumb match, then gets turned a quarter of a turn, with the tab or extension of the ring, if it is so shaped, facing toward the outer end of the thumb. It must be snug but not too tight; it should take some difficulty to get the ring on the thumb. In antiquity, archers would have two rings, one for summer and another for winter to accommodate the swelling and shrinking of the thumb. Size also needs to be adjusted over a period of time as the thumb changes from the strain of much shooting. So buy a ring from someone who knows how to read and fit sizes. The shooter may still have to make adjustments by filing or applying leather on the inside of the ring, or you may have to send it back to the maker more than once to get it right.

The thumb release technique is ancient but has gained much recent exposure and usage. The thumb ring developed in the Middle East, Egypt, and central Asia. Whether the technique developed independently in each one of these regions or originated in one of them and spread, we do not know for sure. All we know is that we can find depictions of this style of shooting in many forms of early artwork from the period, primarily in Egyptian and Syrian. The three-finger style of shooting probably existed along-side the thumb release, but eventually was abandoned as warfare developed with the mounting of the horse and the birth of horseback archery. In later periods, in the eastern part of the world, the thumb ring technique ruled supreme.

Live demonstrations of the thumb release would be so much clearer but the verbal description with supporting pictures and sketches will have to do. All descriptions here are from the perspective of the right handed archer; left handed persons have to reverse the process entirely. Before we describe the actual technique, we should compare this style of shooting to the three finger or Mediterranean technique. The most obvious difference is that the draw is by the thumb and index finger. The three finger shooter discharges the arrow from the left side of the bow, whereas the thumb shooter generally releases the arrow from the right side of the bow. For the three finger shooter, the contact with the string by the three fingers is just on the finger tips about at the first joint, as an L-shaped hook. The rest of the hand, wrist, and arm are in a perfectly straight line. When the finger grip is correct, and the release is imminent, the tips of the fingers are rolling the string slightly toward the bow thus keeping the arrow on the bow. The arrow keeps falling off the bow for the beginner because of clutching the string too deeply (between the two joints) in the three fingers thus turning the arrow away from the bow, or possibly moving the whole hand slightly to the left.

Before nocking the first arrow, a word about the bow. Bows designed for horseback archery are the most appropriate, but a beginner may be able to get by for a while on a simple recurve bow. It is better not to have a shooting shelf, which most recurves have, because it is just another thing to get in the way. The bow must be light, around 30 pounds for the small shooter and up to 40 pounds for the larger and stronger person.

Apparently now we are truly ready to nock an arrow. Please follow the explanations carefully to understand how to do this correctly. There are several ways to shoot with a thumb ring and thumb lock based on an Arabic finger typology. Latham and Paterson (1970) illustrate six variations of the Arab thumb lock. The one labeled Pillion is closest to the one described here in detail. Lukas is describing here the one he likes best and is most comfortable with. Study the picture on page 163 carefully. As you see you will form a fist with your middle, ring and small finger. Keep the index finger and your thumb open. Next, bring the thumb towards your middle finger and rest the

www.lrgaf.org

tip of it on the side of the second joint of the middle finger. Now close your index finger over the thumb itself. The index finger should only rest over the thumbnail. You will see that the first joint of your thumb is at right angles to the middle finger. This is important; it gives you a better more secure hold. Before we go any further, it is important to note, that during the drawing itself you should always keep the other three fingers closed as well. If your thumb and index finger are locked over the string, so should the middle, ring and small finger be clenched in to the fist, not necessarily tight but closed. Otherwise the muscles and tendons in your hand will not work in unison as you draw the bow.

Let's move on to the second step. Knowing how to form a thumb lock will now allow us to draw a bow. Repeat all the steps we have learned so far including hooking your thumb around the string and locking over it with your index finger. Do this without an arrow. Before you can actually draw the bow there are a few more important things to mention. In addition to performing a thumb hold correctly you will also have to straighten your wrist a little bit. It does not have to be perfectly straight.

The last thing to do is to rotate the wrist so that the index finger is parallel to the string and the flat of our wrist, the upper part, is also parallel to the ground. This rotation is very important. If not performed properly, you will have a problem keeping the arrow up against the bow and the string will catch the tip of your index finger as your release the arrow. Also notice that pressure is applied with your index finger in the nock area of the arrow. This is achieved with a proper rotation mentioned above. To be more precise the pressure is applied with a middle section of your third segment of the index finger. This pressure is very important; this is the last element of the thumb lock and how much pressure you apply will actually affect the arrow flight. If you do not apply enough pressure, the arrow will not stay on the bow and you probably did not rotate your wrist correctly to lock the arrow. Too much pressure will actually flex the arrow in the bow itself and thus affect the flight of the arrow erratically because it will be harder for the arrow to straighten out after leaving the bow. This is called the flight paradox.

The persistent wind on the Great Plains of central United States plus the air movement created by the canter both push the arrow even more securely against the bow. This is true only for the thumb ring shooter taking shots to his or her left which are by far the most frequent shots, but when the master archer is able to reach over the horse and shoot to the right, the above advantage disappears; the wind will tend to blow the arrow off the bow and the remaining correction is the thumb lock itself.

If you did everything correctly up to this point, you should just think of the release and the fingers will open on their own. You will notice that this technique will allow you to lengthen your draw and if the bow allows, quite considerably with ease and comfort. When you anchor you can do so anywhere you wish. The favorite spot for Lukas is at the end of the jaw and just below the ear lobe. It is a very good and solid anchor. Since the draw can be much longer you can also float your anchor above your shoulder. It does take some getting used to though. Make sure that your bow can withstand such a long draw before you do so.

We also need to talk about aiming. Since the thumb ring shooter is shooting from the right side of the bow the picture changes considerably. It may seem awkward at first. There are basically three ways to aim at a target. One is on the left side of the bow, which forces you to be almost entirely instinctive. Instinctive archers differ in how much conscious attention, awareness, or sighting of the arrow actually occurs. It seems to some of us that at least conscious vertical orienttation of the arrow on the target is pretty common, whereas elevation may tend to be more purely instinctual. At any rate, all of the aiming techniques have two things in common—the bow hand is pointed steadily at the heart of the target, and the eyes are glued to that same point. The exception is in the case of a long shot with a light bow; then one learns how much higher one may need to aim. In the point of aim strategy, one learns where the tip of his or her arrow must be on the target to hit at a given distance. The gap method is far more calculated and much less likely to be used in horseback archery. Another option is shooting by looking through the handle of the bow, as it were, if you can imagine that. Experiment and see what works best for you.

The beginning thumb ring shooter will find it very difficult to hit the mark at first. It is best to start very close to the target, perhaps ten feet away. The first arrows will hit far off to the right. A lot of people are taken aback and do not understand why that happens. Let me explain. One of the reasons for the errant shots is that the sight

www.lrgaf.org

picture of the target is quite different from what the three finger shooter is used to. Another difference is the bow hand. Every time a three finger shooter releases an arrow, the bow hand moves ever so slightly to the right; it is imperceptible but significant when you switch to the thumb ring. These are some of the reasons your arrow hits to the right. Steady your bow hand and give your brain time to re-program a new shooting picture. Concentrate on steadying your bow hand. Before you know it you will be hitting the mark.

In closing the releasing discussion, Lukas would like to say that when he started shooting this technique there was nobody out there to teach him. "Many times I just wanted to quit, but I stuck to it and the rewards have been worth it. I do not claim to be a great archer, quite the contrary, but my shooting improved by switching to the thumb ring. It is an alternative to the Mediterranean shooting style and in my opinion rules supreme. It is not easy to learn, especially for those who have been shooting three fingers for many years. Raw beginners have the best results because they have no interference from a former style of shooting. I am sure that with patience and perseverance you will find this new way of shooting rewarding."

Stationary ground exercises

Form is very important, but it can be described briefly. It is closer to Olympic or English long bow form than to the popular open form of many hunting styles. The body and head are held quite upright. Shoulders are almost at right angles to the target, very slightly backed off from "shooting in the bow" of the English style. The full draw position, or anchor point, is slightly below the chin and back toward the ear. It is a floating anchor because the archer is being tossed around as it were on the horse.

Kassai teaches a three step process in shooting. Once the arrow is nocked and the release hand is in position on the arrow nock, one is ready to shoot. The three steps are: 1) bow up and fully in position, 2) draw, and 3) release. This is seen also in formal target archers. Hunters on the other hand make the "bow up" and "draw" steps in one smooth motion called the push-pull. In actual horseback archery it probably does not matter which one is used, but the push pull is much more likely to emerge on the course because it is vastly more efficient. However in the early stages of learning, the distinct three step method is probably good because one can more easily monitor one's self on each of the elements and it tends to slow one down in the early stages which is helpful.

Somewhere along the line after nocking and releasing are nicely confirmed and there is some comfort in the shooting process, speed and varied shooting positions need to be introduced. A nice way to push the archer in a group clinic is to form two or more lines of trainees with their own targets. The first person shoots and then runs around to the right and the back of the line while the next archer runs on the left of the line to the front, takes his position facing forward, and at the instructor's signal, shoots. It adds some sense of action even though one is standing perfectly still when the shot is released. Shooting positions can then be varied to having the shoulders aligned with the target (more natural), and finally have the shooter do an about face when reaching the shooting position in order to take the backward shot. To add motivation for speed, the shooting lines can compete against each other. Complexity can be added by having the trainee mount two bales of hay and shoot from the simulated horse in different positions. Finally one can lie down on a bale of hay on one's back and shoot. The three finger shooter will be very hard pressed to keep the arrow on the bow and will have to adapt a bit of an Indian pinch grip to keep the arrow on — good practice for the ceaseless western winds they call Mariah.

Training in most sports uses shaping or using gradually more demanding goals. Go from easy to difficult and in small steps, always retreating temporarily if the behavior falls apart. In each session, build up speed gradually, and at the end of a session taper the speed off so that one finishes confidently and with good form. Often a drum or drum-like object to beat on is helpful to develop a sense of timing and rhythm. Later one will try to sense the rhythm of the canter so that the release can occur at the top of the undulation—the smoothest point in a single sequence of foot placements in the canter.

Shooting exercises while in motion.

www.lrgaf.org

Motion exercises are an invitation and challenge to all persons potentially interested in horse archery. Furthermore, these drills will enliven all archers' practice routines and skills — whether hunter, competitor, or pleasure shooter or aspiring horseback archer. The objectives of the exercises include flexibility, balance, speed, and accuracy in the context of bodily motion. Many of these basic exercises have come to us through the clinics that Kassai has conducted in the States and Canada, and many others have been designed by Lukas in his training camps.

One way to introduce simulated riding motion into practice sessions is to shoot between doing traditional squats. Nock as you go down into the squat, and draw on the way back up; release the arrow as soon as you are fully up and standing. The goal is to be able to nock without looking and while in motion. This kind of practice is absolutely essential. Directional variations can then be added—facing forward, to the side, and facing backwards necessitating a 180 degree turn when coming up out of the squat in order to shoot. The feet do not move; the body twists, which simulates twisting on the horse for the backward shot.

Shooting while walking, jogging, and running has great potential to simulate the motion of shooting from horseback. Because the standardized European course is such an effective and realistic venue for training, we need to have that picture in mind for the walking and running drills. It is a straight 90 meter course divided by markers into three 30 meter sections. The target sits midway on the 90 meter stretch but 7 meters to the left and has three faces, each about 36 inches in diameter. The middle or second target is placed parallel to the course, whereas the first and third targets are "swung" backward from the course at somewhat more than 45 degree angles. In the first third of the course the approach shot must be taken at the first face of the targets, then the right angle shot, and finally the backward shot in the last third of the course. The approach and backward shot is approximately 30 meters depending on exactly when the shot is released. The approach shot is the second most difficult largely because of the distance, and the backward shot not only has the distance challenge but unnatural position of the rider on the horse and the much greater danger involved. The right angle shot is about 7 meters and is the easiest.

All these shots can be approximated from the ground. Start with the easiest, the right angle shot. Walk past the target, seven meters away, and shoot when closest to right angles to it. The trainee may then speed up the walk, eventually try the jog, or even a faster run. Always move from easy to more difficult, and retreat if the level is too difficult. The approach shot should be practiced next. On your imaginary straight course line determine what would be about a 30 meter shot. That will be your distance goal, but you could start with the shortest shot within the first 30 meter section and gradually move up to the 30 meter distance. If you have just one target, turn it so it is approximately at right angles for this shot. The target will be about 25 degrees off the main course. This means that you will have to twist your torso and especially your right shoulder considerably clockwise to take the shot with proper form. Finally the backward shot can be developed. Begin with the shortest shot possible within the third section of the course, and gradually more up to the longer shot of approximately 30 meters. Again the target can be turned to the appropriate angle if there is only one target face.

One of Lukas's favorite motion exercises is when the trainee mounts two bales of hay without being able to touch the ground. Shoot first stationary, and then have two other trainees intentionally rock the bales from the back to simulate the canter. A mock wooden horse with saddle and bridle may also be used.

To the horse

Nothing beats practicing and training under real conditions. The advanced trainee in a clinic probably spends about one-third of the time in ground exercise but most of the time is on the horse on an outside full-dimension course making many passes down the course in a training day. The novice may spend nearly half the training time on the horse but usually in a far more controlled environment such as an inside arena.

The instructor gives feedback to each participant on good and bad points, but always encouraging. A litany of common faults which usually have to be worked on are: failure to come to a full draw;

bending over and losing the nice upright form and thus constricting one's motions; taking one's eye off the target especially when approaching the backward shot; and becoming rigid probably out of an subconscious sense of fear or apprehension. Learning to shoot from the top of the canter comes later in the trainee's maturation. One should take care that the horse is on the left lead while going down the course. A circular turn into the course (curving from left to right) usually takes care of the lead automatically.

More excitement and challenge can be added by the introduction of rolling, and aerial discs. Rolling them on the ground is a little easier than being slightly elevated in the air. For safety do not throw them more that six feet above the ground and be sure of the background. Safety must always be of paramount importance.

The whistle has blown. Horses and humans are tired and hungry. Horses come first. Before dinner there will be a time of group reflection and evaluation of the events of the day. Hitting the target and everything that leads up to it are difficult but immensely rewarding.

****

References:

Faris, Nabih Amin (Translator). 1945. Arab Archery. Princeton, New Jersey: Princeton University Press. From a rare Arab manuscript of the 1500s.

Gray, David, and Novotny, Lukas. Fall 2002. Mounted Archery from the ground up. Primitive Archer.

Kassai, Lajos. 2002. Horseback Archery. Budapest, Hungary: Puski Kiado Kft.

Klopsteg, Paul E. Originally 1934, current 2001. Turkish Archery and the Composite Bow. Manchester, England: Simon Archery Foundation, The University of Manchester.

Koppedrayer, Kay. 2002. Kay's Thumbing Book. Milverton, Ontario: Blue Vase Press.

Latham, J. D., and Paterson, W.F. 1970. Saracen Archery. London: The Trinity Press.

Chapter 10

In South America

by Holm Neumann and David Gray

The vision of the Mounted Archery Association of the Americas is to promote horseback archery from the northern tip of North America to the southern tip of South America. As accounted for in other chapters, dissemination of the discipline has spread across the United States and has a good hold in Canada, but until very recently we were still awaiting mounted archers south of the Rio Grande.

In the 2003 training school at the International Horseback Archery Festival at Fort Dodge, Iowa, a very fine trainee emerged from Mexico. Miguel Mancera Corcuera is an accomplished rider and faithful practitioner of dressage. With such good equestrian skills in hand, and basic archery as well, his progress was phenomenal in one week of training at Fort Dodge. We hope that training centers can be established in Mexico and that Miguel may play a significant role, although at present his passion is that of dressage.

At this point, the progression of mounted archery has skipped Central America and has landed in South America—Brazil. This large country is almost identical in size to the United States, has about one-half the population, and has two of the world's largest cities. The country stretches from the vast wet Amazon Basin in the north where ocean going vessels can navigate 2,300 miles up the Amazon River, to semi-arid plains, hills and mountains in the south. It is a land rich in minerals, cattle, horses, agriculture, modern technological industries, the Samba, and the Bossa Nova. Our story takes us on a two hour drive northeast of one of those large cities, Rio de Janeiro (12 million) to the Desempenho Equestrian Center.

Meeting the Brazilian contacts: Bjarke and Mara Rink

Some years ago Holm Neuman and his wife Susan were at an equestrian event in California and by chance wandered across the national horse breed of Brazil, the Mangalarga Marchador. They became so enamored and impressed with this horse that they started to work on importing them, as there are so few in the States. This naturally led them to visit Brazil and meet the owners of one of the major Marchador ranches, Mr. Bjarke Rink and Mara Rink.

Mr. Rink, originally from Denmark, came to Brazil as a young child. His wife Mara is a native of Brazil. Bjarke is a "throwback" in a wonderful sense to the Renaissance person. His curious and creative mind, wide reading, robust memory, wide ranging experiences in the worlds of movie directing, advertising, cattle, horses, and facile verbal communication skills all add up to a super productive person. Mr. Rink is the Director of the Homo Cabello Research Institute, which is devoted to the study of human-horse communication, the neurophysiology of human equitation, and the history of the effects of the horse on human history.

His first major equestrian book, The Centaur Legacy, 2004, is a widely acclaimed collection of short essays on the history of the domestication and training of the horse. His extensive command of this literature allows him to compare and contrast the many schools of thought about training from the time of Xenophon in 400 B.C. through the centuries of written equestrian history. Bjarke also has an extensive collection of equine tack illustrating the evolution and development of the saddle, stirrup, bit, and other tools useful in mounted warfare. He regularly gives lectures to students of equine studies on these topics.

Bjarke and Mara direct and manage the International Desempenho Riding School. The School attracts students and expert accomplished riders from around the world. The Center has an extensive teaching staff and a string of over 60 schooling horses. Over a dozen of these intelligent, disciplined, superbly gaited horses have been trained to provide the basic mounts for mastering the art of mounted archery.

Launching mounted archery in Brazil

In May of 2006, Holm returned to Brazil accompanied by Lukas Novotny, a master mounted archer and renowned instructor in this field, and two young mounted archers from Oregon — Jet Cowan and Katie Stearns. An international mounted archery instructional clinic at Desempenho was arranged. Under Mr. Novotny's tutelage, a class in ground archery and mounted archery skill was presented during a weeklong forum, including some reinless riding Utilizing Mr. Rink's trained mounts, the participants developed considerable horseback archery skills. Because several of Mr. Rink's professional equestrian staff, Andre, Sathy, and Rafael, have acquired the basics of mounted archery and will continue to advance themselves, the tradition of mounted archery training will be ongoing. Lukas also continues periodically to go back to Brazil to do formal clinics to advance the discipline. A very active interest in mounted archery has been planted in Brazil and the future looks very bright for our South American associates to further this exciting resurrection of an ancient tradition.

A typical day of training in Brazil would involve a preliminary session of ground archery skills including the practice of rapid nocking of arrows. Static shooting at close and distant targets, lateral, forward, and over the back shooting, and shooting on the move in tag team exercises were practiced. Mounted exercises involved warming the horses on the archery course at a walk, shooting at the trot and then at the canter or gallop. Practice for the traditional Hungarian as well as the Korean styles was performed.

The Korean style course involves first shooting at one target with one arrow. The best hit and time wins. A second similar run at two targets, 30 meters apart, is performed. One arrow is shot at each target with the best score and time winning. A third run is then performed with a series of five targets 30 meters apart and the best cumulative score wins. The Hungarian style course has been described in detail in the Training chapter.

Another striking and gratifying aspect of the equestrian center at Desempenho is the degree to which it draws international clientele. The participants at this very first mounted archery clinic traveled from eight countries — Brazil, The Czech Republic, Denmark, England, Finland, France, Germany, and the USA. You will note that a Korean course and the standard Hungarian course are being employed, and possibly a Japanese Yabusame course will be added in the future because there are many persons of Japanese origin in South America. Even though MA3 is focused on the Americas, the ancient and modern history of mounted archery is international, so the broad outreach here is a happy bonus.

The approach to the horse at Desempenho

Mr. Rink contends that the vast majority of older training techniques were based on mechanical models. The horse was seen as a mechanism or machine which had to be controlled in a similar manner. Instead of wheels, levers, and rods to control an engine, one controls a horse by harsh bits, martingales, tie-downs, and various constraining reins to bend the head at the poll, etc. Most of these methods worked well enough to succeed at war, make a show on the parade grounds, and even to develop complex dressage movements. There were exceptions. Xenophon himself advocated a humane, patient treatment of the horse which was remarkable for his day and many centuries afterward but he did not see the smooth synchronized unity of horse and rider very clearly. Steppe people such as the Mongols were at one with their horses in every way. They massed large numbers of horses moving as one being in fierce sudden military attacks and feigned retreat maneuvers. Bjarke notes that the Mongols never got much credit for their phenomenal equestrian achievements and "were always on the wrong side of history." A few more modern exceptions such as Gustav Steinbrecht in the 19th century were making this breakthrough of stressing the need to feel all the movements of the horse in order for the rider to be in harmony with those movements.

Classical and operant training principles must have been well understood by great circus trainers for many centuries. Those principles were never fully scientifically explored until the onset of modern experimental behavioral psychology, and certainly never put in systematic written form. Nevertheless, even these modern behavioral approaches still tend to veer too far toward the side of mechanical models, or at least are limited to that mentality by many equestrian trainers.

It took modern pioneer equestrians such as Bill Dorrance and Ray Hunt to push us to include the more intuitive and feeling dimen-

www.lrgaf.org

sions to maximally interact with our horses. Note the title of the late Bill Dorrance's book—<u>True Horsemanship Through Feel</u>. Mr. Rink cites Daniel Goleman's concept of emotional intelligence and shows that the emotionality of the rider will come through hands, legs, whole body posture, and voice tone, and the horse is exquisitely equipped to register and understand these emotions. Being an animal of prey, and depending on all the emotionally laden signs of danger to flee and thus survive, the horse's emotional faculties are well developed. Leslie Skipper emphasizes even further the reality of the rich emotional development of the horse, in addition to the horse having generous amounts of traditional intelligence. <u>Inside Your Horses Mind: A study of Equine Intelligence and Human Prejudice</u>, (2001). Some horses visibly grieve and appear depressed when a stable-mate dies. The emotions of pleasure and elation must be driving the apparently rough horseplay in the open pasture. In spite of their fighting over hay and grain, horses have been seen to care for a fellow horse who is sick and down. At the Little Neshannock Stables here in New Wilmington horses in an open paddock even protected the pet goose of the Stables. When a stray dog was chasing the goose in the paddock, the horses surrounded the goose, while one of the horses chased the dog out of the paddock.

     Given the emotional sensitivity of the horse and its relative cognitive ability, it is clear that the horse is not a machine. It may respond to many things mechanically and thoughtlessly just as humans often do under stimulus control. But on the other hand, it is powerful and impressive to see how frequently and strongly Bjarke Rink shows us that we must approach the horse cooperatively and as a living partner rather than trying to dominate as though we were dealing with a mindless machine or lowly animal. See pages 25, 66, 85, 144, 214 of <u>The Centaur Legacy</u>. He furthermore asserts that it is important that the rider designs the training so that it is pleasant, fun, and that force be minimized in order that the horse may sense a voluntary dimension to his or her performance; pages 88, 177-179. Also, when a horse acts up, ride him through it without underlining it in a fight and get on to recapturing what will be pleasant to the horse. This involves a whole sea of emotions of horse and rider which the rider will need to analyze very carefully. This partnering attitude should not be confused with the idea of a rider who lacks firmness or fails to correct bad behavior. Rink concludes his book on the Centaur by turning to the human situation and makes a plea that international cooperation must be the most important issue on the global agenda. Our cooperative attitudes to our horses may very well be reflected in our feelings about our fellow human beings.

The national Brazilian horse

The national horse of Brazil is the Mangalarga Marchador. This horse is known for its docility, intelligence, willingness, quickness in learning, and fast smooth gaits. The word Marchador refers to the Marcha which is a special and natural gait between the trot and the canter. The Marcha is a four beat gait with feet moving alternately, laterally or diagonally, with triple support. The smoothness comes from three feet being on the ground at once for a split second. Hendricks (1995) claims this gait of the Marchador is unique in the world. The Marchador does not throw the front legs outward to the side like the Peruvian Paso does in a movement called the termino. The breed stands between 14 and 16 hands. The term Mangalarga was the name of a hacienda or fazenda in Brazil where an important expansion of the breed occurred.

Serious development of this breed began in the early 1800s. The Emperor of Brazil gave a Senior Junqueira an Alter Real stallion named Sublime. Real in Portuguese means "royal" and Alter refers to a breeding farm in Portugal. The Alter Real has been and still is the second most likely breed used for Haute Ecole after the joint first place held by the Andalusian and the Lusitano, from which the Lipizzaners are derived. Other Alter Real stallions and Andalusian stallions were also used. (Espositio, 1999).

The dam side of the breed was based on several types of mares—Andalusians, Argentine Criollos, and Spanish Jennets. Hendricks (1995) thinks the now extinct Jennet mares must have been bred predominately because of their fast smooth ambling gait, whereas Esposito (1999) thinks the Criollo mares played a major role, partially because some of them are gaited. The Criollo is clearly another early strain of Spanish horse known for its exceptional hardiness. Breeding today often has a prerequisite of an endurance ride of 470 miles carrying a standard back weight of 238 pounds, with a 30 mile race at the end. No food or water is provided beyond what can be found on the ride.

If the breeding record is pushed back further to the foundation of all the Spanish breeds mentioned above, the Sorraia undoubtedly emerges, perhaps with lesser strains of the small Garrano. The Sorraia lived in the wilds of southern Iberia, largely Portugal. It is truly a horse rather than a pony and may be as typically Iberian as possible. It apparently is the predominate breed that came first to the new world on the *Pinta* on Columbus's second voyage of 1493. The Lusitano, Andalusian, and other breeds came later (Gray and Red Hawk, 2006).

There is much reason to celebrate the migration of mounted archery into South America. The potential for growth and appreciation of the discipline is exciting.

****

References:

Bennett, D. 1998. Conquerors: The Roots of New World Horsemanship. Solvang, California: Amigo Publications.

Dorrance, Bill. 2001. True Horsemanship Through Feel. Guilford, Connecticut: The Lyons Press.

Draper Judith. 1996. The Book of Horses and Horse Care. New York: Barnes and Noble.

Esposito, Lin (Editor). 1999. Giant Book of the Horse. London: Quarto Publishing.

Gray, David, and Red Hawk, Jay. 2006. Spanish Mustangs and the Lakota Sioux. Under review for magazine publication.

Hendricks, Bonnie. 1995. International Encyclopedia of Horse Breeds. Norman, Oklahoma: University of Oklahoma Press.

Martinez, Maria del Carmen. November 2006. Of Criollos and Cracker Horses. Equus.

Miller, R. M., and Lamb, Rick. 2005. The Revolution in Horsemanship. Guilford, Connecticut: The Lyons Press.

Rink, Bjarke. 2004. The Centaur Legacy: How Equine Speed and Human Intelligence Shaped the Course of History. Glasgow, Kentucky: The Long Rider's Guild Press.

Skipper, Lesley. 2001. Inside Your Horse's Mind: A Study of Equine Intelligence and Human Prejudice. London: Clerkenwell House.

Chapter 11

The Bows for Horseback Archery

By Lukas Novotny

The composite bow has been around for thousands of years, on the battlefield and in the hunting camps. During its time it helped to define boundaries of Empires that have since come and gone. In North Africa, Asia Minor, Central Asia and the Far East, it played a major role as a weapon of choice for armies of mounted archers that swept through vast spaces of these continents imposing the will of their leaders through the sting of an arrow. Their designs varied and changed as they evolved over centuries. We are notably familiar with bows of the Scythians, Mongols and Turks to name just a few among so many.

These bows are known for their power, efficiency and durability. We know that Turks have shot incredible distances with their short recurved flight bows. One of those shoots stands out more than others. It was 972 yards shot by Sultan Selim in 1793.

History of the Asian-type bow

Let us take a brief tour into the history of these bows. Their remarkable qualities can be attributed to their unique design and materials used for their construction, hence the composite bow. We also know them as horn bows, because one of the components in the bow is a horn from a hoof animal like water buffalo, cattle or wild sheep. The basic premise of their construction is simple, yet complex. The weapon consist of four basic materials: horn for compression, sinew for tension, wood as foundation or as a skeleton of the bow, shall we say, and glue, which holds everything together.

Often times we ask ourselves the question, how did the ancients come up with such an advanced weapon? Well, it did not happen overnight. It took hundreds of years of trial and error. The evolution which the composite bow has undergone takes us through ancient places and civilizations which have long faded into the dusty and forgotten pages of history. We can most certainly trace its origins

www.lrgaf.org

to somewhere in Central Asia, where the domestication of the horse took place. These two aspects, horse and the bow, go hand in hand. Had it not been for the horse, perhaps we would not have the composite bow as well. Archery, in this part of the world, danced to the beat of the horse's hoofs.

A few terms may need to be clarified for the reader just entering the discipline. When a bow is drawn, the belly (the side next to the archer) undergoes compression or crunching, whereas the back of the bow (the side away from the archer) undergoes tension or stretching. An additional factor called sheer is where the two forces of compression and tension meet in the central vertical line of the bow from a side view.

Some of the first composite bows were of wood construction merely reinforced by a layer of sinew to prevent the bow from breaking under tension. Such bows were still in wide use by Arabs for many centuries. As time went on, their construction became more involved; now the weapon consisted of several pieces of wood differing in stiffness and elasticity, all enveloped by one or several layers of sinew. Naturally, the qualities of the horn for compression were discovered and came into use soon after. Here, we can finally see a full-fledged "horn bow". The depiction of such articles is clearly seen in the artwork from the period. One does not need to look any further than ancient Assyria and Egypt, although, this type of bow came to Egypt via Central Asia. We recognize two types of bows dating to this period of about 2500 BC to around 800 to 700 BC. One is a angular bow, the original reflex/deflex bow, clearly depicted in paintings and stone carvings as well as a few specimens surviving in museums today, like the ones found in the tomb of King Tut. This composite was quite particular to Egypt, but we can also see its wide use in ancient Syria and Assyria where it probably originated. There was another design, used especially throughout Persia of a less complex D shape of the same construction.

The bows began to change with improvements in metallurgy. The iron first and then steel, carbonized iron, came on to the scene in about 1000 to 800 BC. With that, the defenses against weapons developed as well. The armor became tougher to penetrate and therefore the bows needed to change to be able to penetrate such armor. Tremendous changes happened in bow designs, and for the next several

www.lrgaf.org

hundred years we see that the composite horn bow is taking on its classical shape we so admire today. It began with strongly double curved bows of the tribes of Scythia and evolved into static tip bows of China and Turkic tribes of Central Asia. From there it spread with nomads to Persia and Anatolia. Subsequently it was adopted by Romans and Byzantines as well.

The superior mechanics of the Asiatic horn bow

We can easily emphasize what makes these bow designs so special. It is the actual working limb and the employment of the static tip for improved leverage that sets them apart from the plain wood bow. It is also the composition of the materials that is so unique. The selfbow is made of a single piece of wood or two pieces spliced in the center. It can only take so much stress, both in tension and compression, that one needed to make the bow either long enough to lessen the stresses or be robbed of the draw length when made shorter; otherwise the bow would break. To overcome these problems the ancient peoples looked for alternative materials. It was the sinew that helped prevent breakage under tension. Some of the wood thickness was replaced by sinew, which is far more flexible than wood and has a better memory to retain its original shape. It can stretch and contract at a greater rate, and wood became thinner because some of its thickness was replaced by sinew. The result was that the wood core could bend more easily. This concept allowed for much shorter bows with greater flexibility.

The next stage in development employed the use of horn for compression. Horn is far superior to wood under compression and the strip of horn applied to the belly reduced the thickness of the wood even further, now allowing it to be even more flexible. In this case the wood no longer undergoes both tension and compression; those forces were handled by sinew and horn. The wood core became a platform or a skeleton onto which, like muscle and tendon, the horn and sinew were attached. Now, wood had to endure the sheer stress only.

With this final improvement, we have a weapon that is far more efficient than anything before its conception. With such a combination of materials, one is able to build bows of reduced length with much shorter working limbs allowing easy handling when mounted on the horse. The other advantage of the reduced length is that the bending radius is greatly reduced producing a much faster recovery upon release. This gives us not only greater speed but better efficiency as well.

Let us go into greater detail, describing the actual working limb and comparing it to its predecessor, the wooden bow. Unlike any other bow, the horn composite has little or no taper in the limbs (when viewed from either the belly or the back). That alone is a key ingredient of efficiency, contributing to the shorter bending radius of the limb. This is an ultimate combination creating speed, efficiency and a hand shock-free bow, normally associated with other bows with tapered limbs. The last unwanted behavior in the bow limb can be best explained by illustrating this example. As the wooden bow is being drawn and then ultimately the arrow released most of the energy is transferred into the arrow and the energy that is left in the form of vibration has to travel through the limb. It is the direction of the travel in which the energy leaves the bow that determines more than anything, whether the bow will be hand shock-free or not. The wooden bow limb bends at the tip first and the bending slowly progresses toward the handle section. Upon release, the limb springs forward, the energy that has not been transferred into the arrow then travels back from the tip into the handle in a form of vibration, thus producing the hand-shock effect. In a composite bow, the flow of energy is totally reversed. The limb starts to bend, upon drawing, closer to the handle and then towards the tip. Therefore, when the arrow is released, the vibration travels from the riser or handle to the tip, where it disappears in to thin air.

There are other factors that influence the degree of the hand-shock, like the physical mass of the bow limb. This is not, however, always applicable, especially in the composite or at least in some designs of these bows. Many bowyers would argue that less weight in the tip gives more speed and less hand shock, but in a horn bow, it is not entirely true. Surely, there must be equilibrium in the weight proportions of the bending and non-bending portion of the limb, but because of the way the bow transfers energy through the limb upward upon release, these factors are pretty much negated, even if there is a bit more weight in the static portion of the limb. This extra weight in the static tip also helps to create better efficiency. It is true that a lighter bow tip will affect the speed at which the bow limb recovers after release, but only with the arrow that is carefully matched to it. It does not have enough mass to push heavier arrows and the speed of the arrow is greatly reduced. Hence it is less efficient. The static tip, therefore, gave us not only leverage but better efficiency as well. The shorter bending limb with its faster recovery more than compensates for the additional weight in the tip.

We have covered just about everything in regard to mechanical properties of bow limbs, both in a simple wood bow and a composite. We must mention the invention of a static tip in a horn composite bow which provides leverage. There are actually two reasons for this static tip called a siyah. One of them is very simple, to obtain a sufficient length on the bow. In some areas, it was probably difficult to obtain horn strips long enough. The long static tip made up for that deficiency, but before it was realized, it served another function as well; this function is most important. The long static tip or the long rigid section of the non-bending portion of the limb simply made the bow easier to pull. It was the application of leverage. It either happened entirely by an accident or it was invented.

We know for a fact that these types of composites started to show up on the battlefield soon after the time of improvements in metallurgy. As mentioned before, it was the discovery of iron and then steel production. As the armor became tougher, there was a need for better penetration. The limbs became shorter, stiffer and the addition of the long static tip made it possible to bend such weapons with ease. These tips or rigid sections of the limbs are often as long as the bending limb itself, and it was the length and the angle (from a side view) at which they sweep off the bending limb that determines the degree of leverage itself. All we have to do is look at a couple of examples. One is a "crab" bow of northern India and the other is a Chinese bow of the Manchu period. It is very interesting to see the force draw curve of these bows. You might go as far as saying that this is a predecessor to a modern compound bow with its pulleys, because to a certain degree it fulfills the same function. Innovation in our world happens out of necessity. It is a reaction to an action. Improvements in defenses forced the ancient people to come up with better offensive weapons and so the struggle for the dominance on the battlefield continues today.

Our modern composite bows, used for mounted archery, are different from anything else on today's market, because the designs have evolved from the historic roots of Asiatic composite bows. The appearance alone sets them apart. The unique limb design of these bows is the culmination of many years of not only study, but also the painstaking process of recreating authentic horn bows. This kind of deep understanding can only be gained from the experience of building horn bows of Turkish, Scythian and Mongolian origin. They are a direct derivative of their ancient cousins.

Modern horseback bows

We have just described the physical properties of horn bows and what makes them function so efficiently, but here is a new challenge. How do we transfer these properties into a bow built from modern composites? I have been constantly in search of the most efficient design, using modern materials, and it is an ongoing process. Horn bows have been my motivation from the beginning, and the rich history they have left behind has become a constant source of inspiration to me. I like to think that the use of the most technically advanced materials in combination with outstanding historical tradition sets the modern horsebows apart from the rest, in their performance, efficiency and their gracefulness.

Our modern horseback archery bows can not duplicate but only simulate the workings of their ancient predecessors. Perhaps we may come to the conclusion that we are somewhat limited in trying to simulate the horn bow with these new materials of wood and fiberglass, but that poses new challenges to myself as a bow maker. We have to realize that materials used in both types of bows are inherently different. The reason we can not duplicate the shape of an unstrung horn bow in fiberglass is two-fold. First of all, fiberglass is an artificial substance and it will not stretch as much as sinew will, although it is very strong. Secondly, it will be very unstable if too much reflex is designed into such a bow, due to the lack of mass in the limb. They are simply too thin to not twist. Also, because the material has an incredible memory, it will not take a set. The horn bow on the other hand was initially made with a lot of reflex simply because of its tendency to take a set. To compensate for this, the bow had to be made in such manner, otherwise it would lose its performance with too much string follow. These bows were also left strung for long periods of time

www.lrgaf.org

and the strong reflex helped to maintain its shape and tautness for months at a time. After the use, either a hunting expedition or war, the bow was unstrung and depending on the length of time it was used, the bow was allowed to rest in a dry warm place to regain its original shape. Sometimes, warming cabinets were used to speed up the drying process.

There are other qualities in modern Asian-type composites which are lacking in horn bows. It is not their durability, but rather how easy they are to string and take care of which is a big advantage to a modern archer who does not have the experience to handle a horn bow. The replicas of bows made of natural materials are susceptible to many conditions in our natural environment. One of them is weather. The poundage in a horn bow will fluctuate from summer to winter by as much as five pounds. That is because heat and cold affects the bow as much as it does us. After all, the weapon is made of the same components as our body: tendon and glue, which are actually forms of protein, and horn, which is basically the same thing as hair. We all get somewhat stiff when it is cold and loosen up when it is hot, so does such a bow. It becomes quite supple in summer and stiff in the winter.

On the other hand, we do not experience the same phenomena with our modern composites. They are affected very little by temperature. They also do not need to be properly balanced after the initial stringing. That alone can be a problem for many people who are not familiar with this type of bow. As far as comparing longevity of the two, we know from old records that the horn bow had a life span of well over one hundred years, even if used on regular basis. We simply can not say that about its modern cousin. The fiberglass has only been around for about fifty years now. It is so true that horn bows are extremely durable. I have seen these bows in horseback archery related accidents and they came out perfectly intact. The same can not be said about fiberglass composites. They, on the other hand, can be quite fragile, especially in such accidents. Just to give you an example, I have watched a wreck where a horse fell down with the rider and rolled over the horn bow. I saw limbs twisting in every direction, but to my surprise the bow was all right, a little bit dirty perhaps but otherwise undamaged. A few minutes later, the next rider took a very similar fall and his fiberglass bow broke under the weight of the horse.

There is something to be said about the boundless flexibility of a true horn composite. Each weapon has its pros and cons. One just has to decide which is more suitable for his or her needs. It really comes down to whether we want instant gratification or whether we are willing to put up with some inconveniences that in the end will bring their own rewards. It is like fly-fishing. Do we use graphite or bamboo. Both fulfill the same purpose, but in my book I would pick the bamboo. I suppose I'm a romantic. Although, I have to be honest with you, most of the time I practice my horseback archery with one of my fiberglass bows, precisely for the reason of instant gratification. I just string the bow and go.

There is a cost consideration involved here as well. That alone usually tips the scale in the favor of the modern composite. Horn bows are very expensive, because they are difficult to make and only very few people are competent enough to make them. It also takes a long time to make one. The fiberglass bows can be had for a fraction of the cost and fulfill the same purpose.

Choosing and shooting your horsebow

Whatever bow you choose, make sure it is the right bow for you. One should not select based on looks of the weapon alone. It is important to choose the bow according to ones stature, draw length and strength level. If you're a tall person, do not get a bow that is fifty- two inches long; it will not accommodate your draw length. For beginners, it is wise to get a longer bow. They are more forgiving. Concern yourself with learning the proper technique of shooting as the main goal. It is important that the bow is comfortable for you to shoot. The style of the bow at this point is not important at all. Later on, one may choose to emulate a certain style of archery, but not until your shooting is proficient enough; then perhaps you can choose the style of bow you really like. I have already touched on the subject of the length. This is very important indeed. The shorter the bow, the more difficult it is to master. As I said before, they are not as forgiving. Many people imagine horse bows as being very short and having limitless draw: not so. The short bows will feel stiffer in hand and not as smooth;. that in turn will impede your shooting. Therefore to avoid any frustration as a beginner, heed my advice and take the path of least resistance.

www.lrgaf.org

The poundage of the bow is equally important. Many archers make mistakes by acquiring bows that are too heavy for them. They are simply "overbowed"! That is especially important in mounted archery. Few realize that shooting from a horse's back is an entirely different affair. On the ground, our whole body works in unison pulling the bow which makes it easier to handle bows of higher weights. It is an entirely different feeling shooting from the horse's back. Your lower body, from the hips down, has to work in unison with the moving horse and your upper body with the bow. You're divided in half, so to speak. Shooting this way is therefore more difficult, especially on the backward shots. Believe me when I tell you if you can pull sixty pounds standing on the ground it will feel like eighty on the horse. You simply can not use your whole body to brace yourself for the shot. Most horseback archers today use bows that do not exceed forty pounds, the average being about thirty-five.

I have also been asked a question whether there is any difference between symmetrical and asymmetrical bows. Frankly, the only small advantage I see in the shorter lower limb of a asymmetrical bow is when it comes to maneuvering it off the horse's back. It definitely made it true in the case of Japanese bamboo composites, which were about seven and a half feet long. Here, it was a necessity to make a lower limb one-third of the length of the whole bow to be able to use it while mounted. Other than that, I do not believe there are any noticeable advantages to bows of an asymmetrical shape.

One area we should explore more thoroughly is the actual profile of the bow. It is very important to us primarily because of today's style of shooting. As we know, the Hungarian form of shooting during competition requires us to hold the arrows in the bow hand along with bow itself. It eliminates the need for pulling and nocking the arrows from the hip quiver. This form of shooting brings forth the need for suitable profile and the style of handle to accommodate such an endeavor. Bows that have too much set back in the handle section, so called double curved bows, prevent holding arrows comfortably and force them to protrude into the site window, thus interfering with aiming and shooting itself. It is especially true in thumb ring shooting. The shape and size of the handle is just as important. You should always select a handle that fits your hand, meaning not too big, nor too small. The reversed handle styles of Turkish bows do not lend themselves very well to holding arrows in one's bow hand. Any low to medium high set back in the handle will do. Just stay away from the bows which have too much set back in the handle if you're looking for versatility. The handle should not have any style of pistol grip or shelf cut into it. It is not traditional and it also is a hindrance while shooting. Besides, it is prohibited by competition rules.

If you choose not to hold your arrows in your bow hand and rather pull them directly from the hip quiver, then the profile or the style of handle is not important. This style of shooting became prominent later on, as it is evident in the pictorial record of antiquity. It allowed for a greater safety while riding and shooting. When arrows are contained in the quiver one is less likely to impale oneself in a fall. It is not so when you hold arrows in your bow hand, as I can attest to that from my own experience. One time during competition the horse under me tripped and as I began to fall forward the arrows in my hand fell out and spilled in front of me, going in every direction. In horror and slow motion, I realized that I was falling directly towards the arrows and that I could possibly get impaled on one of them. When I hit the ground, the only thing imbedded in me was a mouthful of dirt between my teeth. I was lucky. This experience only reinforced my theory about why the horseback archers of the later period chose to use the hip quiver and nock the arrows from it, instead of holding them in their bow hand. The issue is safety first. Yes, this technique is slower, but safer. I have not stopped using Kassai's method of shooting because of my fall, but I'm careful now and more conscious of how to get rid of my arrows, should I fall again. Just toss them off to the side. That is one thing I reinforce in my student's mind.

Today's horseback archer should be flexible in using many techniques and should choose the bow that will be most versatile to fulfill the needs required by competitions today. I personally teach both thumb ring and three finger styles of shooting. They have their place, not just in history, but in our contemporary endeavor as well. Lastly, whether you choose to shoot with three fingers or a thumb ring, it will not have any effect on what type of bow you choose.

We all have to agree on one point. Archery has played a major role in our civilizations. From East to West, the bow and arrow, to a lesser or greater degree symbolized human prowess on the battlefield or in the sport of shooting. It served to protect and ward off enemies or put food on the table. It also meant a whole lot more to some particular cultures. There, the bows were involved in religious ceremonies and everyday rituals. Next to the horse, the bow was the most sacred thing to possess. In Indian cultures of North America, women were not allowed to step over the bow. The weapon was treated with utmost respect. In legends, the arrows shot from a bow by national heroes established boundaries of Empires. In Islamic cultures, according to the Koran, the shooting of the bow amounted to a noble deed and everybody was encouraged to participate it. The Bible itself mentions the bow and arrow on many occasions. I could go on and on in greater detail about the importance of the bow and arrow, but it would probably amount to a book just on this subject alone. Even after the bow lost its importance as a weapon on the battlefield, it survived until today. That alone is evidence in itself of how it impacted our cultures. The lore of the bow and arrow is still alive and thriving.

Our revival of horseback archery is the latest addition to the survival of the most noble discipline in archery. The combination of horse, man and the bow makes it by far the greatest achievement of skill. The impact of the horseback archer on our modern world can not be underestimated. The mounted warriors of the past changed the landscape of our cultures. With the death and destruction they brought on their ponies, they also opened new routes for the cultures to exchange goods and ideas from East to West. Perhaps had it not been for Genghis Khan, we would never have experienced the Renaissance. Thanks to Lajos Kassai of Hungary, we now ride again and continue that tradition. The bow, arrow and a horse will forever stay as a reminder of our great past and the warrior inside of us.

References:

Faris, N.A. and Elmer, R. P. (Translators and Editors) 1945. Arab Archery: An Arabic Manuscript of about 1500. Princeton, New Jersey: Princeton University Press.
Grayson, B. 1993. Composite Bows. In Traditional Bowyer's Bible, Volume II. Azle, Texas: Bois d'Arc Press.
Heath, E. G. 1971. The Grey Goose Wing. Especially Chapter 2, The Great Composite Bow: The First 2000 Years. Greenwich, Connecticut: New York Graphic Society Ltd.

Karpowicz, A. 2006. Ottoman Bows in the Topkapi Palace Collection. Journal of the Society of Archery-Antiquarites.

Klopsteg, P. E. Originally 1934, current 2001. Turkish Archery and the Composite Bow. Manchester, England: Simon Archery Foundation.

Latham. J.D. and Paterson, R. N. (Translators and Editors) Originally 1368, current 1970. Saracen Archery. London: The Holland Press.

Lawrence, L. September/October, 2003. History's Curve. Saudi Aramco World. This reference is primarily the story of the old and modern horseback archery bow focused on the bow making work of Lukas Novotny.

Selby, S. 2003. Archery Traditions of Asia. Hong Kong: Hong Kong Museum of Coastal Defense.

Chapter 12

Horses in Horseback Archery of the Americas

by Dana Hotko

In this chapter we cover the horse, your partner, in this horse archery sport. We will briefly cover its origins in the Americas and then come up to modern times to describe some of the breeds or types and some of their characteristics as well as what to look for in a good horse archery mount. Hopefully some of your more major questions will be answered.

Re-entry of the horse into the Americas

To begin with, one must understand that the prehistoric horse became extinct on the American continents thousands of years ago. The horse as we know it today was first brought to the United States in the form of Portuguese and Spanish breeds (such as the Marchador and Barb) in the 16th and 17th centuries. With interest in the "New World" among other European nations came some of the Northern European breeds and types. It is also speculated that during the slave trade of the 17th and 18th centuries, that a few examples of the Arabian horse came over from North Africa and the Middle East.

Through those Spanish and Portuguese imports we now have that blood, primarily, in our Marchadors, of South America, Paso Finos, Barbs, Andelusians, of the North and South Americas, and of course our famous Mustangs of the North American West. All have maintained a fair degree of breed or type consistency except the Mustang, which resulted from the wild, open range survival of Spanish horses that escaped human captivity. In becoming a free-ranging animal, the mustang lost some of its Spanish refinement and in most cases, through natural selection, became a rougher, hardier horse.

Concerning Arabians in the Americas, one needs to consider that there are several strains and many sub-strains. A majority of these were started in this country in the late 1800's and throughout the 1900's. One of the few exceptions to this is the theory that pertains to the first Morgan horse possibly being part Arabian or a strain of Arabian that was and is a more muscular, masculine type.

When the subject of Northern European breeds comes up, the primary breeds thought of pertain to work type or larger-boned, taller horses. However, the thoroughbred type horses were bred in Europe and brought over to America also because racing was taking place in Europe and in early America as well.

The breeds or types being used for mounted archery in America today include Marchadors, Paso Finos, Quarter horses, Mustangs, Arabians, Tennessee Walkers, and the Appendix (Thoroughbred/Quarter cross). This does not exclude other breeds because this writer considers it only a start, as many other breeds or types can be used and are used in other parts of the world.

Choosing a horse

The horse-archer must choose a horse according to what is available in the area and what he or she can afford financially. This area of the chapter is meant to help guide the prospective horse archer into, hopefully, choosing the right horse. Within each horse breed are the characteristics that make it a type or particular breed, characteristics that are physical as well as mental. These characteristics are not to be taken as "gospel" as there are exceptions to every rule, these are only generalizations. There is also great variation within each breed.

We will start with the Arabian, what some consider the most versatile of all the breeds, a breed that has existed for many hundreds of years. The reason it is considered the most versatile is that there are seven basic strains which differ greatly in muscle mass, roundness, basic build, and temperament. Being bred by isolated groups in the desert for different purposes, different builds of Arabian horse emerged. The strains vary from the most muscular "masculine" Hamdani and Kuhaylan strains to the finest boned effeminate Saglawi and Obayaan strains. In general, the Arabian has very good, strong hooves and legs without very many problems. The spine has one less vertebrae; as a result, the overall back length is a little shorter. One must be aware when fitting a saddle to an Arabian horse that it must be a little shorter.

Temperament can be a problem with some of the Arabian horses available as many of them are derived from "show lines" and do not tolerate objects like arrows and bows around their heads. One must be very careful in the Arabian selection process or make it simpler by selecting from "old" bloodlines that have much more stable individuals much more consistently. As a horse archer, I prefer the older "Blue List" or "Blue Star" bloodlines for equestrian martial arts.

When a person says Quarter-horse, does any one type come to mind? It shouldn't. Quarter-horses can be of almost any body build and size. A large percentage of the time when one is dealing with a Quarter-horse we are speaking of a horse that can be a mixture of other breeds but is part Arabian, Turk, or Barb blood and is a more muscular, well-rounded horse. Quarter-horses are considered by some to be the American breed. There is not a common body type for Quarter-horses as there are so many sizes and shapes. Quarter-horses, in the mid-west to western U.S., tend to be working horses and appear to be very tough and hardy. In the Eastern U.S., many are used as trail horses and show horses – the "Pleasure Horse." The original Quarter-horse bloodstock was brought about by the breeding of the finest horses in the North American continent. Those horses were a mixture of Turk, Barb, and/or Arabian bloodlines. Theses horses were then bred with horses brought to the "New World" by north and central Europeans into the colonies.

During the Spanish conquests of South America, several differrent types of horses were brought over and bred or cross-bred. Some of these breeds, now, are known as Andalusians, Spanish or North American Barbs, Paso Finos, and Marchadors. Of these, the Marchadors in South America and the Paso Finos have been used for horse archery. As with most of the horses that originated from the Iberian Peninsula area of the Mediterranean, they are renowned for being easily trained and people-pleasing horses. Some contend that the Marchador was already a breed before coming to the Americas from Portugal and others state the Marchador was developed from crossing different types of horses originating from the Iberian Peninsula after they came to South America. Paso Finos were also developed by crossing breeds already brought to the "New World."

Today's Thoroughbred is renowned as a racehorse in the Americas. However, in recent years Thoroughbreds are becoming more and more available to the average horse owner through race tracks at very

www.lrgaf.org

reasonable prices. The first Thoroughbreds were a result of bringing two Arabian sires and a Turkish sire to England from the Mediterranean region or Middle East around the turn of the 17th century. These sires, being bred to native English breeds at the time resulted in horses with the ability to carry more weight, and be faster over longer distances than before.

Mustangs today are being used by a few horse archers. Primarily the Mustang is a more accessible horse to people who reside in areas of the western United States. However, occasionally, through projects supported by the Bureau of Land Management, people in the Eastern U.S. are also able to get hold of them. One of the more prominent horse archers in the U.S., Pat Stoddard, took an antelope with a bow from the back of a Mustang some years ago during a long and rapid chase. Jay Redhawk, in South Dakota, also has killed buffalo from the back of a Quarter/Mustang type horse, after quite a chase, with a traditional bow and arrows with flint heads. The Mustang is obviously a very hardy and durable animal partly due to the natural breedings and the habitat in which it survives in the wild. It has thrived in parts of the American West since the times when its ancestors arrived in the Americas. These ancestors would be horses from the Iberian Peninsula as well as Barbs and Middle-Eastern horses that the Spaniards and Portuguese brought with them in the 1500's. Some of the smaller, isolated groups of Mustangs even retain, to some degree, some of the individual characteristics of the breeds of their ancestors. For instance, some bear strong resemblance to Barb horses of North Africa and Spain even today.

The Appendix is also used in horse archery today in America. It is a result of crossing a Quarter-horse with a Thoroughbred, the result being a little bit more "level-headed" durable type of horse than the traditional Thoroughbred.

I had the pleasure of watching a large draft horse during a competition in Ft. Dodge, Iowa, some years ago. Aside from the fact that the horse wasn't really built for doing 90 meter sprints up and down the track, it did hold a rather long but definitely rhythmic stride conducive to shooting from horseback.

In actuality, we see that many different breeds are being used in horse archery circles with great success. When the average horse archer chooses a horse, the general characteristics of different horse breeds need to be considered more than the availability of horses in the area. The following are some of the criteria I go through when looking for a suitable horse archery mount. Some of these criteria may pertain just to my area of the United States and some are country-wide. You must understand that choosing this prospective horse archery mount is not unlike choosing a friend. Some mounts can easily be your friend and some will never be your friend.

One of the first things to catch your eye when you look at your prospective mount is the way the horse carries itself. That is, observe its attitude and how it reacts to its surroundings. Is this horse afraid, curious, angry, or friendly? Does the horse move with confidence or indifference or is it even aware of its surroundings? Some of the most intelligent horses out there will look for a way to get out of work, similar to people. The object is to pick out a horse that one can bond with so that both horse and rider can perform to the best of their abilities – understanding always that a horse is an unpredictable being and can, in the wrong situation, react adversely.

Also, one of the things I consider is the health of the horse. There is an old saying, "Never buy a lame racehorse," that applies here as well. Lameness does not only apply to physical well-being but also to mental well-being. Some horse injuries can heal without permanent damage and some cannot. Know the difference! For instance, in my area, we have quite a few horseracing tracks. It is not unusual to be able to obtain a Thoroughbred horse for a very low price because it doesn't run well on the track. Look at the feet and legs for chronic problems! Also, racehorses can have a hard-to-work-with mentality when it comes to doing more controlled tasks. Horses can also have mental scarring that impairs performance, perhaps from previous abuse or neglect. There are a million trainers out there and some use rather traumatic methods of training that can affect the attitude a horse has toward doing anything new.

Another few points for me to look at as a practicing horse archer are the body-build, speed, and rhythm of the prospective mount. I personally prefer a mid-sized, more slightly-built horse with a differrent rhythm or speed than what I have already in a mount. The more experienced horse archery student will seek out horses that differ in rhythm and speed so that he or she may expand equestrian skills.

In summary, what matters concerning the horse archery mount is that it is physically able to do the work and has the attitude and willingness to work with new surroundings. For the person who wishes simply to do archery as a hobby from the horse's back, there are horses out there to choose from, even for the novice of this particular sport. If a person takes his or her own time and pays attention to the rules, a good horse can be obtained at a very reasonable price. For the novice, do not go for the "green broke" horse or the horse that no one has ridden for many years. Get a horse suitable to your abilities and needs. Those of us who shoot off the horse regularly are constantly looking for that physically and mentally suitable horse to obtain and add to the stable, and it need not be expensive. My last one was free; I'll have to train him myself, but that is completely within my abilities. I passed up a very well-trained Andalusian stallion with dressage training for free last year because I didn't have the space. Now I am watching a 14.2 hand Quarter-Horse mare, waiting for her to have a foal so that I can obtain the mare after weaning for $400. The horses exist, just be patient for the right one. Think: 4-H kids go off to college; where do their horses go?

Training the horseback archery horse

In training a horse archery mount, we will consider, for the hobbyist, that the horse is already trained to ride. There are a whole set of new situations to train the horse to accept. In the beginning, the horse has to become accustomed to the sound of the bow being shot and arrows flying at all directions from you on its back. This can be started by shooting ground archery, in a confined paddock at a target, with the horse wandering comfortably around the paddock. Do not accidentally shoot the horse! In the next step, tie the horse to a post or some other secure object close by while you shoot at the same target, watching carefully for the horse's reaction. If things are consistently good, saddle the horse and shoot on the ground at the same target. This serves to connect the shooting with the horse being saddled for work. At this point, shooting should occur from many positions around the horse, being very aware of the horse's attitude. The final step in the beginning is to sit on the horse, while it is saddled, and shoot from the horse as it stands or walks calmly around the paddock. Always be aware that you can take a step back and rework a particular step as you go if the horse reacts adversely.

In the mid-stage of training a horse-archery mount, most work has to do with riding the course or along a fence-line in order to give the horse a sense of something to follow in its line of sight. We start this exercise at a walk repeatedly many times (10 to 20), then at a trot, the same number of times, then at a canter many times. Build up to cantering the course with the reins dropped. If the horse does not respond appropriately to each step as it progresses, back up and start over at the previous step. Each step may take hours, days, or even weeks. Every horse is different. If training is progressing well, the horse should be ready to try out on the 90 meter course.

In the final steps of training, your horse archery mount should do most of its work on the course. A curved entry into the traditional Hungarian course should aid the animal to be in the left lead and stay in that lead for stability of rhythm. The rider should do all of the necessary things to encourage the horse to maintain a steady rhythm and speed. Some horses will run the 90 meter course in 15 to 16 seconds, while others will run very fast, in seven to eight seconds. Try to develop a rate of speed that is comfortable for you both. Once a manageable speed and rhythm have been established, the rider may consider shooting at a side target, always taking into consideration the horse's attitude. If all goes well, the rider may then consider forward shots. If good progress is still being made, move to the back shots last, as this leaves the rider at his or her most vulnerable position for injury. The horse must accept the rider in any position, shooting any direction.

One of the common denominators for all archery horses is that they are schooled to maintain a constant performance. This maintains the consistency necessary to perform well for both rider and horse. After all, training a horse does not stop when you get off the horse; it continues always. When you are in the presence of the horse, you must always have that horse's attention, to some degree. This is how you bond with the horse and get the horse to respond to your needs. Even when you walk the horse from one location to another, you must have that horse's attention; otherwise you'll get run over or stepped on. Bluntly, you either train the horse not to step on you or invade your space, or the horse trains you to get the hell out of the way. Training and conditioning must go on continuously.

www.lrgaf.org

In conclusion, the horse that does the best job is not a horse of a particular breed, but a horse that is worked with often. It's not a horse of a particular color, but a sturdy, even-tempered horse that is willing to work and be exposed to different things with acceptance.

References:

Bennett, D. 1998. Conquerors: The Roots of New World Horsemanship. Solvang, California: Amigo Publications Inc.

Draper, J. 1996. The Book of Horses and Horse Care. New York: Barnes and Noble.

Hendricks, B. L. 1995. International Encyclopedia of Horse Breeds. Norman Oklahoma: University of Oklahoma Press.

Miller, R. M. and Lamb, R. 2005. The Revolution in Horsemanship. Guilford, Connecticut: The Lyons Press.

Skipper, L. 2001. Inside Your Horse's Mind: A Study of Equine Intelligence and Human Prejudice. London: J.A. Allen.

Chapter 13

Saddles and Tack:
From Early Man to Modern Mounted Archer

by Barbara Leeson

Man's relationship with the horse and development of tack was born out of need to control a herd animal. The horse soon evolved into an important mode of transportation, vehicle of war and indicator of one's status and wealth, with tack evolving to suit each need. Today the horse is still seen as such by different cultures, as well as being a form of personal expression of a rider's identity, life and beliefs. Tribal lines of the horse cultures are no longer defined by territory but by our riding discipline. It is our tack which identifies us, whether it is dressage, team penning or mounted archery.

The Early Beginnings of Horse Tack

It is important to understand that some aspects of the history of equine domestication and early development of tack are hotly debated. And until irrefutable proof of dates and locations are uncovered they will continue to be so. The earliest example of one of these debates is where and by whom the first horses were domesticated. Most agree that this event happened between 3000 BC and 2300 BC, some claiming by the farmers of China, others suggest that it was by a nomadic steppe people living near the Black and Caspian Seas. It is also very possible that there was parallel development in both places, and others, at the same time.

There is also emerging evidence and research from the Institute for Ancient Equestrian Studies that would throw off the commonly agreed timeline. Horse bones along with those of domesticated sheep and cattle have been found deposited in human graves dating from 5000 BC on the Ukrainian steppe. Their further research also indicates skeletal remains of horses from the Botai site in Kazakstan, 3500 BC, show signs of wear on the teeth consistent with the use of soft bits.

www.lrgaf.org

What is certain is that man learned that he could keep horses much like he had been keeping cattle and used them for many of the same purposes: meat, milk from mares, and hides for tents and clothing. Early restraints were twisted fiber ropes wrapped around the nose or a nose ring, as was used by the Mesopotamians. Both systems were borrowed methods used to restrain cattle. These methods evolved into the use of a rope or leather thong wrapped around the lower jaw, a technique used much later by the Native Americans.

Horses also followed cattle into the role of draught animals, resulting in the need for better control, which led to the creation of a basic bit and bridle. Made out of leather this bridle would have included a thong passed through the mouth and attached to something resembling today's halter. Over time the bits were made out of thicker and stiffer material, and bone or antler terminals added to the ends to keep the bit in place.

It was not until after man had mounted up (around 2000 BC) that metal bits were developed and by 1500 BC two types of bits where in use. Both easily recognizable as forerunners to today's snaffle, one used a straight bar as a mouthpiece the other a jointed bar. Their use quickly spread across Eurasia and beyond both east and west. By 600 BC further control was added to these bits by using spikes on the inside of the bit terminals that would press into the soft sides of the horse's face when the reins where pulled. The bridles themselves had also become richly decorated and a sign of status and wealth.

Two hundred years later, the next major development came from the Celts of Gaul who had by 400 BC developed the curb bit which was imported to Rome after Caesar conquered them. It was the Romans who developed spades and ports on the basic curb bit, sharpening the action of it. After the curb was introduced the external spikes used on a bit fell from use. However, they were sometimes added to the inside of the bit as pikes, rollers or sharp disks. Greek General Xenophon endorsed this practice though did allow that "you must refrain from pulling at his mouth with this bit".

"Civilized" man's search for more control is not surprising. Horses were being carefully bred by some cultures for size and spirit, and maintained on a diet of corn and other grain. Lacking the benefit of a supportive saddle, the rider would want to maximize control of a strong, hot horse, especially when used during shock tactics in war by a

www.lrgaf.org

Roman heavy cavalry. It should be noted that the nomads of the steppe used a snaffle almost exclusively throughout their history. This is possibly due to their use of light cavalry tactics in war, the temperament of their horses, and the diet they provided to their mounts.

The development of the saddle parallels man's growing use of riding for travel and war and his need for comfort and security astride. By 600 BC, riders used a basic saddle cloth with a girth and breast strap and sometimes breeching around the hindquarters. It was the Scythians who took this basic idea one step further. The Pazyryk burial mounds, located in the Altai Mountains and dated 500 BC, contained examples of their well thought-out saddle pad design. This design consisted of two stuffed felt pads which would lie on either side of the horse's spine, joined together at the front and back by leather straps and held in place by a girth, breast strap and breeching. This pad would sit atop a saddle cloth, both highly decorated in embroidery and appliqué work.

The Pazyryk tombs are an important find of note; the site has given us a better and deeper understanding of the Scythian culture and beliefs. Not only did they contain many full skeletons of horses and fine examples of their tack, but also examples of textiles and domestic goods of these steppe people.

The Sarmatians, neighbors of the Scythians to the west, took the Scythian advancement and added a wooden arc-shaped frame to the front and the back of the pads. This would hold the pads together and keep it in place over the horse's withers and spine more firmly while giving the rider more security while mounted. It was also the first step towards a saddle tree. Native Americans would also develop saddles along these ancient lines after the re-introduction of the horse in America by the Spanish. First using a saddle cloth then developing a saddle pad and ultimately a saddle tree, all would have been richly decorated with beading and dye work.

Further developments of a wooden tree spread through war and trade in all directions covering the area from Japan to Rome, and began to show regional and cultural differences. One feature all saddles developed, in various forms, was a prominent cantle and pommel to keep a rider, without the benefit of stirrups, securely in the saddle.

Stirrups also have a cloudy history with many cultures and countries claiming to have originated them. Not surprising, as it greatly improved mounted war tactics for both heavy and light cavalry. Our first indication of the stirrup comes from India around 100 BC, a simple loop in which the big toe was placed was used, and it is not unreasonable to think this idea spread and was changed and enlarged to accommodate the foot.

There is also some well borne evidence that the stirrup was first developed as an aid in mounting a horse, not to support a rider. A pottery figure of a cavalry member from the Western Jin Dynasty (265 – 316 AD) is shown with a single stirrup on one side of his saddle. Far to the west, the Romans rode with a pair of "skala" meaning step or stair attached to their saddles, and the Old High German, Old Saxon and Old English words for stirrup are based on words for climbing, although they were introduced to stirrups later than the near and far East.

No matter why the stirrup was initially developed, mounted warriors and cavalry quickly grasped the significance of a stirrup that could be used to mount then braced against while riding. Both light and heavy cavalry where able to ride faster and cover longer distances without tiring as quickly and when engaged in battle they had more security and stability in the saddle.

The use of stirrups reached Europe in the mid to late 5th century, certainly helped along the way by the Huns' occupation of Hungary and raids into Western Europe. By the 10th century the stirrup was widely used. Saddles had reached a fairly sophisticated level in construction, design and ornamentation, as had bits and bridles, and all three continued to evolve in sophistication of design and ornamentation.

At this point in history, development of tack, through the advancements in training ideas, slowly swings from the east to west with Europe making further contributions towards what would become standard in today's tack. The crusades gave birth to ideals of chivalry and spawned jousting tournaments which in turn introduced the idea of pageantry. By the 16th Century Renaissance period, young well-born men were expected to take an interest in horsemanship, and baroque riding schools were established beginning the "classical" riding movement and further advances in tack design.

The early eastern saddle influenced the saddles of the fully armored knight in Western Europe and beyond to the saddles used in the dressage and jumping rings today. Meanwhile, western riders today enjoy the foundation laid down by the early Moors who used a saddle with a horn that was refined by the Spanish before being brought to the Americas.

Man's use of the horse and development of tack has been an interesting journey, 5000 years in the making. Today's rider enjoys the benefits of this journey, which defines what tribal discipline we belong to, while being comfortable, and practical.

Tack of the Mounted Archer Cultures

Most saddles from the different mounted archery cultures look very similar. All share a simple four-piece construction, consisting of two saddle bars, with a pommel and cantle joining them at front and back. The seat of these saddles would be a carved wood insert, or rawhide stretched between the pieces. These similarities are not surprising due to the exchange of goods between cultures and tribes, from trade and war. However, differences in their construction or decoration will usually indicate their origin.

The following is by no means the definitive description of the saddles used by these different cultures during the same time period. Provided here is an overview of some of the best examples history has left us, of the individual style of saddles, at their peak of development and ornamentation.

Mongolian, Chinese and Tibetan

The saddles used by the people now living in Mongolia, Tibet, China and surrounding areas would usually be built with a high, upright pommel, in the shape of a curved inverted "V" or "U". The cantle might be a more rounded arch or echo the shape of the pommel. Depending on the saddle's use, the cantle would be positioned upright or angled back, and in some cases almost flush, with the back of the saddle tree. The people of Mongolia showed the greatest variation in the shape of pommel and cantles. Tibet saddles the least variation; they were usually built with a thick, inverted "U" shaped pommel and cantle.

Mongolian steppe herders still use these types of saddles and display an interesting form of decoration. Large silver buttons are used on the seat cushions and to decorate the saddle bars as a display of the owner's wealth and status. These buttons are referred to as "whites", and saddles are categorized by the number of "whites" they display, i.e. a saddle with four of these large silver buttons on it would be called a "four whites" saddle.

Regional and cultural variations determined the mode and style of decoration on the saddles. Pierced, gilded or enameled metal work, ivory inlay, and sometimes ray or shark skin coverings on the tree were all used. Saddle pads tended to be felted or woven in bright colours and patterns. The Mongolians particularly favored long pads that extended down the sides of the horse. A leather covering, carved or embossed, was sometimes used overtop of the saddle pad.

Stirrups tended to be basic in construction, a metal arch or circle with a footplate. A common ornamental theme on Chinese stirrups was two dragon heads on either side of the mount where the stirrup leather passed through.

Bridles could be very plain or highly decorated with pierced or enameled metalwork, depending on the occasion and owner's status and wealth.

Japan

By the Edo period the warriors of Japan had developed their stylized "Kura"; these saddles are the most easily recognizable of the Asian saddle types. Both pommel and cantle are in pleasing round arches symmetrical to each other, angled outwards from the seat and extend several inches down past the side-bars. Covered by lacquer, the saddles usually feature understated decorations such as a family crest on the outside of the pommel in gold leaf.

The stirrups, or "Abumi", used with these saddles are easily identifiable. They are cast iron, sculptured platforms that the entire foot rests on, with the front sweeping up and over the toe and back to a buckle that attaches to the stirrup leather. They sometimes feature exquisitely executed inlay designs.

Breeching and breast straps were often used, made with long, thick fringes that would dance with the horse's movement. Bridles were also often festooned with fringe and tassels. This elaborate tack can still be seen during many Japanese mounted archery ceremonies today.

The Moors and Middle East

India, Persia, Turkey, and North African regions developed saddles with the cantle usually in a rounded arch low to the back of the saddle offering a very shallow seat. The pommel rises in a sculptured inverted "V" and ends in a rounded upright horn which is sometimes carved to resemble a knot. These saddles were usually lacquered in brilliant colours, sometimes with inlayed pearl shell. Another variation from these areas is a saddle style more resembling an Asian type with a high pommel and cantle.

Saddle pads would have been finely woven, with geometric or zoomorphic designs. If owned by the wealthy, these saddles would be completely draped by a velvet saddle cover that had been richly embroidered using silver or gold thread. Tassels were used to trim bridles, saddle pads and embroidered cloths that extended over the horse's back.

It is interesting to note that Moorish and Japanese stirrups did for a period resemble each other. Both types of stirrups were a solidly constructed platform of metal on which the entire foot rested. However, the Moorish stirrup is joined to the stirrup leather in the more conventional fashion.

Hungarian

Due to the Huns' occupation and influence, the Hungarian and Eastern European saddles emulated those of the eastern steppe in design. The pommel and cantle mirror each other in angling away from the seat. The cantle being of the round arch style and the pommel an inverted curved "V". Both may end with a small knob or horn used to suspend a rawhide seat, on which a leather or fabric seat cushion was attached.

The Hungarians also had a love for rich fabric and embroidery to display their wealth while mounted. They would incorporate both into decorative seat cushions and protective "saddle holders", a cloth fitted over the saddle. Pierced and repousse metalwork would be used to decorate the front, back and edges of the pommel and cantle. These types of embellishments would carry over to the fine bridles these horses wore, as well as quivers and bow cases.

Modern Mounted Archery Tack

Modern horse archers have a huge selection of tack available to them today, made in different styles and different materials; it can be a little overwhelming when starting out.

The English Saddle

There are many variations to the English saddle, all purpose, dressage, and jumping being the main types. Jumping, and to a lesser degree, "all purpose" saddles have the benefit of being built to supporting the leg with a shorter stirrup in the modified two-point position sometimes taken when shooting astride. Dressage saddles, although not as supportive to the leg in the two-point position are built to support the leg down and around the horse and tend to be more deep seated, which offers the riders a more secure and balanced seat.

The Western Saddle

Even more so than the English saddle, the western saddle has many variations based on its intended use. Roping, reining, barrel racing and western pleasure saddles all have slight design variations. Add to this the regional variation from Spain, Brazil, Mexico, Australia etc; and you have an overwhelming set of choices. Western saddles, due to their uses, offer riders great support while riding and doing other tasks at the same time. They tend to be deep seated and offer novice riders a greater feeling of security while they develop a balanced seat. Experienced riders enjoy the comfort of the saddles and the security offered when performing the high speed maneuvers needed in roping, reining, and shooting. The only drawback of some western saddles is that due to the large stirrup fenders and its construction a novice rider might find it difficult to keep their leg in a supportive position while shooting in a two-point stance. This is certainly not the case in all western saddles but may occur in some.

Mounted Archery Bareback and with Pads

Mounted archery done bareback is the ultimate test of horsemanship and marksmanship, there is no replacing the feeling of a horse striding out beneath you once you have mastered the balance and skill required. Bridging the gap between saddles and bareback riding are "bareback pads", usually a saddle pad type cushion with a girth. They offer a measure of extra padding between the horse and rider, but little in the way of support or security. Some bareback pads come with stirrups; however this is more of a dangerous hindrance than a support tool, especially when used by a novice or unbalanced rider. Without a rigid tree the saddle pad can easily slip sideways or completely roll when uneven weight is even briefly applied in the stirrups.

Traditional Mounted Archery Saddles

A dressage rider uses a dressage saddle, a cowboy ropes from a western saddle. Form follows function in any riding discipline includeing mounted archery. It would be hard to try and improve upon saddle designs that were developed by the ancient mounted archers whose lives depended on a secure saddle that afforded maximum support and maneuverability while shooting. A lesser reason for investing in a traditional saddle is for competitions, demonstrations and displays. It completes the picture of a mounted archer and the pageantry of the art.

From time to time truly exceptional saddles become available online, usually on auction or Asian antique websites. Either antiques or contemporary saddles brought out from a country still using traditional tack can be a once-in-a-lifetime find. Investing in one should be done as one would invest in art. Buy it for the appreciation of its workmanship, decoration and design, for it is questionable if it will fit the types of modern horses currently used for mounted archery in America. Cheap traditional styled saddles are often available from Asia from online auctions. These fall into the strictly decorative category or to be bought to study their design as they are often cheaply built without the horses' conformation in mind.

Luckily for today's mounted archer, functional reproductions of traditional mounted archery saddles are available from other sources. Lajos Kassai has for many years been building and selling saddles based on a traditional Hungarian style and he was the first to seriously undertake recreating saddles specifically for mounted archery.

In the United States, Lukas Novotny, owner of the Saluki Bow company, has been designing and crafting saddles that reflect a number of Asian and eastern European mounted archery designs. They are often embellished with beautiful traditional cut work in brass, bronze, and silver. From Canada and apprenticed under Lukas is the author of this chapter, also providing mounted archery saddles of traditional design, as well as bits and stirrups.

Stirrups & Girths

Both stirrups and girths should suit the saddle you are using. Stirrups should be large enough that the rider's toes and lower foot cannot become wedged in or stuck when the foot is placed properly. A wide variety of safety stirrups are now available, some which break away if the rider falls off with the foot stuck in the stirrup, others that have a covering over the front of the stirrup which prevents the foot from slipping through and getting caught.

There is a wide range of girths on the market today and many new innovations in design and materials have been made to make them more comfortable for the horse. Choose a girth of the appropriate length for your horse, and check after the first few rides that it is not causing rub marks or sores.

Cruppers and Breastplates

As mentioned in the saddle fitting section, these are sometimes needed to keep a saddle in place. However they can also be used purely as decorative costuming.

Bits and Bridles

There is a stupefying array of both western and English bits available to riders today, each one of which can be an aide or, in the wrong hands, a punishing tool. A bit and bridle should allow the rider to guide and control the horse along with leg and seat aids, regarding direction and speed, without pain or damage inflicted on the horse.

Most bits fall into two categories: the curb bit and the snaffle bit, each of which have many variations, and although a curb bit is considered more severe then a snaffle, variations in both can change that.

The snaffle bit may have a jointed bar mouthpiece which attaches to two rings outside of the horse's mouth to which the reins and headstall are fastened. It acts mainly on the horses tongue, lips and exposed gums between the incisor and molar teeth when the reins are pulled. The curb bit can also have a jointed or solid mouthpiece and is positioned the same way in the horse's mouth, but the mouthpiece is attached to a vertical shank instead of rings and uses leverage action instead of direct force. The headstall is attached to the top of the shank with the reins attached to the bottom. Sometimes a curb chain is also attached so that it rests in the horse's chin groove. When the reins are pulled, the bottom of the shank is pulled back, levering the upper shank forward and putting pressure on the horse's sensitive poll, (area behind the ears), via the headstall. A port or spade shaped piece rising in the middle of the mouthpiece, will increase the action of this bit by putting pressure on the roof of the horse's mouth.

When choosing an appropriate bit the rider must take into account his or her own riding skill, and the horse's level of training. Louis Taylor points out that a given bit must be coupled with appropriate use. Riders are sometimes tempted to upgrade to a more severe bit when facing control issues. However, upgrading to a severe bit can cause a downward spiral where one severe bit is exchanged for something more severe and onward. This strategy can cause other behavior problems and will deaden the horse's mouth and attitude when being ridden. It is far better to examine the rider's skill and horse's suitability and training for the work it is being asked to do, then seek knowledgeable help to work through issues. Horses can perform quite happily with a severe bit when ridden by a knowledgeable person, but in general it is far better to start with a mild bit, good advice and good training practices.

Bridles come in a variety of styles, English and western. Since the function of a bridle has not changed in thousands of years, the main difference is in the style and decoration. Choose a bridle that fits your horse and complements him and you cannot go wrong.

Hackamores, Bosels and Bitless Bridles

These types of horse headpieces work by way of pressure to the nose and poll of the horse in concert with leg and seat aids. Although they seem less aggressive than bitted bridles, they can still be abusive in the wrong hands and care must be taken when using them. Much like Dana Hotko's Arab mare Murphy, some horses are more comfortable being ridden without a bit and with proper training will do just as well, or better.

Reins

Most bridles come complete with reins. For the purpose of mounted archery they should be of a length that drop comfortably in front of the saddle, or if using a western or traditional saddle behind the pommel or horn, without too much excess. English reins will need a knot tied in them to prevent the excess from dragging to one side of the horse where the horse could potentially put a foot through and trip. Western pommel and split reins are unsuitable for this reason. Reins adjusted too short can travel up the horse's neck and be difficult to reach after shooting, so care must be taken when finding the right length.

Western barrel racing reins are ideal for mounted archery. They are of a one piece construction with no center buckle or knot. Their length can be adjusted on the ends which attach to the bit and they are available in a variety of styles and colours that complement both English and western bridles.

Martingales, draw reins and the like may be classified as training aides. These are effective only if the rider's hands are on the reins and their use is limited on a mounted archery course.

The Importance of Saddle & Tack Fitting

No matter what type of tack is ultimately chosen it is a priority that it fits the horse and rider, in that order, correctly. A horse wearing a saddle that fits through the withers and a bridle that is adjusted correctly with the appropriate bit, will be a much happier partner to train and shoot from. We will take a brief look at tack fitting; however this overview should not replace expert advice when choosing your tack.

Fitting a Bridle

The crown piece is used to hold the bit in the horse's mouth and should be adjusted so that the bit sits in the mouth between the teeth on the jaw bars. A good indication of this is that 2 "wrinkles" appear in each corner of the horse's mouth. The throat latch is to stop the bridle from slipping forward over the horse's head. As such, it should be tight enough to prevent that, but never so tight as to interfere with the horse's breathing and flexion. The brow-band or ear piece stops the bridle from slipping back on the horse's neck. Neither should rub on the ears nor pull the bridle forward tightly. The noseband, if used, should be loose enough that the horse can flex its jaw. When tightened it should allow two fingers to be inserted between it and the horse's nose and sit mid-way between the corners of the mouth and cheekbone.

Saddle Fitting

A saddle that correctly fits a horse should distribute the rider's weight evenly on both sides of the horses' spine and not interfere with its natural movement. One way to check for even weight distribution is to remove the saddle after riding and see if there is an even and symmetrical sweat pattern on the horse's back. This indicates a saddle that distributes the rider's weight evenly. An asymmetrical or spotted sweat pattern would indicate that the saddle doesn't spread the weight uniformly. It shows that the saddle is "bridging", not in contact with the horse's back uniformly. The uneven sweat pattern also indicates that there are areas where the saddle is concentrating too much weight onto that one area, forming a pressure point.

There should be no direct weight on the horse's spine or as far back as the loins in order to avoid soreness. The gullet must be wide enough to clear the spine when a rider's weight is applied. A saddle should not pinch the withers or bind the shoulders, it should sit comfortably behind the shoulder and conform to the horse's side, not perched on top or slumped onto the top of the withers. Distribution of stuffing in a saddle or padding used underneath it can also affect saddle fit. Inappropriate padding can position a rider so that he or she feels they are riding uphill and behind the horse's motion, putting excessive weight on the back of the saddle, or have a rider sitting downhill riding into the horse with disproportiate pressure on the withers. Neither situation will help the horse or rider and can cause soreness in both.

Cruppers and breastplates are sometimes needed to prevent a saddle from slipping forward or back. Sometimes both are used to keep a saddle from rolling. This rolling can be due to an improper fitting saddle or to the horse's own conformation. Wither pads, shims and lift pads can be used to adjust a saddle to a horse. However, a well fitting saddle is preferable and these pads cannot fix all problems.

Tack Maintenance

Tack can be a major expenditure. Keeping it clean and well-maintained will insure many years of use from your investment. Clean any dirt or sweat off after each ride and giving it a thorough cleaning at least twice a year using a leather conditioner and saddle soap. This will extend the life of your tack beyond years. A rider will also do well to be especially vigilant about the condition of his or her girth, stirrup leathers and reins, and should check their condition and stitching regularly. Should one of these break, especially while riding at speed, serious injury can follow.

Leather or Synthetic?

Most pieces of tack, including saddles, are available in the traditional leather or in synthetic materials, both have pros and cons. Leather is traditional, long wearing, and ages beautifully. However it can be weakened by environmental conditions especially if the rider does not take care to maintain it. Synthetic materials do not suffer much from environmental conditions and are easy to clean but can show signs of wear and tear more rapidly depending on the materials.

www.lrgaf.org

Buying Used Tack

Well made tack is often available second hand at tack stores, auctions and online outlets giving riders the option of paying less while still getting quality tack. The key is to make sure the used tack is of good quality, has been maintained well over the years and most importantly will fit you and your horse. Check the quality and condition of the material and stitching. To make sure that the saddle tree is still intact, pick up the saddle and place the cantle of it against your stomach, grab the pommel with your hands and try to bend the saddle back towards you. If there is significant movement in any direction then the tree is likely broken and the saddle unusable. The one exception to this test is if you've picked up a spring tree saddle, this type of saddle will flex when tested this way. However, it will flex smoothly and evenly, springing back to its original position when the pressure is released.

A less obvious flaw in used tack is a twisted tree; in this case the rigid tree has literally twisted. This requires careful eye-balling from the back and front of the saddle making sure the centre of the cantle lines up with the centre of the pommel and vice versa. Buyers should inquire if there is a return policy or trial period on the tack, new or used, in case it proves not to fit the horse and rider or shows other flaws after it has been tried the first time. Auctions are unlikely to provide this option but many tack stores do.

In the end.....

The tack you choose will (for better or worse) affect you and your horse's comfort and skill at mounted archery. Choose wisely and with knowledge. There is no "wrong tack" as long as it is functional and comfortable to you and your horse.

References:

Atlas of the World, Third Compact Edition. 2000. New York: Random House.

Dennis, G. T. (translator), 1984. Strategikon. Philadelphia: University of Pennsylvania Press.

www.lrgaf.org

Edwards, E. H. 1995. <u>The Encyclopedia of the Horse</u>. Toronto, Canada: Reed Books.

Henderson, C. (Consulting editor). 2002. <u>The New Book of Saddlery and Tack</u>. New York: Sterling Publishing Co.

Hyland, Ann. 1994. <u>The Medieval Warhorse: From Byzantium to the Crusades</u>. Gloucestershire: Sutton Publishing Limited.

<u>Imperial China: The Art of the Horse in Chinese History, Exhibit Catalogue</u>. 2000. Kentucky: Harmony House Publishers.

Internet. The Institute for Ancient Equestrian Studies. http://users.hartwick.edu/iaes/index.html

Karasulas, A. 2004. <u>Mounted Archers of the Steppe, 600 BC to 1300 AD</u>. Oxford: Osprey Publishing.

Taylor, L. 1966. <u>Bits.</u> Hollywood: Wilshire Book Co.

Chapter 14

The Mounted Archery Association of the Americas (MA3)

By the Association Officers

The two main associations in this section on mounted archery organizations have a lot in common as well as having distinct differences. Both organizations have a deep commitment to promote the great potential of mounted archery. Both organizations owe a debt of gratitude to the founder of the standardized European discipline— Kassai Lajos. Kassai has left a major mark upon us on two counts, namely his vision of the positive inner mentality of the discipline, as well as the outer visible standards for training and performance. Kassai's book, <u>Horseback Archery</u>, presents both the inner and outer parts of the discipline effectively and artfully. Kassai's interest in seeing his program and rules promoted in the United States is furthered by Kassai USA and his official representative, Todd Delle. Todd resides in the beautiful Flathead Lake area of Montana which provides a wonderful context for training and competitions; that story is given in the next chapter.

Probably the biggest difference in the two associations is the degree of strict adherence to the European standards of competition versus a more eclectic set of competitive events. The Mounted Archery Association of the Americas (MA3) builds on the standardized Kassai competition course with some target and scoring modifications, but entirely new events are added to the formal competition schedule. The MA3 disciplines and rules are presented at the end of this chapter. Individual records for competitions are posted on the association website. Another difference is that MA3 focuses on all the Americas, from Canada to the southern tip of South America.

Expanding participation

The long-range purpose of MA3 is to introduce the sport via mass demonstrations and mass media to a wide audience, while continuing to recruit and cultivate a relatively modest body of committed performers. Since the introduction of the discipline into the United States in 1998 the purpose has been to nurture a small core of trained mounted archers in order that they could disseminate the message and share the sport with others in an initial building stage. In other words the initial goal has been training, whereas the objective needs to shift to include mass exposure. There is no illusion of expanding to the scale of golf or tennis, much less the major sports. At the writing of this book, the discipline is generally unknown on any broad scale, but this is changing. Exposure has largely been to archers and equestrians via repeated articles in Primitive Archer magazine, and to the fervent but modest audiences and participants at the International Horse Archery Festival in Fort Dodge, Iowa. The more recent goal of establishing decentralized, scattered training sites throughout the Americas is being accomplished. At this point we owe much gratitude to our lead trainer Lukas Novotny for his dedicated and skillful training to ever extended clinic sites in Canada, Iowa, Ohio, Oregon, Hawaii, and Brazil, not to mention his international outreach beyond the Americas.

Mounted archery is a great activity and so it is just natural to want to share it and get the story told. As outlined in the Introduction, the stimulation of the discipline is unique in coupling the mind and body of the archer using the bow with the innate dynamics of a large intelligent mount. The great potential for inner personal growth and development also needs to be noted repeatedly. In reaching out to mass audiences, we want to do two things. We want to multiply the number of persons training for the discipline, and we want to super multiply the spectator and general support base. The spectator vicariously reaps a portion of the stimulation and growth of the performer. In turn spectator activity can facilitate the support needed for mass media exposure and publicity. The modest fees for membership are used to fund either development of events or publicity for those events.

www.lrgaf.org

Incorporation and funding

The Mounted Archery Association of the Americas, Inc. is indeed incorporated and is completing the requirements of the non-profit 501 (C) (3) Internal Revenue code. The Association is controlled by a board of directors elected by the membership at large. The four traditional officers are elected by the board of directors. On any given year, when there is a major national event staged by the Association, a live face-to-face annual meeting will be held during that time; otherwise the annual meeting for business and elections will be conducted electronically.

Organizational income consists of membership fees, gate fees at demonstrations and competitions, and fees from trainees registered for clinics. Grants may be pursued as well, especially for special efforts such as a targeted educational exhibit. Typical expenditures often include items such as insurance fees, horse rentals, and deposits for demonstration sites, etc., but these change as conditions and needs change. Because this is a young organization, there will be unanticipated problems to solve in spite of good advanced planning.

The role of the website

The website for the association is playing a critical step in reaching a wider audience. Links to our website from archery and equestrian sites are proving to be an effective connection. Events for a given year are listed and described for everyone with access to the Internet. Data about clinics, demonstrations, seminars, and competetions are fully presented so readers can do advance planning. Dates, places, fees, deadlines, event descriptions, and accommodations are presented for easy access. The administration of the association is on a volunteer basis but we will try to answer all inquiries as quickly and efficiently as possible.

The officers and board of directors and their locations are listed so that the reader can get a better picture of the scope of the organization. Membership is focused on North and South America, but is open to any applicant anywhere. Membership is open to all ages but voting privileges begin for members over 18 years. Members are kept

www.lrgaf.org

fully informed of the ongoing business aspects of the organization. A yearly outside audit is conducted and reported to the members.

The well developed association website has been very helpful in conveying the progress, maturity, and well-established nature of the organization. It is a great tool for both business and educational objectives. The developmental aspects of business such as exploring and securing new sites for demonstrations, securing insurance coverage, negotiation with banks, and bargaining for equipment and horse transportation have all been greatly facilitated. Educationally, both mounted archers and spectators should be well served. Frequently occurring questions and concerns of mounted archers are answered in a Q and A section. An array of select published and unpublished articles and essays are available to all persons perusing the website. Relevant books are listed and reviewed periodically. This book is easily available via amazon.com, but sources for less accessible books are noted.

Pageantry

The development of some appropriate pageantry for opening parades and closings at demonstrations is another current objective of the Association. Lukas presents several beautiful costumes and some nice saddle adornments, but most of our riders in the ceremonies are still working on this part of our mission. The emerging philosophy about costuming is that each rider chooses his or her own costume; it should be inspired by one of the Asian tribal groups which entered and integrated into the cultures of eastern Europe, but we do not want to get hung up on strict period authenticity. Bright colors, and dramatic display are paramount, building loosely on the spirit of the chosen period or tribe. Each horse and tack should likewise be adorned with a theme of color, motif, and style chosen by the owner. For competitions, plans may move toward one uniform robe-like garment or kaftan of one color for all, with skill levels being distinguished by the color of the sash around the waist or over the shoulder.

As opening ceremonies and closings evolve, some simple choreographed movements will enhance the pageantry. For example, from a formation of a group of horses standing abreast facing the audience, one or two mounts could step forward and do side-passes in unison first to one side and then to the other. The equestrians in the audience may recognize that we appreciate their various special interests. It would not be claiming that we incorporate dressage, but would offer some respect to horse people similar to learning some words and phrases of a different language when visiting outside one's country.

As the reader can see, MA3 is a growing organization with a strong foundation, but with much pioneering work still ahead. It welcomes your membership and participation in strengthening a great discipline and making it accessible to a greatly expanded audience.

Competition rules

Qualifying to compete

All MA3 competitors or horses new to our competitions must pass the following tests. 1) Riders must be able to show control at the walk, trot, and canter. 2) Riders must demonstrate care and control while making one side shot on the course at the canter. 3) Horses must be calm and manageable at the canter while a rider is making a side shot on the course.

General rules

The following rules apply to all competition disciplines or events unless otherwise stated.
1) The competitor's horse must be in a canter or gallop and remain on course for a score to be taken.
2) Each competitor will have three passes at each discipline which will determine his or her final score.
3) Competitors will have opportunity to do warm-up prior to the running of a competition or discipline as dictated by the competition Judge.
4) Bows cannot be compound, or crossbow types, nor have mechanical triggers or sights. They have to be of traditional style such as Asian, Middle Eastern, or Native American with simple handles and without arrow shelves, shooting windows, or pistol grips.
5) The Judge's decision will be final on all scoring and judging matters as they unfold on the course.

www.lrgaf.org

The three disciplines

Discipline One, standard Hungarian-type course.

Each competitor will canter down a 90 meter course divided by four 12 foot high posts which divide the course into three equal sections. A three-faced target is placed at the center of the course (45 meters) but seven meters off to the left side of the course. The competitors will shoot as many arrows as possible at the appropriate target face as designated by his or her position between the posts. The course must be completed in 16 seconds or less, otherwise no score will be recorded for any targets hit during that pass.

The targets and scoring are as follows. The targets are standard school and recreational 32 inch Styrofoam forms covered with a skirted target face of five colors and are widely available. Scoring of the three targets is according to the difficulty of the shot.

Forward or approach shot: gold = 6; red = 5; blue = 4; black = 3; white, = 2.
Side shot: gold = 5; red = 4; blue = 3; black = 2; white = 1.
Parting or backward shot: gold = 7; red = 6: blue = 5; black = 4; white = 3.

In addition, time remaining under the 16 second limit on the stop watch when a run is completed will be added to the points scored (1 second = 1 point). If no targets are hit during the pass, no "time points" will be awarded. See the layout of the course in the diagram on page 170.

Discipline Two, moving targets.

Each competitor will canter the 90 meter course and attempt to shoot at three moving disks. The throwers (three of them) will stand 4 meters from the center of the course, and 5 meters down-course from each of the three respective drove posts. For the standardized competition with formally recorded scores, the disks are rolled on the ground. The course again must be completed in 16 seconds or no score will be recorded regardless of the number of hits. The self-made 6-ply corrugated cardboard disk target will be 1 foot in diameter and painted

www.lrgaf.org

and scored as follows. Red center = 7 points; white outer ring = 5 points. Bonus points for speed of the horse are exactly the same as in the "Hungarian course" described in the discipline immediately above this one. A faulty throw can be called by the Judge followed by a corrected throw requiring an additional pass by the competitor.

Discipline Three, alternating targets.

Each competitor will canter down the 90 meter course with 5 targets presented — 3 on the left, and 2 on the right side of the archer. The targets are inspired by the Japanese Yabusame, 1 foot square of breakable material such as cedar shingles, cardboard, or flexible plastic. Left-hand targets are positioned 4 meters from the center of the course and with the center of the target being 2 feet (61cm) above ground level. Right-hand targets are 2 meters from the center of the course and with the center of the target being 2 feet (61 cm) above ground level. All targets are placed 45 degrees to the course. The sequence of shooting this discipline, where L = left, and R = right, is L, R, L, R, L. All arrow points in this discipline must be rubber blunts for safety's sake. See the three-discipline diagram. Hits for the left-hand targets have a value of 5 points, and hits on the right-hand target have a value of 7 points. (See diagram on page 171.)

The number of warm-up runs will be decided by the judge at each event and may vary with the experience of the body of competitors, the condition of the course, and especially the training level of the horses. Each competitor is scored on three runs of the course for each discipline, for a total of 9 runs in a formal competition. As stated above in the general rules, the total score for a complete competition is the simple sum of the three discipline scores.

Informal non-standardized demonstrations and competitions may be staged in indoor arenas on shortened courses but none of these scores would be entered in the Association record book because the conditions are totally different and are not comparable to the standardized course. On the other hand informal scoring would be possible in order that competitors could see their relative standing for that particular occasion.

www.lrgaf.org

Safety and course layout

All equestrian sports are high risk activities. The accident rate however for this discipline is low if safety rules are carefully followed. At all times safety will be in the forefront of any competition and rules can be modified as needed by the circumstances of the location. We encourage all riders to use helmets and competitors under 18 years of age are required to do so.

Separation of spectators from the shooting action is critical. A 75 meter space behind the targets must be totally blocked off from all spectator traffic. On the spectator side of the course, a 10 meter safety buffer from the center of the course must be well barricaded. Even though bright colored rope would seem to be good material to demarcate areas, it should not be used anywhere on the course. If a horse panics, bolts and gets twisted into a rope, panic is likely to increase and the rope can burn or cut like a knife. Use standard 3 inch traffic tape. There should be two strands on the fence to separate spectators from the course. Permanent standardized courses may use a ditch-like formation with 10 inch high earth berms on the sides to help guide the horses down the track which is one meter wide. An alternative is to use flexible plastic posts with one strand of traffic tape on each side of the course. Posts must be flexible in case a rider falls on a post. The full 3" tape will flutter in the wind and some horses may have trouble adapting to it. A solution is to split the tape down the middle to a 1 ½ inch width (or twist the tape), the wind cannot catch it nearly as much and it is still strong enough to be durable.

The backdrop is partially a safety feature, but is more a matter of facilitating arrow retrieval. On a permanent course, it should be built as an earth mounding. Because the center of the targets for Discipline One are 2 meters above ground, the top of the earth mound should be 4 meters high at the center, should extend laterally 17 meters each way from center, tapering to 0 elevation at the ends of the extensions. The whole mound structure should form a slight semi-circle from the top view; the extension tips come in toward the track slightly.

If a competition is staged on a more temporary course, the backstop may be constructed of a wood frame covered with flakeboard or arrow netting. The total frame consists of five segments 4 feet wide and 12 feet high. One 4 foot by 12 foot segment will face the course and will hold the right angle or side shot target. Two other 4 foot by 12 foot sections will flair or "swing" back 15 degrees from the right-angle target on either side of it. The targets are centered vertically on these winged segments. An additional 4 foot by 12 foot section is then added to each of the flaired wings in order to catch more of the errant arrows. Please note that these additional 4 by 12 foot extension sections have not been drawn in on the diagrams of the course.

If one is constructing a more permanent course with an earth mound, the spacing of the three targets can be deduced from the dimensions just mentioned. In this case the three targets are usually mounted on one strong 6 inch by 6 inch timber, with steel or wood framing in the back in order to present the targets at the correct height, correct angles, and at the correct distances from each other.

Code of conduct

Competitors are to act professionally at all times, mindful that the public, event sponsors, facility management, and staff are deserving of respect. On the course or off, any competitor acting in an unsafe manner, one that is detrimental to the running of the competition, or one that reflects badly on other competitors, event host, or official may be eliminated from the competition without any monetary refund of the entrance fee.

Other organizations

The International Horse Archery Festival based in Iowa will continue to champion the discipline. New efforts to promote and sponsor mounted archer events are emerging independently. These organizations are springing up spontaneously and testify to the desire for the discipline and its dispersion at the grass-roots level. War Horse Challenge is a good example, as well as mounted archery events within the Creative Anachronism organization. There may be others.

Although this book focuses on the Americas, we are very mindful of the strong organizations around the world. Yabusame groups have been on the scene for centuries. Kassai's international organization is well established and growing. The Society for the Promotion of Traditional Archery in England has been active in mounted archery. There is a growing group in Hong Kong, and the International Horse Archery Federation based in Korea is drawing international participation.

****

References:

Gray, David. Winter 2005. Mounted Archery at Seven. Primitive Archer.
Kassai, Lajos. 2002. Horseback Archery. Budapest, Hungary: Puski Kaido, kft.

www.lrgaf.org

Chapter 15

Horseback Archery World Association (HAWA) and Kassai USA

by Todd Delle

Kassai USA is the American branch of The Kassai School of Horseback Archery and represents the Horseback Archery World Association (HAWA) in the United States. HAWA is the association that connects some fifteen Kassai Schools together across the globe. Each of the individual schools, referred to as a Törzs or Kánság, is led by a person who has fulfilled the requirements set by the association. These include not only showing proficiency in competition but also successfully completing examinations and demonstrating a working knowledge of the rules and training methods forming the foundation of the Kassai style. These leadership positions are elected by the membership. I currently fill two positions, Törzsfö and Országfo. As Törzsfö, I have the responsibility of providing training opportunities for members, hosting competitions, and conducting examinations of members earning their degrees. As Országfo, I simply have the responsibility of making certain all matters concerning HAWA in the United States are carried out correctly and efficiently. This position also includes a seat on the board of HAWA, where I represent the United States.

The Kassai School of Horseback Archery teaches horseback archery as a martial art. This involves both ancient and modern techniques. The common thread weaving throughout these techniques is that the keys unlocking the doors to each new level of competence are found within the individual. Archery, when practiced in its purest form, involves a bow with no mechanical aids, an arrow, and a person. The person will not become an archer until he can reach inside himself to solve the problem of putting the arrow in the target. As this understanding of the bow and arrow becomes deeper, the arrow finds its way into the target under more and more difficult situations.

The art of riding is much the same; the solutions come from within. Instructors can offer suggestions and guide you to the answers but they cannot crawl inside you and show you how it feels to move in harmony with a horse. Timing, feel, and balance come from within the individual; there is no way to mechanically substitute for these feelings. Those who are fortunate enough to gain an understanding of either the discipline of archery or riding will tell you that this understanding leaks into other areas of life until it becomes a part of their lives. Those who combine the arts of riding and archery into horseback archery find something more. One leak becomes two. The leaks combine to become a flow. This flow then finds its way into every corner of life until it becomes not a "part," but a "way" of life. It is this way of life that has captured the spirit of a few people each generation for thousands of years. It is also this way of life we pursue within the Kassai School of Horseback Archery.

As the most prominent horseback archer of our time, Kassai's work and dedication to the development of horseback archery as a martial art is unmatched. It is because of this dedication that I have the opportunity to bring the Kassai School of Horseback Archery to the United States. It is impossible to separate the schools in any of the different countries from each other, or from the head school in Hungary. We share a common training format developed in Hungary by Kassai Lajos. The scores of the competitions held in each nation are submitted annually in our World Cup series. The scores of each member competing in more than one competition are averaged to determine ranking. (For example, in 2006 I competed in Hungary, Canada, and the United States.) Examinations are standardized and members who have earned any of the degrees or titles are able to train in any of the schools, with confidence that basic exercises and form drills are consistent. As a Törzsfö I know that a member who visits me from another Törzsfö or Kan will be ready to fulfill any responsibility befitting his rank.

I met Kassai Lajos at the first International Horse Archery Festival, held in Fort Dodge, Iowa, in September of 2000. From this first meeting two things became very clear to me. First, Kassai had a vision for developing and spreading a modern version of the ancient discipline of Horseback archery. Secondly, this was something I wanted to be a part of. It was impossible at that time to know the seeds planted then would take almost four years to sprout.

In August of 2004, I had the honor and privilege of bringing to the United States the first sanctioned Kassai Horseback Archery competition held outside of Europe. This also included a small training camp where I began to introduce the training methods developed by Kassai Lajos in Hungary. Each year since then I have hosted two international competitions and training camps during the summer. I also offer on-going training opportunities for members of the Kassai School here in the United States.

Start of the Kassai School

The Kassai School began in Hungary in the mid 1980's, but the vision had started many years before, with one child's interest in not only learning about, but also experiencing the ways of his ancestors. Childhood dreams and play rarely manifest anything more than sweet memories, but, Kassai Lajos has held onto the dreams of his childhood to ride the Steppes with bow in hand. The visions of the child are not quite what the reality of the man has become. Instead of riding over the Steppes leading in battle, Kassai travels the world sharing an almost forgotten art. Although he does not lead countless warriors, he does lead a small group of dedicated people who study the system of training and competition he has developed.

It is my opinion, labeling this style of Horseback Archery a "system" is not only incorrect and misleading, but also completely unfair to its founder. A system implies that if you follow the steps correctly and in the proper order, you will arrive at the designated result each and every time. What Kassai has created is a style of horseback archery. This style is taught and practiced in a manner causing it to become a personal journey, or "way," and when we cross the line dividing "system" from "way," we have crossed the line dividing sport from martial art. Kassai's story of how he developed his approach to horseback archery is chronicled in his book, Horseback Archery.

For Kassai Lajos what started as an exploration into the ways of his ancestors has grown into an international association, the Horseback Archery World Association. This association is based on his methods of training and competition. One man, with a horse rescued from the slaughter house, has transformed an idea into an association of hundreds of members, with representation in twelve countries (as of 2006) spread throughout Europe, North America, and New Zealand. Schools are developing rapidly in other nations.

www.lrgaf.org

The beginning of Kassai U.S.A.

The development and practice of Kassai USA parallels the development of schools in other nations. We who have started a Kánság or Törzs of the Kassai School in our home countries share a love of history and horses. For me, this lifelong interest in both archery and history included collecting antique weapons. My research included the use of replicas of many different weapons, including bows.

My study of the history of horsemanship brought things full circle. I was able to combine history, weapons, and horses. My first attempts at shooting from the back of the horse were standing, or at the walk, while hunting whitetail deer in Montana's forests. Using the horse allowed me to approach within eight to ten yards of the deer while mounted. This method was useful for me, but not exactly what I would consider a sport for the masses.

Through the efforts of David Gray, I was introduced to Kassai Lajos. That introduction dramatically changed my approach to Horseback Archery. Earlier in this book David Gray gave the history of how he met Kassai and his arrangements for bringing him to the United States and introducing his style of Horseback Archery. It was David's effort and others' which resulted in the International Horse Archery Festival where I met Kassai.

During the years 2000-2004, I spent a large amount of time getting to know Kassai and learning more about his method of training. This included training with him here, at IHAF, and traveling to Hungary two to three weeks each year for both training and competition. My first trip, in the spring of 2002, was an exercise in patience for both of us. I had no idea what to expect. After attending two training sessions here in the United States and being able to exchange letters, I was still completely unprepared for my first training camp in Hungary, both physically and mentally.

Looking back on that first visit to Kassai's Valley, it was no more than an audition. The Magyars are a very close knit group of people and membership into the Kassai School requires that at least three current members recommend you. Finding acceptance into the family there is not difficult, but you must be willing to put your best into everything you do while at the school. This means not only during training but also during work time or preparing meals. Each person who trains on the school property has a responsibility to maintain it and share the workload.

As each year passes and I return to the Valley, I always seem to find another person who speaks English better than I thought and knows me better than I would have expected. It is a family that keeps growing in my absence. The result of this is that each time I return, more and more knowledge is shared with me from an ever-increasing number of horseback archers. I am able to learn from not only Kassai directly, but from many of those fortunate enough to have contact with him on a daily or weekly basis. By keeping an open mind and listening, I am able to learn from other students of all ability levels. Personal contact and training with Kassai is supplemented in this way.

Direct contact is of course the best teacher-student relationship and has been essential to developing my understanding of Kasai's teaching and philosophies. Conversations about how a technique can be improved, or how solving an internal tension will be reflected in the release of an arrow, are best shared from the back of a horse. It was during one of our rides that Kassai shared with me his vision for a new martial art form, Horseback Archery.

Discussions while on horseback are a natural venue for sharing thoughts and I have been fortunate enough to share many hours in this setting with Kassai. The transfer of knowledge that takes place while building a relationship forged through shared experiences becomes very personal. I have come to understand that the mental training and internal preparation are essential if the physical training is to have meaning. It is this "way" of training that I bring back with me to share with others.

Understanding the passion Kassai has for Horseback Archery is difficult to put into words. This discipline has been practiced for more than 2000 years, and the people of the Eurasian Steppes still carry this in their culture and their blood. This passion is easy to recognize and is very contagious.

During my trips to Hungary, I have had the opportunity to train and share thoughts with many different teachers of Horseback Archery. All of these teachers bring with them a slightly different solution to the same problem. The variations that exist always seem to surprise me. When individuals reach inside themselves to solve the same external problem, it is truly amazing to see the results. The wealth of knowledge and experience that is shared during my stays in Hungary always sends me home overflowing with new challenges, and with fresh ideas about solving them. As a group of leaders, we share the common goal of returning to our respective nations and building on the foundation started by Kassai in Hungary. On top of this foundation, we each add a part of ourselves. By accumulating the knowledge of others, and blending that with our own experience, we are able to keep this "way" from becoming a "system." This insures that the Kassai method of Horseback Archery will continue to grow and evolve.

The formation of HAWA

During these same trips to Hungary, I established my relationships with others in the international community rapidly developing in Europe. Johannes Fischnaller (who also attended IHAF 2000), of Austria, and Pettra Engeländer, of Germany, were both establishing schools in their own countries at this same time. We worked together under the guidance of Kassai and started laying the groundwork for the formation of HAWA. Since that time we have added groups in Canada, New Zealand, and Norway. Greece and Bulgaria are developing and there are rumblings in England and China of a start. We all share a common goal, to bring the Kassai style of Horseback Archery to our respective nations. The most important thing we share is a common spirit. This spirit binds us together across the globe and across our cultures.

The international experience I have been able to gain has helped tremendously in the development of Kassai USA. Language and culture are always potential problems when there are people from many different nations. It takes a strong commitment from each of us to work together efficiently. Sometimes it is not unlike trying to get an idea through to your horse. Make it simple, clear, and send it from the heart. Take the time to make certain it is understood. This is part of the commitment that the leadership circle of the Kassai School of Horseback Archery has to each other. We have a commitment to Kassai Lajos, to share the knowledge given to us. As a group we are dedicated to bringing this way of Horseback Archery to our home countries. This dedication extends to helping each other establish the international organization and school. It is also a dedication to those training with us, to make certain those we train will surpass our achievements and teach the next generation. It has been my experience that the proficiency level of beginning horseback archers grows twice as fast now as it did five years ago when I started training in earnest, and my scores in competition rose faster than those who started five to ten years before me. This I see as proof that the training methods we use are not only working, but improving all the time. It also speaks well of the teachers and their willingness share what they have learned without holding back for fear of competition from their students.

When I train with the international group, it is easy to see the connection many of these people have with their ancestors. It shows very clearly in the way they practice this discipline. The training regimen within the Kassai School is very demanding and is designed for those who are looking at Horseback Archery as more than just a way to have some fun. Horseback Archery becomes not a game or sport; it becomes a way of life. It is this way of life that Kassai has been able to share with me over the years, made possible because of a connection we share through the love of the horse and bow. I am not sure that I will ever be able to understand this connection completely; I only know it exists.

About the school

The leadership of the Kassai School is based in Hungary. All leadership positions are elected from the Kagan (leads HAWA), and are elected by the Országfo (leaders of the nations), who are elected by the Kans and Törzsfö, who are elected by the members. These positions are built on trust and respect upon the premise that it is impossible to lead if there is no one to follow. The community of Horseback Archers is built on the idea of leading by example. Those who find themselves in positions of leadership have shown the ability to serve others. This ability to provide for others is part of the age-old tradition of horseback archers. In the past great Khans led the clans and leadership was tested in battle; now the leaders provide places to train and warriors are tested in competition. Leaders are not only chosen by their ability to provide, but also by the ability to teach and guide others along the path of Horseback Archery.

www.lrgaf.org

Each year the leaders of every nation gather for the international training camps held in Kaposmérö, Hungary, under the direction of Kassai. We spend time strengthening the connections we have with each other while working with the horses, practicing archery skills, and maintaining the school grounds. Sometimes this even includes practicing horseback archery, although it can be said that everything done during one of these camps relates to horseback archery. The training of the mind, body, and spirit takes many forms and it takes an open mind to see the relationship between tasks and performance. Cutting grass or gathering walnuts can be monotonous tasks. They can also be times of learning. Each person makes his own decisions of how to apply these tasks. For myself, gathering walnuts becomes a way to exercise my eyes. The faster I can scan the ground and identify my target, the walnut, the faster I can pick a spot on a moving target and send the arrow. This is Horseback Archery training as a way of life.

The relationships between the leaders and their ability to work together are key factors in the success of the international school. We spend the time required to build these relationships in many ways. Training camp is spent living together as family. This means we work, eat, sleep, train, laugh, and cry together. On the outside, the practice of horseback archery appears an individual experience and the truth is, it can be. What is also true is that this individual experience can become collective. When a group shares a common objective, the performance of the individual is enhanced. Building relationships among the members of the school is just as important as learning to nock an arrow. We build these relationships at both the student and teacher levels. The success of each Törzs, or Kánság, depends on the relationships between their respective members and their ability to work together. From a martial perspective this means going into battle with those you trust and respect, as your life may depend on them. The success of the organization at the national and international levels depends on the relationships built between those in the leadership positions.

Each member within the school has a responsibility as both a student and a teacher. One of our responsibilities as teachers is to never stop learning, to always be a student. The other is to never stop passing this knowledge to others. It is only when we can accept our dual roles as students/teachers that we can fulfill our responsibilities to the other members within the school. From the time a student passes the first examination, he has gained enough knowledge to help others start along their own paths of Horseback Archery. What is considered the most basic knowledge to some may be true wisdom to another. I do not often have to answer the question, "Which is the bow and which is the arrow?" I very often answer the question, "How do I hold them?" This basic transfer of knowledge must be given and received with as much respect, as though a person's life depends on it. In the world of weapons and horse, it just might.

Membership in the school is by invitation or recommendation. Those interested in joining are asked to attend an "Open Day." Open days are training days when the school invites visitors to watch the training. The format varies for each location but the purpose is the same, providing a way for people to become familiar with the requirements for training within the Kassai School. It also allows those who are interested in joining the school the opportunity to see what lies ahead. There are always members training at different levels of experience. This allows visitors to see first-hand the transitions and steps forming the path of the horseback archer.

All training starts on the ground, and ground training never stops. This applies to archery, riding, and horses. Open days are also the best way to meet the horseback archers and ask questions about the school and how it functions.

The training is physically demanding. There is a basic fitness test required that involves running, riding, and shooting. The examination system provides a way to show progress or achievement in the system of degrees offered. Competition is a way of testing knowledge and ability. Those who have earned the title of Kan and Törzsfö are responsible for providing these opportunities for the membership.

Examinations

The school has an examination system that starts with basic archery form. The first test establishes the foundation of the form needed to shoot from horseback. Timing, balance, and rhythm are the building blocks supporting the horseback archer throughout his career. Mastering the basic fundamentals of shooting and timing is the object of this examination.

www.lrgaf.org

The second test is a riding examination demonstrating ability and balance. This is conducted at both the trot and canter while bareback. Riding simple patterns and performing different tasks, the rider shows the control and ability necessary on the competition course. Most of the training on horseback is conducted without the aid of a saddle.

The third examination is a combination of archery and riding. First is an archery test of shooting speed and accuracy, followed by a riding test exhibiting control of the bow. Theoretical knowledge of the training system, as well as the regulations of competition and examination system, must also be shown.

After successful completion of the first three examinations, the student may apply for the first student degree. Here the student is tested at proficiency on the competition course. This test is conducted under the rules for competition, with the student riding bareback. It is only after the successful completion of these first three examinations, and once the first degree is earned, that a member of The Kassai School earns the right to be called Horseback Archer.

The Kassai School of Horseback Archery recognizes three levels to the first student degree and twelve degrees for the Horseback Archer: three Student, three advanced, and six Master. These degrees are earned through scores achieved in international competition, followed by examinations of proficiency.

Training

Training starts with the body. One of the core principles of the Kassai School is that participating in the art of horseback archery will change you as a person, both inside and out. The physical demands of riding and shooting can greatly influence the mental ability of those who are not prepared to spend long periods of time on horseback or shooting. It is when we are pushed beyond our physical limits that we start to make mistakes. In the archery portion of horseback archery, this is not so critical — a few missed targets or a few sore muscles. For the mounted portion of training, this can be a disaster, and possibly fatal. Physical ability and mental clarity are essential for safety in any riding discipline. Later, the horseback archer pushes beyond the physical limits as a way to break through mental blocks, but this is only after proper training and preparation.

The first training test within in the Kassai School is one of fitness and endurance. The Warrior Test is a combination of running, riding and shooting. The requirements for men/women are a 10/5k timed cross country style run, completed in 72/36 minutes. Next are 2/1 hours of trotting bareback, finishing with 500/250 arrows in 90/45 minutes scored on a 60cm target at 20 meters. Having the ability to complete this test requires a great commitment to yourself.

Archery training starts on the ground without the bow. The basic form of drawing and release are combined with proper body positions for shooting forward, sideways, and backward, and practiced statically. Next, using a series of exercises designed to enhance timing, rhythm, and balance, the same forms are practiced in motion. The object is not only to develop agility but to also help develop the separation of upper and lower body movements needed to successfully shoot from the back of a moving horse. These exercises are then repeated with the bow.

Archery practice itself is taught many different ways, with exercises and games designed to develop the different qualities essential to horseback archery. Aerial targets, flight shooting, and speed shooting are all ways of developing an understanding of the abilities and limits of yourself and your equipment. By using both drills and games, archers relax and have fun while, at the same time, honing the skills needed to shoot a minimum of 3 arrows in less than 6 seconds, with accuracy.

Again, riding starts on the ground and without the horse. Proper posture and the feel for the reins are developed with exercises helping the new rider find balance and a feel for the horse's movements. This gives the new rider a better understanding of what the horse feels, to understand how the rider's balance or lack thereof affects the horse. Horses are also worked from the ground, helping the rider understand how a horse moves and responds to pressure and release. By having a better understanding of how the horse moves and responds, the rider is better prepared to work with the horse, both on the ground and while mounted.

Mounted work is a combination of games and drills. Mounted games are some of the most valuable practices we can use as riders.

They bring our anxiety levels down, allowing us to ride without our minds getting in the way. We step back and learn like children, letting our bodies learn for themselves. These games can be as simple as tossing a ball or as complex as trying to identify the horse's footfalls while riding blindfolded.

All these different exercises develop skills needed by the horseback archer. The idea of using many different methods of training for archery and riding is to sharpen specific skills. Archers, throughout history, have carried more than one type of arrow point in their quivers. Some arrows work better for certain jobs than others.

Competition

Competition is the time when we gather more for sharing and celebrating with each other, instead of boasting about our scores. There is a spirit between the competitors that is hard to explain. Each of us performs to the best of our ability; there is no question about this. We are there supporting the other competitors so they may achieve their best as well. In essence the competition is within each of us. By gathering together in a competitive setting, we test our true understanding of Horseback Archery.

Desiring to be the world's best horseback archer is the goal we all hold in our dreams. In reality, we must first reach our own true potential. It is only when we have realized this level of competence that we can truly know how we compare to others. Sadly, most people will fall short of this first goal and quit. The ones who stay with this discipline realize there is no finish. The art of Horseback Archery is one which no person will ever completely master. There is always room for improvement. When a perfect score is achieved, then the challenge will be repeating it, at faster speeds. Our competition is no more than a way of measuring some of this progress and is also an outward manifestation of internal change.

Todd Delle, Törzsfö

Kassai USA provides training, equipment, and international competition for the horseback archer. The training methods I share have been developing for more than twenty years and continue to

www.lrgaf.org

evolve. Each year I return to Hungary, training with Kassai and the leaders of other nations. This group forms the core of the Horseback Archery World Association. It is impossible to separate one school or nation from the others. We work as a team, supporting each other in every possible way. Those at the leadership level travel, whenever possible, to other schools making certain new schools have experienced students on hand. This helps insure a smooth start for new schools. Members of any Kassai school are welcome in any Kassai school throughout the world. This is only possible because we keep our commitment to each other, to the school, and to the founder, teaching as we have been taught. We can be sure that a member has earned his rank and, by this rank, we know what level of training and responsibility to expect.

The Kassai School of Horseback Archery takes its place within the tradition of the older schools of martial arts.

Reference:

Kassai, Lajos. 2002. Horseback Archery. Budapest, Hungary: Puski Kaido, kft.

www.lrgaf.org

Our Current List of Titles

Abdullah, Morag Mary, *My Khyber Marriage* - Morag Murray departed on a lifetime of adventure when she met and fell in love with Sirdar Ikbal Ali Shah, the son of an Afghan warlord. Leaving the comforts of her middle-class home in Scotland, Morag followed her husband into a Central Asia still largely unchanged since the 19th century.

Abernathy, Miles, *Ride the Wind* – the amazing true story of the little Abernathy Boys, who made a series of astonishing journeys in the United States, starting in 1909 when they were aged five and nine!

Beard, John, *Saddles East* – John Beard determined as a child that he wanted to see the Wild West from the back of a horse after a visit to Cody's legendary Wild West show. Yet it was only in 1948 – more than sixty years after seeing the flamboyant American showman – that Beard and his wife Lulu finally set off to follow their dreams.

Beker, Ana, *The Courage to Ride* – Determined to out-do Tschiffely, Beker made a 17,000 mile mounted odyssey across the Americas in the late 1940s that would fix her place in the annals of equestrian travel history.

Bey, A. M. Hassanein, *The Lost Oases* - At the dawning of the 20th century the vast desert of Libya remained one of last unexplored places on Earth. Sir Hassanein Bey, the dashing Egyptian diplomat turned explorer, befriended the Muslim leaders of the elusive Senussi Brotherhood who controlled the deserts further on, and became aware of rumours of a "lost oasis" which lay even deeper in the desert. In 1923 the explorer led a small caravan on a remarkable seven month journey across the centre of Libya.

Bird, Isabella, *Among the Tibetans* – A rousing 1889 adventure, an enchanting travelogue, a forgotten peek at a mountain kingdom swept away by the waves of time.

Bird, Isabella, *On Horseback* in *Hawaii* – The Victorian explorer's first horseback journey, in which she learns to ride astride, in early 1873.

Bird, Isabella, *Journeys in Persia and Kurdistan, Volumes 1 and 2* – The intrepid Englishwoman undertakes another gruelling journey in 1890.

Bird, Isabella, *A Lady's Life in the Rocky Mountains* – The story of Isabella Bird's adventures during the winter of 1873 when she explored the magnificent unspoiled wilderness of Colorado. Truly a classic.

Bird, Isabella, *Unbeaten Tracks in Japan, Volumes One and Two* – A 600-mile solo ride through Japan undertaken by the intrepid British traveller in 1878.

Blackmore, Charles, *In the Footsteps of Lawrence of Arabia* - In February 1985, fifty years after T. E. Lawrence was killed in a motor bicycle accident in Dorset, Captain Charles Blackmore and three others of the Royal Green Jackets Regiment set out to retrace Lawrence's exploits in the Arab Revolt during the First World War. They spent twenty-nine days with meagre supplies and under extreme conditions, riding and walking to the source of the Lawrence legend.

Boniface, Lieutenant Jonathan, *The Cavalry Horse and his Pack* – Quite simply the most important book ever written in the English language by a military man on the subject of equestrian travel.

Bosanquet, Mary, *Saddlebags for Suitcases* – In 1939 Bosanquet set out to ride from Vancouver, Canada, to New York. Along the way she was wooed by love-struck cowboys, chased by a grizzly bear and even suspected of being a Nazi spy, scouting out Canada in preparation for a German invasion. A truly delightful book.

de Bourboulon, Catherine, *Shanghai à Moscou (French)* – the story of how a young Scottish woman and her aristocratic French husband travelled overland from Shanghai to Moscow in the late 19th Century.

www.lrgaf.org

Brown, Donald; *Journey from the Arctic* – A truly remarkable account of how Brown, his Danish companion and their two trusty horses attempt the impossible, to cross the silent Arctic plateaus, thread their way through the giant Swedish forests, and finally discover a passage around the treacherous Norwegian marshes.

Bruce, Clarence Dalrymple, *In the Hoofprints of Marco Polo* – The author made a dangerous journey from Srinagar to Peking in 1905, mounted on a trusty 13-hand Kashmiri pony, then wrote this wonderful book.

Burnaby, Frederick; *A Ride to Khiva* – Burnaby fills every page with a memorable cast of characters, including hard-riding Cossacks, nomadic Tartars, vodka-guzzling sleigh-drivers and a legion of peasant ruffians.

Burnaby, Frederick, *On Horseback through Asia Minor* – Armed with a rifle, a small stock of medicines, and a single faithful servant, the equestrian traveler rode through a hotbed of intrigue and high adventure in wild inhospitable country, encountering Kurds, Circassians, Armenians, and Persian pashas.

Carter, General William, *Horses, Saddles and Bridles* – This book covers a wide range of topics including basic training of the horse and care of its equipment. It also provides a fascinating look back into equestrian travel history.

Cayley, George, *Bridle Roads of Spain* – Truly one of the greatest equestrian travel accounts of the 19th Century.

Chase, J. Smeaton, *California Coast Trails* – This classic book describes the author's journey from Mexico to Oregon along the coast of California in the 1890s.

Chase, J. Smeaton, *California Desert Trails* – Famous British naturalist J. Smeaton Chase mounted up and rode into the Mojave Desert to undertake the longest equestrian study of its kind in modern history.

Chitty, Susan, and Hinde, Thomas, *The Great Donkey Walk* - When biographer Susan Chitty and her novelist husband, Thomas Hinde, decided it was time to embark on a family adventure, they did it in style. In Santiago they bought two donkeys whom they named Hannibal and Hamilcar. Their two small daughters, Miranda (7) and Jessica (3) were to ride Hamilcar. Hannibal, meanwhile, carried the baggage. The walk they planned to undertake was nothing short of the breadth of southern Europe.

Christian, Glynn, *Fragile Paradise: The discovery of Fletcher Christian, "Bounty" Mutineer* – the great-great-great-great-grandson of the *Bounty* mutineer brings to life a fascinating and complex character history has portrayed as both hero and villain, and the real story behind a mutiny that continues to divide opinion more than 200 years later. The result is a brilliant and compelling historical detective story, full of intrigue, jealousy, revenge and adventure on the high seas.

Clark, Leonard, *Marching Wind, The* – The panoramic story of a mounted exploration in the remote and savage heart of Asia, a place where adventure, danger, and intrigue were the daily backdrop to wild tribesman and equestrian exploits.

Clark, Leonard, *A Wanderer Till I Die* – In a world with lax passport control, no airlines, and few rules, the young man from San Francisco floats effortlessly from one adventure to the next. When he's not drinking whisky at the Raffles Hotel or listening to the "St. Louis Blues" on the phonograph in the jungle, he's searching for Malaysian treasure, being captured by Toradja head-hunters, interrogated by Japanese intelligence officers and lured into shady deals by European gun-runners.

Cobbett, William, *Rural Rides, Volumes 1 and 2* – In the early 1820s Cobbett set out on horseback to make a series of personal tours through the English countryside. These books contain what many believe to be the best accounts of rural England ever written, and remain enduring classics.

Codman, John, *Winter Sketches from the Saddle* – This classic book was first published in 1888. It recommends riding for your health and describes the septuagenarian author's many equestrian journeys through New England during the winter of 1887 on his faithful mare, Fanny.

Cunninghame Graham, Jean, *Gaucho Laird* – A superbly readable biography of the author's famous great-uncle, Robert "Don Roberto" Cunninghame Graham.

Cunninghame Graham, Robert, *Horses of the Conquest* – The author uncovered manuscripts which had lain forgotten for centuries, and wrote this book, as he said, out of gratitude to the horses of Columbus and the Conquistadors who shaped history.

Cunninghame Graham, Robert, *Magreb-el-Acksa* – The thrilling tale of how "Don Roberto" was kidnapped in Morocco!

Cunninghame Graham, Robert, *Rodeo* – An omnibus of the finest work of the man they called "the uncrowned King of Scotland," edited by his friend Aimé Tschiffely.

Cunninghame Graham, Robert, *Tales of Horsemen* – Ten of the most beautifully-written equestrian stories ever set to paper.

Cunninghame Graham, Robert, *Vanished Arcadia* – This haunting story about the Jesuit missions in South America from 1550 to 1767 was the inspiration behind the best-selling film *The Mission*.

Daly, H.W., *Manual of Pack Transportation* – This book is the author's masterpiece. It contains a wealth of information on various pack saddles, ropes and equipment, how to secure every type of load imaginable and instructions on how to organize a pack train.

Dixie, Lady Florence, *Riding Across Patagonia* – When asked in 1879 why she wanted to travel to such an outlandish place as Patagonia, the author replied without hesitation that she was taking to the saddle in order to flee from the strict confines of polite Victorian society. This is the story of how the aristocrat successfully traded the perils of a London parlor for the wind-borne freedom of a wild Patagonian bronco.

Dodwell, Christina, *Beyond Siberia* – The intrepid author goes to Russia's Far East to join the reindeer-herding people in winter.

Dodwell, Christina, *An Explorer's Handbook* – The author tells you everything you want to know about travelling: how to find suitable pack animals, how to feed and shelter yourself. She also has sensible and entertaining advice about dealing with unwanted visitors and the inevitable bureaucrats.

Dodwell, Christina, *Madagascar Travels* – Christina explores the hidden corners of this amazing island and, as usual, makes friends with its people.

Dodwell, Christina, *A Traveller in China* – The author sets off alone across China, starting with a horse and then transferring to an inflatable canoe.

Dodwell, Christina, *A Traveller on Horseback* – Christina Dodwell rides through Eastern Turkey and Iran in the late 1980s. The Sunday Telegraph wrote of the author's "courage and insatiable wanderlust," and in this book she demonstrates her gift for communicating her zest for adventure.

Dodwell, Christina, *Travels in Papua New Guinea* – Christina Dodwell spends two years exploring an island little known to the outside world. She travelled by foot, horse and dugout canoe among the Stone-Age tribes.

Dodwell, Christina, *Travels with Fortune* – the truly amazing account of the courageous author's first journey – a three-year odyssey around Africa by Landrover, bus, lorry, horse, camel, and dugout canoe!

Dodwell, Christina, *Travels with Pegasus* – This time Christina takes to the air! This is the story of her unconventional journey across North Africa in a micro-light!

Duncan, John, *Travels in Western Africa in 1845 and 1846* – The author, a Lifeguardsman from Scotland, tells the hair-raising tale of his two journeys to what is now Benin. Sadly, Duncan has been forgotten until today, and we are proud to get this book back into print.

www.lrgaf.org

Ehlers, Otto, *Im Sattel durch die Fürstenhöfe Indiens* – In June 1890 the young German adventurer, Ehlers, lay very ill. His doctor gave him a choice: either go home to Germany or travel to Kashmir. So of course the Long Rider chose the latter. This is a thrilling yet humorous book about the author's adventures.

Farson, Negley, *Caucasian Journey* – A thrilling account of a dangerous equestrian journey made in 1929, this is an amply illustrated adventure classic.

Fox, Ernest, *Travels in Afghanistan* – The thrilling tale of a 1937 journey through the mountains, valleys, and deserts of this forbidden realm, including visits to such fabled places as the medieval city of Heart, the towering Hindu Kush mountains, and the legendary Khyber Pass.

Gall, Sandy, *Afghanistan – Agony of a Nation* - Sandy Gall has made three trips to Afghanistan to report the war there: in 1982, 1984 and again in 1986. This book is an account of his last journey and what he found. He chose to revisit the man he believes is the outstanding commander in Afghanistan: Ahmed Shah Masud, a dashing Tajik who is trying to organise resistance to the Russians on a regional, and eventually national scale.

Gall, Sandy, *Behind Russian Lines* – In the summer of 1982, Sandy Gall set off for Afghanistan on what turned out to be the hardest assignment of his life. During his career as a reporter he had covered plenty of wars and revolutions before, but this was the first time he had been required to walk all the way to an assignment and all the way back again, dodging Russian bombs *en route*.

Gallard, Babette, *Riding the Milky Way* – An essential guide to anyone planning to ride the ancient pilgrimage route to Santiago di Compostella, and a highly readable story for armchair travellers.

Galton, Francis, *The Art of Travel* – Originally published in 1855, this book became an instant classic and was used by a host of now-famous explorers, including Sir Richard Francis Burton of Mecca fame. Readers can learn how to ride horses, handle elephants, avoid cobras, pull teeth, find water in a desert, and construct a sleeping bag out of fur.

Glazier, Willard, *Ocean to Ocean on Horseback* – This book about the author's journey from New York to the Pacific in 1875 contains every kind of mounted adventure imaginable. Amply illustrated with pen and ink drawings of the time, the book remains a timeless equestrian adventure classic.

Goodwin, Joseph, *Through Mexico on Horseback* – The author and his companion, Robert Horiguichi, the sophisticated, multi-lingual son of an imperial Japanese diplomat, set out in 1931 to cross Mexico. They were totally unprepared for the deserts, quicksand and brigands they were to encounter during their adventure.

Hanbury-Tenison, Marika, *For Better, For Worse* – The author, an excellent story-teller, writes about her adventures visiting and living among the Indians of Central Brazil.

Hanbury-Tenison, Marika, *A Slice of Spice* – The fresh and vivid account of the author's hazardous journey to the Indonesian Islands with her husband, Robin.

Hanbury-Tenison, Robin, *Chinese Adventure* – The story of a unique journey in which the explorer Robin Hanbury-Tenison and his wife Louella rode on horseback alongside the Great Wall of China in 1986.

Hanbury-Tenison, Robin, *Fragile Eden* – The wonderful story of Robin and Louella Hanbury-Tenison's exploration of New Zealand on horseback in 1988. They rode alone together through what they describe as 'some of the most dramatic and exciting country we have ever seen.'

Hanbury-Tenison, Robin, *Mulu: The Rainforest* – This was the first popular book to bring to the world's attention the significance of the rain forests to our fragile ecosystem. It is a timely reminder of our need to preserve them for the future.

Hanbury-Tenison, Robin, *A Pattern of Peoples* – The author and his wife, Marika, spent three months travelling through Indonesia's outer islands and writes with his usual flair and sensitivity about the tribes he found there.

Hanbury-Tenison, Robin, *A Question of Survival* – This superb book played a hugely significant role in bringing the plight of Brazil's Indians to the world's attention.

Hanbury-Tenison, Robin, *The Rough and the Smooth* – The incredible story of two journeys in South America. Neither had been attempted before, and both were considered impossible!

Hanbury-Tenison, Robin, *Spanish Pilgrimage* – Robin and Louella Hanbury-Tenison went to Santiago de Compostela in a traditional way – riding on white horses over long-forgotten tracks. In the process they discovered more about the people and the country than any conventional traveller would learn. Their adventures are vividly and entertainingly recounted in this delightful and highly readable book.

Hanbury-Tenison, Robin, *White Horses over France* – This enchanting book tells the story of a magical journey and how, in fulfilment of a personal dream, the first Camargue horses set foot on British soil in the late summer of 1984.

Hanbury-Tenison, Robin, *Worlds Apart – an Explorer's Life* – The author's battle to preserve the quality of life under threat from developers and machines infuses this autobiography with a passion and conviction which makes it impossible to put down.

Hanbury-Tenison, Robin, *Worlds Within – Reflections in the Sand* – This book is full of the adventure you would expect from a man of action like Robin Hanbury-Tenison. However, it is also filled with the type of rare knowledge that was revealed to other desert travellers like Lawrence, Doughty and Thesiger.

Haslund, Henning, *Mongolian Adventure* – An epic tale inhabited by a cast of characters no longer present in this lackluster world, shamans who set themselves on fire, rebel leaders who sacked towns, and wild horsemen whose ancestors conquered the world.

Heath, Frank, *Forty Million Hoofbeats* – Heath set out in 1925 to follow his dream of riding to all 48 of the Continental United States. The journey lasted more than two years, during which time Heath and his mare, Gypsy Queen, became inseparable companions.

Hinde, Thomas, *The Great Donkey Walk* – Biographer Susan Chitty and her novelist husband, Thomas Hinde, travelled from Spain's Santiago to Salonica in faraway Greece. Their two small daughters, Miranda (7) and Jessica (3) were rode one donkey, while the other donkey carried the baggage. Reading this delightful book is leisurely and continuing pleasure.

Holt, William, *Ride a White Horse* – After rescuing a cart horse, Trigger, from slaughter and nursing him back to health, the 67-year-old Holt and his horse set out in 1964 on an incredible 9,000 mile, non-stop journey through western Europe.

Hopkins, Frank T., *Hidalgo and Other Stories* – For the first time in history, here are the collected writings of Frank T. Hopkins, the counterfeit cowboy whose endurance racing claims and Old West fantasies have polarized the equestrian world.

James, Jeremy, *Saddletramp* – The classic story of Jeremy James' journey from Turkey to Wales, on an unplanned route with an inaccurate compass, unreadable map and the unfailing aid of villagers who seemed to have as little sense of direction as he had.

James, Jeremy, *Vagabond* – The wonderful tale of the author's journey from Bulgaria to Berlin offers a refreshing, witty and often surprising view of Eastern Europe and the collapse of communism.

Jebb, Louisa, *By Desert Ways to Baghdad and Damascus* – From the pen of a gifted writer and intrepid traveller, this is one of the greatest equestrian travel books of all time.

Kluckhohn, Clyde, *To the Foot of the Rainbow* – This is not just a exciting true tale of equestrian adventure. It is a moving account of a young man's search for physical perfection in a desert world still untouched by the recently-born twentieth century.

Lambie, Thomas, *Boots and Saddles in Africa* – Lambie's story of his equestrian journeys is told with the grit and realism that marks a true classic.

Landor, Henry Savage, *In the Forbidden Land* – Illustrated with hundreds of photographs and drawings, this blood-chilling account of equestrian adventure makes for page-turning excitement.

Langlet, Valdemar, *Till Häst Genom Ryssland (Swedish)* – Denna reseskildring rymmer många ögonblicksbilder av möten med människor, från morgonbad med Lev Tolstoi till samtal med Tartarer och fotografering av fagra skördeflickor. Rikt illustrerad med foto och teckningar.

Leigh, Margaret, *My Kingdom for a Horse* – In the autumn of 1939 the author rode from Cornwall to Scotland, resulting in one of the most delightful equestrian journeys of the early twentieth century. This book is full of keen observations of a rural England that no longer exists.

Lester, Mary, *A Lady's Ride across Spanish Honduras in 1881* – This is a gem of a book, with a very entertaining account of Mary's vivid, day-to-day life in the saddle.

MacDermot, Brian, *Cult of the Sacred Spear* – here is that rarest of travel books, an exploration not only of a distant land but of a man's own heart. A confederation of pastoral people located in Southern Sudan and western Ethiopia, the Nuer warriors were famous for staging cattle raids against larger tribes and successfully resisted European colonization. Brian MacDermot, London stockbroker, entered into Nuer society as a stranger and emerged as Rial Nyang, an adopted member of the tribe. This book recounts this extraordinary emotional journey, regaling the reader with tales of pagan gods, warriors on mysterious missions, and finally the approach of warfare that continues to swirl across this part of Africa today.

Maillart, Ella, *Turkestan Solo* – A vivid account of a 1930s journey through this wonderful, mysterious and dangerous portion of the world, complete with its Kirghiz eagle hunters, lurking Soviet secret police, and the timeless nomads that still inhabited the desolate steppes of Central Asia.

Marcy, Randolph, *The Prairie Traveler* – There were a lot of things you packed into your saddlebags or the wagon before setting off to cross the North American wilderness in the 1850s. A gun and an axe were obvious necessities. Yet many pioneers were just as adamant about placing a copy of Captain Randolph Marcy's classic book close at hand.

Marsden, Kate, *Riding through Siberia: A Mounted Medical Mission in 1891* – This immensely readable book is a mixture of adventure, extreme hardship and compassion as the author travels the Great Siberian Post Road.

Marsh, Hippisley Cunliffe, *A Ride Through Islam* – A British officer rides through Persia and Afghanistan to India in 1873. Full of adventures, and with observant remarks on the local Turkoman equestrian traditions.

MacCann, William, *Viaje a Caballo* – Spanish-language edition of the British author's equestrian journey around Argentina in 1848.

Meline, James, *Two Thousand Miles on Horseback: Kansas to Santa Fé in 1866* – A beautifully written, eye witness account of a United States that is no more.

Muir Watson, Sharon, *The Colour of Courage* – The remarkable true story of the epic horse trip made by the first people to travel Australia's then-unmarked Bicentennial National Trail. There are enough adventures here to satisfy even the most jaded reader.

Naysmith, Gordon, *The Will to Win* – This book recounts the only equestrian journey of its kind undertaken during the 20th century - a mounted trip stretching across 16 countries. Gordon Naysmith, a Scottish pentathlete and former military man, set out in 1970 to ride from the tip of the African continent to the 1972 Olympic Games in distant Germany.

Ondaatje, Christopher, *Leopard in the Afternoon* – The captivating story of a journey through some of Africa's most spectacular haunts. It is also touched with poignancy and regret for a vanishing wilderness – a world threatened with extinction.

Ondaatje, Christopher, *The Man-Eater of Punanai* – a fascinating story of a past rediscovered through a remarkable journey to one of the most exotic countries in the world — Sri Lanka. Full of drama and history, it not only relives the incredible story of a man-eating leopard that terrorized the tiny village of Punanai in the early part of the century, but also allows the author to come to terms with the ghost of his charismatic but tyrannical father.

Ondaatje, Christopher, *Sindh Revisited* – This is the extraordinarily sensitive account of the author's quest to uncover the secrets of the seven years Richard Burton spent in India in the army of the East India Company from 1842 to 1849. "If I wanted to fill the gap in my understanding of Richard Burton, I would have to do something that had never been done before: follow in his footsteps in India…" The journey covered thousands of miles—trekking across deserts where ancient tribes meet modern civilization in the valley of the mighty Indus River.

O'Connor, Derek, *The King's Stranger* – a superb biography of the forgotten Scottish explorer, John Duncan.

O'Reilly, Basha, *Count Pompeii – Stallion of the Steppes* – the story of Basha's journey from Russia with her stallion, Count Pompeii, told for children. This is the first book in the *Little Long Rider* series.

O'Reilly, CuChullaine, (Editor) *The Horse Travel Handbook* – this accumulated knowledge of a million miles in the saddle tells you everything you need to know about travelling with your horse!

O'Reilly, CuChullaine, (Editor) *The Horse Travel Journal* – a unique book to take on your ride and record your experiences. Includes the world's first equestrian travel "pictionary" to help you in foreign countries.

O'Reilly, CuChullaine, *Khyber Knights* – Told with grit and realism by one of the world's foremost equestrian explorers, "Khyber Knights" has been penned the way lives are lived, not how books are written.

O'Reilly, CuChullaine, (Editor) *The Long Riders, Volume One* – The first of five unforgettable volumes of exhilarating travel tales.

Östrup, J, *(Swedish), Växlande Horisont* – The thrilling account of the author's journey to Central Asia from 1891 to 1893.

Patterson, George, *Gods and Guerrillas* – The true and gripping story of how the author went secretly into Tibet to film the Chinese invaders of his adopted country. Will make your heart pound with excitement!

Patterson, George, *Journey with Loshay: A Tibetan Odyssey* – This is an amazing book written by a truly remarkable man! Relying both on his companionship with God and on his own strength, he undertook a life few can have known, and a journey of emergency across the wildest parts of Tibet.

Patterson, George, *Patterson of Tibet* – Patterson was a Scottish medical missionary who went to Tibet shortly after the second World War. There he became Tibetan in all but name, adapting to the culture and learning the language fluently. This intense autobiography reveals how Patterson crossed swords with India's Prime Minister Nehru, helped with the rescue of the Dalai Lama and befriended a host of unique world figures ranging from Yehudi Menhuin to Eric Clapton. This is a vividly-written account of a life of high adventure and spiritual odyssey.
Pocock, Roger, *Following the Frontier* – Pocock was one of the nineteenth century's most influential equestrian travelers. Within the covers of this book is the detailed account of Pocock's horse ride along the infamous Outlaw Trail, a 3,000 mile solo journey that took the adventurer from Canada to Mexico City.
Pocock, Roger, *Horses* – Pocock set out to document the wisdom of the late 19th and early 20th Centuries into a book unique for its time. His concerns for attempting to preserve equestrian knowledge were based on cruel reality. More than 300,000 horses had been destroyed during the recent Boer War. Though Pocock enjoyed a reputation for dangerous living, his observations on horses were praised by the leading thinkers of his day.
Post, Charles Johnson, *Horse Packing* – Originally published in 1914, this book was an instant success, incorporating as it did the very essence of the science of packing horses and mules. It makes fascinating reading for students of the horse or history.
Ray, G. W., *Through Five Republics on Horseback* – In 1889 a British explorer – part-time missionary and full-time adventure junky – set out to find a lost tribe of sun-worshipping natives in the unexplored forests of Paraguay. The journey was so brutal that it defies belief.
Rink, Bjarke, *The Centaur Legacy* – This immensely entertaining and historically important book provides the first ever in-depth study into how man's partnership with his equine companion changed the course of history and accelerated human development.
Ross, Julian, *Travels in an Unknown Country* – A delightful book about modern horseback travel in an enchanting country, which once marked the eastern borders of the Roman Empire – Romania.
Ross, Martin and Somerville, E, *Beggars on Horseback* – The hilarious adventures of two aristocratic Irish cousins on an 1894 riding tour of Wales.
Ruxton, George, *Adventures in Mexico* – The story of a young British army officer who rode from Vera Cruz to Santa Fe, Mexico in 1847. At times the author exhibits a fearlessness which borders on insanity. He ignores dire warnings, rides through deadly deserts, and dares murderers to attack him. It is a delightful and invigorating tale of a time and place now long gone.
von Salzman, Erich, *Im Sattel durch Zentralasien* – The astonishing tale of the author's journey through China, Turkistan and back to his home in Germany – 6000 kilometres in 176 days!
Schwarz, Hans *(German)*, *Vier Pferde, Ein Hund und Drei Soldaten* – In the early 1930s the author and his two companions rode through Liechtenstein, Austria, Romania, Albania, Yugoslavia, to Turkey, then rode back again!
Schwarz, Otto *(German)*, *Reisen mit dem Pferd* – the Swiss Long Rider with more miles in the saddle than anyone else tells his wonderful story, and a long appendix tells the reader how to follow in his footsteps.
Scott, Robert, *Scott's Last Expedition* – Many people are unaware that Scott recruited Yakut ponies from Siberia for his doomed expedition to the South Pole in 1909. Here is the remarkable story of men and horses who all paid the ultimate sacrifice.
Shackleton, Ernest, *Aurora Australis* - The members of the British Antarctic

Expedition of 1907-1908 wrote this delightful and surprisingly funny book. It was printed on the spot "at the sign of the Penguin"!

Skrede, Wilfred, *Across the Roof of the World* – This epic equestrian travel tale of a wartime journey across Russia, China, Turkestan and India is laced with unforgettable excitement.

The South Pole Ponies, *Theodore Mason* – The touching and totally forgotten story of the little horses who gave their all to both Scott and Shackleton in their attempts to reach the South Pole.

Stevens, Thomas, *Through Russia on a Mustang* – Mounted on his faithful horse, Texas, Stevens crossed the Steppes in search of adventure. Cantering across the pages of this classic tale is a cast of nineteenth century Russian misfits, peasants, aristocrats—and even famed Cossack Long Rider Dmitri Peshkov.

Stevenson, Robert L., *Travels with a Donkey* – In 1878, the author set out to explore the remote Cevennes mountains of France. He travelled alone, unless you count his stubborn and manipulative pack-donkey, Modestine. This book is a true classic.

Strong, Anna Louise, *Road to the Grey Pamir* – With Stalin's encouragement, Strong rode into the seldom-seen Pamir mountains of faraway Tadjikistan. The political renegade turned equestrian explorer soon discovered more adventure than she had anticipated.

Sykes, Ella, *Through Persia on a Sidesaddle* – Ella Sykes rode side-saddle 2,000 miles across Persia, a country few European woman had ever visited. Mind you, she traveled in style, accompanied by her Swiss maid and 50 camels loaded with china, crystal, linens and fine wine.

Trinkler, Emile, *Through the Heart of Afghanistan* – In the early 1920s the author made a legendary trip across a country now recalled only in legends.

Tschiffely, Aimé, *Bohemia Junction* – "Forty years of adventurous living condensed into one book."

Tschiffely, Aimé, *Bridle Paths* – a final poetic look at a now-vanished Britain.

Tschiffely, Aimé, *Mancha y Gato Cuentan sus Aventuras* – The Spanish-language version of *The Tale of Two Horses* – the story of the author's famous journey as told by the horses.

Tschiffely, Aimé, *The Tale of Two Horses* – The story of Tschiffely's famous journey from Buenos Aires to Washington, DC, narrated by his two equine heroes, Mancha and Gato. Their unique point of view is guaranteed to delight children and adults alike.

Tschiffely, Aimé, *This Way Southward* – the most famous equestrian explorer of the twentieth century decides to make a perilous journey across the U-boat infested Atlantic.

Tschiffely, Aimé, *Tschiffely's Ride* – The true story of the most famous equestrian journey of the twentieth century – 10,000 miles with two Criollo geldings from Argentina to Washington, DC. A new edition is coming soon with a Foreword by his literary heir!

Tschiffely, Aimé, *Tschiffely's Ritt* – The German-language translation of *Tschiffely's Ride* – the most famous equestrian journey of its day.

Ure, John, *Cucumber Sandwiches in the Andes* – No-one who wasn't mad as a hatter would try to take a horse across the Andes by one of the highest passes between Chile and the Argentine. That was what John Ure was told on his way to the British Embassy in Santiago – so he set out to find a few certifiable kindred spirits. Fans of equestrian travel and of Latin America will be enchanted by this delightful book.

Warner, Charles Dudley, *On Horseback in Virginia* – A prolific author, and a great friend of Mark Twain, Warner made witty and perceptive contributions to the world of nineteenth century American literature. This book about the author's equestrian adventures is full of fascinating descriptions of nineteenth century America.

Weale, Magdalene, *Through the Highlands of Shropshire* – It was 1933 and Magdalene Weale was faced with a dilemma: how to best explore her beloved English countryside? By horse, of course! This enchanting book invokes a gentle, softer world inhabited by gracious country lairds, wise farmers, and jolly inn keepers.

Weeks, Edwin Lord, *Artist Explorer* – A young American artist and superb writer travels through Persia to India in 1892.

Wentworth Day, J., *Wartime Ride* – In 1939 the author decided the time was right for an extended horseback ride through England! While parts of his country were being ravaged by war, Wentworth Day discovered an inland oasis of mellow harvest fields, moated Tudor farmhouses, peaceful country halls, and fishing villages.

Von Westarp, Eberhard, *Unter Halbmond und Sonne* – (German) – Im Sattel durch die asiatische Türkei und Persien.

Wilkins, Messanie, *Last of the Saddle Tramps* – Told she had little time left to live, the author decided to ride from her native Maine to the Pacific. Accompanied by her faithful horse, Tarzan, Wilkins suffered through any number of obstacles, including blistering deserts and freezing snow storms – and defied the doctors by living for another 20 years!

Wilson, Andrew, *The Abode of Snow* – One of the best accounts of overland equestrian travel ever written about the wild lands that lie between Tibet and Afghanistan.

de Windt, Harry, *A Ride to India* – Part science, all adventure, this book takes the reader for a thrilling canter across the Persian Empire of the 1890s.

Winthrop, Theodore, *Saddle and Canoe* – This book paints a vibrant picture of 1850s life in the Pacific Northwest and covers the author's travels along the Straits of Juan De Fuca, on Vancouver Island, across the Naches Pass, and on to The Dalles, in Oregon Territory. This is truly an historic travel account.

Woolf, Leonard, *Stories of the East* – Three short stories which are of vital importance in understanding the author's mistrust of and dislike for colonialism, which provide disturbing commentaries about the disintegration of the colonial process.

Younghusband, George, *Eighteen Hundred Miles on a Burmese Pony* – One of the funniest and most enchanting books about equestrian travel of the nineteenth century, featuring "Joe" the naughty Burmese pony!

We are constantly adding new titles to our collections, so please check our websites: **www.horsetravelbooks.com** and **www.classictravelbooks.com**